THE POLITICS OF CLIMATE CHANGE

Books by Anthony Giddens:
Capitalism and Modern Social Theory
Politics and Sociology in the Thought of Max Weber
The Class Structure of the Advanced Societies
New Rules of Sociological Method
Studies in Social and Political Theory
Emile Durkheim
Central Problems in Social Theory
A Contemporary Critique of Historical Materialism
Sociology: A Brief but Critical Introduction
Profiles and Critiques in Social Theory
The Constitution of Society
The Nation-State and Violence
Durkheim on Politics and the State
Social Theory and Modern Sociology
The Consequences of Modernity
Modernity and Self-Identity
The Transformation of Intimacy
Beyond Left and Right
Reflexive Modernization (with Ulrich Beck and Scott Lash)
Politics, Sociology and Social Theory
In Defence of Sociology
The Third Way
Runaway World
The Third Way and its Critics
Where Now for New Labour?
Europe in the Global Age
Over to You, Mr Brown
Sociology Sixth Edition

Edited Works:
Emile Durkheim: Selected Writings
Positivism and Sociology
Elites and Power in British Society (with Philip Stanworth)
Classes, Conflict and Power
Classes and the Division of Labour
Social Theory Today
Human Societies
On the Edge: Living with Global Capitalism (with Will Hutton)
The Global Third Way Debate
The Progressive Manifesto
The New Egalitarianism (with Patrick Diamond)
Global Europe, Social Europe (with Patrick Diamond and Roger Liddle)

THE POLITICS OF CLIMATE CHANGE

Second Edition, Revised and Updated

Anthony Giddens

polity

First published in 2011 by Polity Press

Polity Press
65 Bridge Street
Cambridge CB2 1UR, UK

Polity Press
350 Main Street
Malden, MA 02148, USA

ISBN-13: 978-0-7456-5514-7
ISBN-13: 978-0-7456-5515-4(pb)

A catalogue record for this book is available from the British Library.

Typeset in 11 on 13pt Palatino
by Servis Filmsetting Ltd, Stockport, Cheshire
Printed and bound in Great Britain by MPG Books Ltd, Bodmin, Cornwall

The publisher has used its best endeavours to ensure that the URLs for external websites referred to in this book are correct and active at the time of going to press. However, the publisher has no responsibility for the websites and can make no guarantee that a site will remain live or that the content is or will remain appropriate.

Every effort has been made to trace all copyright holders, but if any have been inadvertently overlooked the publisher will be pleased to include any necessary credits in any subsequent reprint or edition.

For further information on Polity, visit our website: www.politybooks.com

CONTENTS

ACKNOWLEDGEMENTS

This work grew out of my involvement in a project organized under the auspices of the think-tank Policy Network and the Centre for the Study of Global Governance at the London School of Economics. I should like to thank my colleagues in both institutions for their help and advice during the writing process. My gratitude is due in particular to Roger Liddle, Olaf Cramme, Simon Latham and Jade Groves at Policy Network; and to David Held at the Centre. Anne de Sayrah helped the project in more ways than I can count. Karen Birdsall did a marvellous job for the first edition, checking footnotes and assembling the bibliography. Olaf Corry provided some important feedback on a draft manuscript. I owe an especially large debt to Hugh Compston, who commented in a meticulous way on an early version of the book; and to Johanna Juselius, who did the same at a later point. Victor Philip Dahdaleh generously provided the funding for the collective project, so a big vote of thanks to him. I am indebted to everyone at Polity Press, including especially John Thompson, Gill Motley (as always), Sarah Lambert and Emma Hutchinson. I would like to thank Emma in particular for her attention to detail and for the amount of work she put into the project. Sarah was unfailingly helpful in preparing this new edition. Olaf Corry provided further critical comments. Special gratitude is due to Anna Wishart, whose help and involvement were invaluable; Anna made a major contribution in particular to the section on the US in chapter 4. Tom Hale provided a very valuable critical reading of the manuscript. Sarah Dancy has done an excellent copy-editing job on both editions. I dedicate the work to Indie and Matilda, definitely members of the younger generation, in the hope that it might contribute a little to making the world in which they will grow up less daunting.

INTRODUCTION

This is a book about nightmares, catastrophes – and dreams. It is also about the everyday, the routines that give our lives continuity and substance. It is about the warming of our planet – a phenomenon which, if it proceeds unchecked, constitutes an existential threat to our civilization. The changes we are wreaking on the world's climate will produce increasingly extreme and erratic weather, subject large areas of the globe to drought and eventually make them uninhabitable. Rising ocean levels will have the same effect upon low-lying coastal zones.

The book is a prolonged enquiry into a single question. Why do most people, most of the time, act as though a threat of such magnitude can be ignored? Almost everyone across the world must have heard the phrases 'climate change' and 'global warming' and know at least a bit about what they mean. The two terms can be used interchangeably. They refer to the fact that the greenhouse gas emissions produced by modern industry are causing the earth's climate to warm up, with potentially devastating consequences for the future. Yet the vast majority of people are doing very little, if anything at all, to alter their daily habits, even though those habits are the source of the dangers in store for us.

It is not as if climate change is creeping up on us unawares. On the contrary, large numbers of books have been written about it and its likely consequences. Serious worries about the warming of the earth's climate were expressed for a quarter of a century or more without making much of an impact. Within the past few years the issue has jumped to the forefront of discussion and debate, not just in this or that country, but across the world. Yet, as collective humanity, we are only just beginning to take the steps needed to respond to the threats that we and succeeding generations are confronting. Global warming is a problem unlike any other, however, both because of its scale and because it is mainly about the future. Many have said that to cope with it we will need to mobilize on a level comparable to fighting a war; but in this case there are no enemies to identify and confront. We are dealing with dangers that seem abstract and elusive, however potentially devastating they may be.

No matter how much we are told about the threats, it is hard to face up to them, because they feel somehow unreal – and, in the meantime, there is a life to be lived, with all its pleasures and pressures. The politics of climate change has to cope with what I call *Giddens's paradox* – a theme that appears throughout this text. It states that, since the dangers posed by global warming aren't tangible, immediate or visible in the course of day-to-day life, many will sit on their hands and do nothing of a concrete nature about them. Yet waiting until such dangers become visible and acute – in the shape of catastrophes that are irrefutably the result of climate change – before being stirred to serious action will be too late. For we know of no way of getting the greenhouse gases out again once they are there and most will be in the atmosphere for centuries.

Giddens's paradox affects almost every aspect of current reactions to climate change. It is the reason why, for most citizens, climate change is a back-of-the-mind issue rather than a front-of-the-mind one. Attitude surveys show that many of the public accept that global warming is a major threat; yet only a few are willing to alter their lives in any significant way as a result. Among elites, climate change lends itself to gestural politics – grandiose-sounding plans largely empty of content.

What social psychologists call 'future discounting' further accentuates Giddens's paradox – more accurately, one could say it is a sub-category of it. People find it hard to give the same level of reality to the future as they do to the present. Thus a small reward offered now will normally be taken in preference to a much larger one offered at some remove. The same principle applies to risks. Why do many young people take up smoking even though they are well aware that, as it now says on cigarette packets, 'smoking kills'? At least part of the reason is that, for a teenager, it is almost impossible to imagine being 40, the age at which the real dangers start to take hold and become life-threatening.

There is a high level of agreement among scientists that climate change is real and dangerous, and that it is caused by human activity. A small minority of scientists, however – the climate change 'sceptics' – dispute these claims, and they get a good deal of attention in the media. Many other, less expert, contributors have taken their side. Someone can always say, 'it's not proven, is it?' if it be suggested that he should change his profligate ways. Another response might be: 'I'm not going to change unless others do.' Yet another reaction could be: 'Nothing that I do, as a single individual, will make any difference.' Or else he could say, 'I'll get round to it sometime', because one shouldn't underestimate the sheer force of habit. I would suggest that even the most sophisticated and determined environmentalist struggles with the fact that, under the shadow of future cataclysm, there is a life to be lived within the constraints of the here-and-now.

Politicians have woken up to the scale and urgency of the problem and many countries have recently introduced ambitious climate change policies. Over the past few years, a threshold has been crossed: most political leaders are now aware of the hazards posed by global warming and the need to respond to them. Yet this is just the first wave – the bringing of the issue onto the political agenda. The second wave must involve embedding it in our institutions and in the everyday concerns of citizens, and here, for reasons just mentioned, there is a great deal of work to do. The international community is on board, at least in principle. Negotiations aimed at limiting global warming have taken place at meetings organized by the United Nations, in an attempt to get global reductions in greenhouse gas emissions. They are still continuing, but have produced little in the way of concrete results so far. There has been far more talk than there has been tangible action.

Much of this book concentrates on climate change policy in the industrial countries. It is these countries that pumped most of the emissions into the atmosphere in the first place, and they have to take prime responsibility for controlling them in the near future. They must take the lead in reducing emissions, moving towards a low-carbon economy and making the social reforms with which these changes will have to be integrated.

We do not as yet have a developed analysis of the political innovations that have to be made if our aspirations to limit global warming are to become real. It is a strange and indefensible absence, which I have written this work to try to repair. My approach is grounded in realism. Some authors say that coping with climate change is too difficult a problem to be dealt with within the confines of orthodox politics. Up to a point I agree with them, since quite profound changes will be required in our established ways of political thinking. Yet we have to work with the institutions that already exist and in ways that respect democracy.

The state will be an all-important actor, since so many powers remain in its hands, whether one talks of domestic or of international policy. There is no way of forcing states to sign up to international agreements; and even if they choose to do so, implementing whatever is agreed will largely be the responsibility of each individual country. Emissions trading markets can only work if the price of carbon is capped, and at a demanding level, a decision that has to be made and implemented politically. The one major supra-national entity that exists, the European Union, is heavily dependent on decisions taken by its member nations, since its control over them is quite limited.

Markets have a much bigger role to play in combating climate change than simply in the area of emissions trading. There are many fields where market forces can produce results that no other agency or framework could manage. In principle, where a price can be put on an environmental good without affronting other values, it should be done, since competition will then create increased efficiency whenever that good is exchanged. However, active state intervention is once again called for. The environmental costs entailed by economic processes often form what economists call 'externalities' – they are not paid for by those who incur them. The aim of public policy should be to make sure that, wherever possible, such costs are internalized – that is, brought into the marketplace.

'The state', of course, comprises a diversity of levels, including regional, city and local government. In a global era, it operates within the context of what political scientists call multilayered governance, stretching upwards into the international arena and downwards to regions, cities and localities. To emphasize the importance of the state to climate change policy is not to argue for top-down government. On the contrary, the most dramatic initiatives are likely to bubble up from the actions of far-sighted individuals and from the energy of civil society. States will have to work with a variety of other agencies and bodies, as well as with other countries and international organizations, if they are to be effective.

One can't discuss the politics of climate change without mentioning the green movement, which has been a leading influence on environmental politics for many years. It has had a major impact in forcing the issue of climate change onto the political agenda. 'Going green' has become more or less synonymous with endeavours to limit climate change. Yet there are big problems. The green movement has its origins in the hostile emotions that industrialism aroused among the early conservationists. Especially in its latter-day development in Germany in the 1970s and 1980s, the greens defined themselves in opposition to orthodox politics. Neither position is especially helpful to the task of integrating environmental concerns into our established political institutions. Most green parties have now joined the mainstream. Yet just what is and what is not valuable in green political philosophies has to be sorted out.

It isn't possible – or so I shall argue – to endorse any approach which tries in some sense to 'return to nature'. Conservationism may be a defensible value, but it has nothing intrinsically to do with combating global warming. Indeed, it may even hamper our efforts. As a result of the advance of science and technology, we have long since crossed the boundaries which used to separate us from the natural world. More of the same will be needed, not less, if we are seriously to confront problems of climate change. Partly for this reason, I reject one of the core ideas of the green movement – the precautionary principle: 'Don't interfere with nature.' Moreover, in seeking to stem climate change, no matter what is often said, we are not trying to 'save the planet', which will survive whatever we may do. The point is to preserve, and if possible enhance, a decent way of life for human beings on the earth.

The word 'green' is in such widespread use that I have no hope of dislodging it. But it is now more of a problem rather than any help when it comes to developing policies to cope with climate change. I shall avoid using the term in what follows.

A whole range of questions has to be asked and answered. I list only a few briefly here. Later in the book, I try to respond to all of them, no doubt with varying degrees of success.

To cope with global warming, a long-term perspective must be introduced into politics, domestically and internationally. There has to be some sort of forward *planning*. 'Planning' is not a word with particularly pleasant connotations, since it conjures up images of authoritarianism on the one hand and ineptness on the other. Planning fell out of favour partly because it was oppressive and partly because it didn't work. If there is to be a return to such an endeavour, what form should it take?

And then there is the issue of coping with *risk* and *uncertainty*. Climate change politics is all about risk and how to manage it, and the notion appears on almost every page of this volume. We can't know the future; the philosopher Karl Popper used to say that if we could, it wouldn't be the future. The long-term thinking needed to counter climate change has to operate against the backdrop of uncertainty. It is often possible to assign probabilities to future events; but there are many contexts where existing knowledge is stretched thin and large areas of uncertainty loom. What political strategies are needed to confront this range of problems?

In democratic countries governments come and go. Moreover, in real-life contexts many issues jostle for attention, including immediate questions of the day, which at the time may seem overwhelmingly important. In such circumstances, how is continuity of climate change policy to be maintained? Climate change, I shall argue, is not a left–right issue. There should be no more talk of 'green being the new red'. A cross-party framework of some kind has to be forged to develop a politics of the long term, but how? Countering climate change will cost money – where will it come from? Countries that are in the vanguard of climate change policy, as the developed countries have to be, could face problems of competitiveness. Their industries could be hampered by having to compete with goods that can be made more cheaply elsewhere where there are no environmental taxes or regulatory restrictions. How big a problem is this likely to be? Certainly, many business firms and employers' groups have used it as a basis for dragging their heels as far as climate change initiatives are concerned.

Finally, there are many difficult questions surrounding technology. Investment in renewable energy resources is crucial in countering climate change. Yet those resources won't develop in some sort of automatic way, nor will they be stimulated by the operation of market forces alone. The state has to subsidize them, in order for them to be competitive against fossil fuels and to protect investment in the face of the fluctuations to which the prices of oil and natural gas are subject. Technological change can only be predicted to a limited degree. How should governments decide which technologies to back? Like climate change, energy has suddenly come into the limelight as a fundamental problem for many nations and for the world as a whole. The underlying causes are to some degree the same. The energy needs of the industrial countries have created most of the emissions that are causing global warming. The rapid economic growth of developing nations, especially China and India, given their immense population size, is putting further strain on available energy sources, as well as increasing the level of greenhouse gases in the atmosphere. Responding to climate change has to be closely integrated with questions of energy security. It has become conventional to say so these days, but I have been struck by how loosely connected in most writings they actually are.

At what point will the world begin to run out of oil? There is intense discussion about when world oil and gas supplies will peak – in other words, when half or more of them will have been consumed. If the peak in world oil supplies is in fact approaching, then serious problems loom. Modern society is very heavily based upon oil not only insofar as energy is concerned, but also because oil figures in so many of the manufactured goods which figure in people's lives. Some 90 per cent of the goods in the shops involve the use of oil in one way or another.

Whether oil production is close to peaking or not, we are living in a civilization that, as far as we can determine future risk, looks unsustainable. It isn't surprising that the past few years have seen the emergence of a doomsday litera-ture, centred on the likelihood of a cataclysmic breakdown. Other civilizations have come and gone; why should ours be sacrosanct?

Yet risk is risk – the other side of danger is always opportu-nity. We must create a positive model of a low-carbon future – and, moreover, one that connects with ordinary, everyday life in the present. There is no such model at the moment and we have to edge our way towards it. It won't be a green vision, but one driven by political, social and economic thinking. It can't be a utopia, but utopian strands will be involved, since they supply ideals to be striven for. A mixture of the idealistic and the hard-headed is required. No quick fix is available to deal with the problems we face – it's going to be a slog, even with the breakthroughs we need, and in fact must have. The prize, as I shall argue below, is huge. There is another world waiting for us out there if we can find our way to it. It is one where not only climate change has been held at bay, but where oil has lost its capacity to determine the shape of world politics.

Where do we stand at the moment in terms of the risks posed by global warming? What are our chances of limiting or containing them? A great deal hangs, of course, upon our assessment of just how serious those risks actually are. Here we are dependent on the findings, and the prognostications, of science. Perhaps the risks have been exaggerated and we haven't got too much to worry about? Could the sceptics be right to say the dangers are much less than the majority of climatologists believe? The possibility does exist, but it is slim. The scientific findings are very robust, and based on many different types of observation. Moreover, as I shall discuss in what follows, it is at least as likely that the dangers of climate change are actually *greater* than the majority of scientists think. Unlike most of the sceptics, disturbingly, those who make such arguments are practising scientists – some of them very eminent ones.

Containing climate change is quintessentially an issue that we cannot put off – and yet at the moment we are doing just that. The volume of greenhouse gases going into the atmosphere continues to mount. Since current trends are out of kilter with what is needed if we are to bring emissions under control, we are essentially looking for breakthroughs. Where might they occur?

They could happen at the *international level*. The role of leaders is to lead, and where necessary to be well ahead of most of the citizens they serve. There are at least some encouraging signs. Until recently, the leaders of the developing countries argued that reducing emissions should be solely a concern of the industrial states, which got rich on the basis of the indiscriminate use of fossil fuels. That attitude has now changed rather dramatically. It is still incumbent on the developed countries to accept the main responsibility. However, the leaders of some of the large emerging economies, most notably China and Brazil, now accept that their countries have a key role to play. It is possible that in some ways they could come to be in the vanguard, as China already is in terms of investment in certain areas of renewable technology.

There might be breakthroughs in the *economic conditions affecting low-carbon technologies*, hence transforming the energy field. The Middle East is the site of about a third of the world's recoverable oil. For a century or so, Western, and then more specifically American, power maintained a certain stability in the otherwise volatile region – and protected the flow of oil. The price of oil never remotely reflected the true economic cost of keeping that flow going – billions of dollars were spent on sustaining that military and diplomatic presence. That situation is currently unravelling, hopefully as part of a process of the democratization of countries that had become frozen in time. The price of oil could rise, and stay high, whether through protracted instability in the region, or other factors. Such an outcome could possibly give a dramatic new impetus to concerns about energy security, and hence to much greater investment in renewable technologies.

There could be breakthrough innovations in various areas of *technology*. Technological innovation, at least of a far-reaching kind, is not itself always, perhaps not even usually, predictable. The history of technology shows that most transformative innovations came out of the side-field. Their inventors initially had no idea of the impact they came to have – this was true of the cluster of innovations that created the internet, for example. So innovation relevant to climate change policy could come from anywhere, and be of a form that no one has even thought of as yet. Short of that, there are some areas where it is known that advances could make a major impact. For instance, if it became possible to store electricity cheaply and on a large scale, it would make an enormous difference, given the intermittent nature of some low-carbon energy sources. If nuclear fusion suddenly became a reality, it could provide endless cheap, renewable energy. A further possibility is so-called geo-engineering, above all discovering some way of removing greenhouse gases from the atmosphere on a large scale.

There could be an event, or set of events, clearly attributable to climate change, that cause a surge in *activism* around the world. These might be weather episodes which, while falling short of the cataclysmic, stimulate a breakthrough in consciousness. It is hard to think how such a scenario could avoid Giddens's paradox; but it is possible that unusual and extreme weather in a particular region could become a driving force of activism there, which could then spread elsewhere.

Finally, these possibilities could combine in various ways. Could, could, could – the 'coulds' indicate the open nature of the future, but no amount of 'could happens' necessarily add up to a 'will happen'. In the meantime, humanity lives in the shadow of risks that are real, unprecedented and all the more dangerous because the changes they signal appear irrevocable. Chapter 1 looks at these risks in more detail.

I

CLIMATE CHANGE, RISK AND DANGER

Our understanding of the origins of global warming in current times dates back to the work of the French scientist Jean-Baptiste Joseph Fourier in the early part of the nineteenth century. Energy reaches the earth from the sun in the shape of sunlight; it is absorbed and is radiated back into space as infra-red glow. When Fourier calculated the differential between the energy coming in and that going out as infrared radiation, he found that the planet should, in theory, be frozen. He concluded that the atmosphere acts like a mantle, keeping a proportion of the heat in – and thus making the planet liveable for humans, animals and plant life. Fourier speculated that carbon dioxide (CO_2) could act as a blanket in the atmosphere, trapping heat and causing surface temperatures to increase.

Later observers, most notably John Tyndall, a scientist working at the Royal Institution in London, worked out just which atmospheric elements trap infrared. The gases that make up most of the atmosphere, nitrogen and oxygen, offer no barrier to heat loss. Those producing what came to be called the greenhouse effect, such as water vapour, CO_2 or methane, are only present in relatively small amounts. Scientists use the calculation of 'parts per million' (ppm) to measure the level of greenhouse gases in the air, since the percentage figures are so small. One ppm is equivalent to 0.0001 per cent. It is because a tiny proportion makes such a large impact that greenhouse gases created by human industry can have profound effects on the climate (CO_2 makes up less than 0.04 per cent of the composition of the air, and the other greenhouse gases even less). Since CO_2 is the most important greenhouse gas in terms of volume, it is sometimes used as a standard of measurement when assessing emissions. The notion of 'CO_2 equivalent' is also often employed. It is the amount of CO_2 emission that would be involved to produce the same output as all the greenhouse gases combined. It is usually written as CO_2e.

Over the past 150 years or so, greenhouse gases in the atmosphere have progressively increased with the expansion of industrial production. The average world temperature has grown by about 0.8 degrees since 1901. The temperature of the earth is not only rising, it is doing so at an accelerating rate. From 1880 to 1970, global average temperature increased by about 0.03°C every decade. Over the period since 1970, the increase has averaged 0.13 degrees per decade. Data released by the National Oceanic and Atmospheric Administration of the US (NOAA) showed that 2010 tied with 2005 as the warmest year since reliable records began in 1880. Every decade since 1950 has been warmer on average than the one before.

We know from geological studies that world temperatures have fluctuated in the past, and that such fluctuations correlate with CO_2 content in the air. The evidence shows, however, that at no time during the past 650,000 years has the CO_2 content of the air been as high as it is today. It has always been below 290ppm. By 2010, it had reached 389ppm and is currently rising by some 2ppm each year.

The growth rate for 2010 was 2.14ppm, as measured by scientists at the Mauna Loa observatory in Hawaii. It was the seventh year out of the previous nine to see a rise of more than 2ppm. This increase was considerably higher than scientists at the observatory had expected. It could indicate that the natural sinks of the earth are losing their capacity to absorb greenhouse gases. Most climate change models assume that some half of future emissions will be soaked up by forests and oceans, but this assumption therefore may be too optimistic. Warming is greater over land areas than over the oceans, and is higher at northern latitudes than

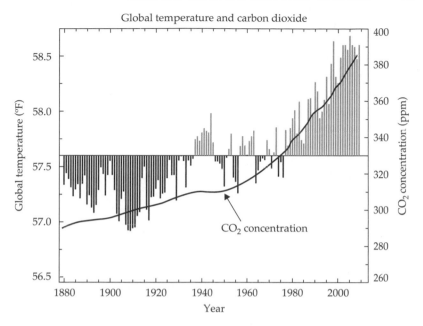

Figure 1.1 The global surface temperature is rising
Global annual average temperature measured over land and oceans. Grey bars indicate temperatures above and black bars indicate temperatures below the 1901–2000 average temperature. The black line shows atmospheric carbon dioxide concentration in parts per million.

Source: NCDC/NOAA

elsewhere. Very recent studies show that the temperatures of the oceans are rising several times faster than was thought likely a few years ago. Higher temperatures produce more acidity in the water, which could seriously threaten marine life. Warmer seas release more CO_2, accelerating the global warming effect.

Satellite data, available since 1978, show that the annual average Arctic sea ice coverage is shrinking by nearly 3 per cent per decade, with larger decreases in the summer of over 7 per cent. The Arctic ice-cap is less than half the size it was 50 years ago. Over that time, average temperatures in the Arctic region have increased by about seven degrees, a result of a specific feedback cycle that exists there. The sun's rays strike the Arctic at a sharper angle than elsewhere over the summer, at a time when the ice is giving way to open water, which

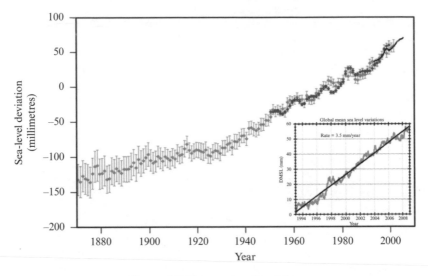

Figure 1.2 The sea level is rising
Annual averages of global sea level. Light grey: sea level since 1870. Dark
grey: tide gauge data. Black: based on satellite observations. The inset
shows global mean sea-level rise since 1993 – a period over which sea-level
rise has accelerated.

Source: NCDC/NOAA

absorbs more solar radiation. Until recently it was thought
that ice-free Arctic summers would occur at some point near
the end of the century. However, the actual melting has been
faster than was anticipated and appears to be accelerating.
Hence summers free of ice might occur much sooner.

Commercial trans-Arctic voyages could then be initiated. It
would be possible to go from Northern Europe to East Asia or
the north-west coast of the US avoiding the Suez and Panama
Canals.

Mountain glaciers are retreating in both hemispheres and
snow cover is less, on average, than it once was. Sea levels rose
over the course of the twentieth century, although there is considerable controversy among scientists about just how much.
Warming is likely to intensify the risk of drought in some parts
of the world and lead to increased rainfall in others. Evidence
indicates that the atmosphere holds more water vapour than
used to be the case even a few decades ago – a major influence
over unstable weather patterns, including tropical storms and

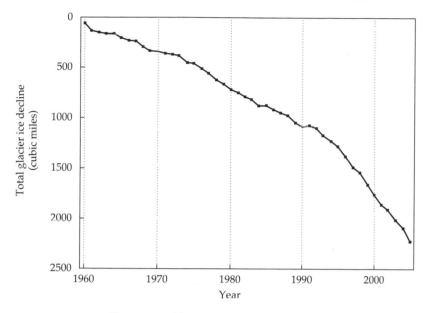

Figure 1.3 Glacier volume is shrinking
Cumulative decline (in cubic miles) in glacier ice worldwide.

Source: NCDC/NOAA

floods. Over the past 40 years, westerly winds have become stronger. Tropical cyclones in the Atlantic have become more frequent and more intense over that period, probably as a result of warming.

The most authoritative body monitoring climate change and its implications is the Intergovernmental Panel on Climate Change of the UN (IPCC), first established in 1988. Hundreds of scientists and reviewers are involved in its major publications; few scientific documents ever can have been subjected to such exhaustive scrutiny. The IPCC has had an enormous impact upon world thinking about global warming. Its declared aims are to gather together as much scientific data about climatic conditions as possible, subject it to rigorous review and reach overall conclusions on the state of scientific opinion. In several authoritative reports, it has mapped the changing world climate in detail, showing that the potential consequences range from the worrying to the disastrous. In the fourth of such reports, published in 2007, the IPCC says, 'warming of the climate

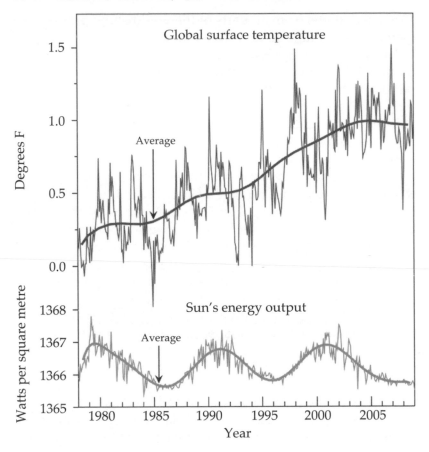

Figure 1.4 Energy from the sun has not increased
Global surface temperature (top, dark grey) and the sun's energy received
at the top of the earth's atmosphere (bottom, light grey). Solar energy has
been measured by satellites since 1978.

Source: NCDC/NOAA

system is unequivocal'. It is the only part of the document
where such a term is used. All the rest is couched in terms of
probabilities. There is a '90 per cent probability' that observed
warming is the result of human activity through the introduction of greenhouse gases into the atmosphere, these coming
from the consumption of fossil fuels in industrial production
and travel, and from new forms of land use and agriculture.[1]
Records of global surface temperature date back to 1850. Since
that date, 11 of the hottest years have occurred during the past

13. Observations from all parts of the world show progressive increases in average air and sea temperatures.

The IPCC assesses the implications of climate change in terms of a number of different possible scenarios for the period up to the end of the current century. There are six different scenario groups – in other words, future possibilities – depending upon factors such as levels of economic growth, resource scarcities, population increase, the expansion of low-carbon technologies and the intensifying of regional inequalities. Under the most favourable scenario, global warming will still occur, within a range of between 1.1 and 2.9°C. Sea levels will rise between 18 and 38 centimetres by the end of the century. If, on the other hand, the world continues to run, as is the case now, on oil, gas and coal, and to strive for high levels of economic growth, world temperatures could increase by more than 6°C by 2100. In these circumstances, the sea level might rise by between 26 and 50 centimetres.

The 'most probable' scenario distinguished by the IPCC, in which fossil fuels are quite widely used, but are balanced by cleaner forms of energy generation, and where population growth is brought under control, is still worrying. In this scenario, temperatures could rise by more than 4°C, with an increase of 48 centimetres in sea levels. There would probably be a decrease in rainfall of 20 per cent in sub-tropical areas, while more rain would fall in the northern and southern latitudes.

The IPCC and the European Commission have both stated that the aim of emissions control policy should be to limit global warming to an average of 2°C, and that to have even a 50:50 chance of achieving this outcome, atmospheric concentrations of greenhouse gases must be stabilized at 450 CO_2e. However, given the existing build-up of emissions, some regard this target as already impossible to achieve.

The effects of climate change are almost certainly already being felt. The 2007 report of the IPCC states that we can assert with 'High Confidence' (an 8 in 10 chance or above of being correct) that global warming has led to more and larger glacial lakes, faster rates of melting in permafrost areas in Western Siberia and elsewhere, changes in some Arctic and Antarctic ecosystems, increased and earlier run-off from glacier and snow-fed rivers, earlier springtimes in northern areas and a movement of some plant and animal species towards the poles.[2]

The IPCC says that resource-based wars could dominate the current century; coastal cities could become flooded, provoking mass destitution and mass migration, and the same could happen as drier areas become more arid. Given their location and lack of resources, the poorer parts of the world will be more seriously affected than the developed countries. Yet the latter will have their share of problems, including more and more episodes of violent weather. The United States, for example, has greater extremes of weather than most other parts of the world and these are likely to intensify further.

The sceptics and their critics

Scenarios are about future possibilities, so it is not surprising that there are those who question them, or who object to the very thesis that current processes of global warming are produced by human activity at all. Since the sceptics are in a minority, they see themselves not only as questioning a broad scientific consensus, but as tilting against a whole industry that has grown up around it.

Fred Singer and Dennis Avery, for example, advance the thesis that 'modern warming is moderate and not man-made'.[3] Their view, they complain, does not get much of a hearing, because of the attention that surrounds the claims made by the IPCC. 'A public relations campaign of staggering dimensions', they say, 'is being carried forward to convince us that global warming is man-made and a crisis . . . environmental advocacy groups, government agencies, and even the media have spared no expense in spreading [the] dire message.'[4]

For them, there is nothing new about the increasing temperatures observed today. The world's climate has always been in flux. A moderate but irregular 1,500-year climate change cycle, driven by shifts in sun-spot variations, is well documented by the work of geologists. We are in the warming phase of just such a cycle at the moment. The chief worry we should have for the long-term future is, in fact, a coming ice age, as our relatively mild period draws to a close.

Other climate change sceptics take a somewhat different tack, while also emphasizing that heretical views don't get much of a hearing, let alone research funding. Patrick Michaels, for instance, claims that the findings and projections of the IPCC are intrinsically flawed.[5] Too many individuals and groups, he says, have a stake in predicting disasters and cataclysms to come. Only about a third of those producing the IPCC documentation are in fact scientists; the majority are government bureaucrats. Facts and findings that don't fit the main storyline are suppressed or ignored.

The Danish author Bjørn Lomborg is often lumped with the sceptics, and indeed entitled his first book on climate change *The Skeptical Environmentalist*.[6] His is an unusual form of scepticism, however. He accepts that global warming is happening and that human activity has brought it about. What is much more debatable, he says, 'is whether hysteria and headlong spending on extravagant CO_2-cutting programmes at an unprecedented price is the only possible response'.[7] Lomborg questions the idea that climate change risks must inevitably take precedence over all others. For the moment, world poverty, the spread of AIDS and nuclear weapons pose greater problems.

The arguments upon which Lomborg builds his case have been examined by Howard Friel, in his book *The Lomborg Deception*. Friel looks at Lomborg's book citation by citation and finds it seriously wanting. Lomborg's main thesis (echoed by some others of the more moderate sceptics) is that climate change 'will not pose a devastating problem for our future'.[8] Friel documents how selective are the materials Lomborg cites, as are his interpretations of them.[9] Presumably partly in response to such critiques, Lomborg has modified his earlier position, or appears to have done so. In a book published in 2010 he says that 'we all need to start seriously focussing, right now, on the most effective ways to fix global warming'.[10]

Other authors, writing about risk more generally rather than only about global warming, have suggested that we live in an 'age of scares', of which climate change is one. Our worries and anxieties, as Christopher Booker and Richard North put it, mark the emergence of a 'new age of superstition', resembling episodes of mass hysteria in the past, such as the witch-hunts of the post-mediaeval period. Scares, nearly all of which have turned out to be unfounded, have become part of our everyday lives, 'from mysterious and deadly new viruses and bacteria in our food, or floating about in the environment, to toxic substances in our homes and workplaces; all culminating in the ultimate apocalyptic visions conjured up by the fear of global warming'.[11]

Should one pay any attention to what the sceptics say, given that they are a small, albeit vocal, minority? Many scientists believe their writings are irresponsible, since they convey to the public that there is extensive space for doubt about the origins, and probable consequences, of warming, when in fact there is little. There was a furore when the UK's TV Channel 4 produced a documentary in March 2007 called *The Great Global Warming Swindle*, which featured several of the most prominent sceptics.

Yet the sceptics do deserve and must receive a hearing. Scepticism is the life-blood of science and just as important in policy-making. It is right that whatever claims are made about climate change and its consequences are examined with a critical, even hostile, eye and in a continuing fashion. There is no doubt that 'big science' can attain a momentum of its own. The IPCC is not simply a scientific body, but a political and bureaucratic one. The sceptics are right to say that in the media, and sometimes in the speeches of politicians, climate change is now often invoked as though it explains every weather episode: 'Whenever there was any kind of unusual weather event, heat-waves, storms, droughts or floods, some broadcaster could be relied upon to describe it as "further confirmation of climate change".'[12]

However, the sceptics do not have a monopoly on critical scrutiny. Critical self-examination is the obligation of every scientist and researcher. The fact that the findings of the IPCC are almost always expressed in terms of probabilities and possibilities gives due recognition to the many uncertainties that exist, as well as gaps in our knowledge. Moreover, the scientists contributing research findings to the IPCC have differences among themselves about the progression of global warming and its likely consequences.

The 'climate wars'

The conflicting views of the sceptics and the mainstream scientific community reached a new level of intensity when emails emanating from the University of East Anglia's Climatic Research Unit (CRU) in November 2009 were hacked and their contents made public.[13] More than 1,000 emails passing between a group of climate researchers working in the UK and the US were leaked in this way. The emails were released only a short while before the UN meetings at Copenhagen, at which world leaders gathered to try to reach agreements on curbing carbon emissions (see below, pp. 185–95). It is not known who hacked into the scientists' computers, or why, but the timing strongly suggests that the endeavour was an attempt to undermine the summit by casting doubt upon the scientific findings underlying it.

To the sceptics, the emails showed that the scientists in question were deliberately manipulating their data to bolster their thesis that humanly induced climate change is occurring. The scientists also seemed to be reluctant to make public the full range of research findings on which their claims were based. In addition, the critics argued, they sought to manipulate the peer review process so as to block the publication of papers critical of their work.

The whole episode received a great deal of attention in the media across the world. Two of the scientists concerned, Professor Philip Jones of the CRU and Michael Mann of Pennsylvania State University in the US, found themselves at the centre of the storm of controversy thus provoked. In both cases, the universities involved were swamped with emails, phone calls and letters accusing the scientists of deception and even fraud.

Each was subject to several investigations. Professor Jones appeared before three such inquiries – the House of Commons Science Select Committee; a committee of inquiry chaired by the scientist Lord Oxburgh; and a tribunal set up by the University of East Anglia. Pennsylvania State University established an investigatory committee to examine the conduct of Professor Mann.

All the inquiries exonerated the scientists from any substantial misconduct. The University of East Anglia report underlined the 'rigour and honesty' of the scientists. The investigatory committee in the US concluded that Professor Mann 'did not engage in . . . any actions that seriously deviated from accepted practices within the academic community for proposing, conducting, or reporting research, or other scholarly activities'.[14]

The scientists didn't escape all censure. The Pennsylvania inquiry commented, for example, that it was 'careless and inappropriate' of Professor Mann to share unpublished manuscripts with third parties without having received permission from the authors of those manuscripts to do so. The East Anglia report criticized Professor Jones and his colleagues for insufficient openness in response to requests for their data sources. The report also made the observation that, in the age of the internet and legislation about freedom of information, there is a 'transformation in the need for openness in the culture of publicly funded science'.

Jones and Mann were among the many scientists contributing to the work that produced the publications of the IPCC. Independently of the affair of the emails, but overlapping in time, the IPCC also became embroiled in controversy. Two errors came to light in the 2007 IPCC report on the progression of, and dangers represented by, humanly induced climate change. It was stated that the glaciers in the Himalayas might disappear by 2035. In another place the claim appears that 55 per cent of the Netherlands lies below sea level, and hence is particularly susceptible to flooding if and when overall sea levels rise across the world.

In fact, were the Himalayan glaciers to vanish by 2035, they would have to melt 25 times faster than currently is the case. In the case of the Netherlands, the report should have read that 55 per cent of the country is prone to flooding – 26 per cent of the country is at risk because it lies below sea level, while a further 29 per cent is at risk of being vulnerable to river flooding.

Partly because the discovery of the mistakes coincided with the debate over the leaked emails, they also provoked something of a furore, and were very widely reported. To many of the sceptics, they confirmed suspicions about the lack of objectivity in the IPCC procedures – in spite of the fact that these were isolated errors in a very large and detailed volume.

The Netherlands Environmental Assessment Agency launched an investigation into the 2007 IPCC report in order to see if further questionable statements could be unearthed. The Agency found nothing that would place in question the main conclusions drawn by the IPCC. The IPCC methods and findings were found to be 'robust' and 'well-founded'. The inquiry noted, however, that the summaries in the IPCC report 'tended to single out the most important negative aspects of climate change'. For instance, the possibly positive implications of climate change for forestry in North Asia are indicated in the body of a chapter, but are not referred to in the summary that appears at the end. The investigators concluded that more could be done in future IPCC publications to heighten transparency and clarity as to how the experts had reached their specific judgements and assessed different risk scenarios.

It seems unlikely that the IPCC procedures will remain intact – not because of the errors or other problems that have come to light, but because of their cumbersome and slow-moving character. The IPCC's vast reports appear about every six years. For the 2007 volume, governments and reviewers submitted some 90,000 comments on the draft text, all of which had to be assessed by the expert panels. Some scientists have called for shorter reports, to be produced more frequently, and which would therefore be more able to keep abreast of the flow of new research and data. Others have proposed a review process based upon Wikipedia, allowing free access to data. Yet it is difficult to see how entries could be scrutinized and monitored for reliability or accuracy.

Since the episode of the leaked emails, not just Jones and Mann, but other prominent climate scientists too have received emails and other communications threatening them and their families.[15] In a television interview, Michael Mann described the following as typical of some of the emails he had been receiving: 'Six feet under with the roots is where you should be. I was hoping I would see the news that you'd committed suicide. Do it, freak.' Jones received many death threats, as well as other highly aggressive emails, and at one point he felt so much under attack that he contemplated killing himself. A well-known climate scientist based at Stanford University, in California, stated that he received 'hundreds' of abusive emails when the debate about the leaks was at its height. Together with other climate scientists, his name figured on a neo-Nazi website where threats were made against them because of their Jewish ancestry. Clive Hamilton has described comparable hate mail received by climate scientists in Australia.[16]

In response to such attacks, groups of climate scientists have published statements affirming the need to defend science and the scientific method. In Britain, scientists from 121 universities and scientific institutions signed a statement 'from the UK science community'. It stated that they 'have the utmost confidence in the observational evidence for global warming and the scientific basis for concluding that it is due primarily to human activities'. 'The evidence and the science', they continued, 'are deep and extensive . . . coming from decades of painstaking and meticulous research, by many thousands of scientists across the world who adhere to the highest standards of professional integrity.'[17]

A similar statement was put out by members of the US National Academy of Sciences. It declared:

> We are deeply disturbed by the recent escalation of political assaults on scientists in general and climate scientists in particular . . . Many recent assaults on climate science . . . are typically driven by special interests or dogma, not by an honest effort to provide an alternative theory that credibly satisfies the evidence. . . . There is compelling, comprehensive, and consistent objective evidence that humans are changing the climate in ways that threaten our societies and the ecosystems on which we depend.[18]

The activities of at least some of the sceptics have been not only funded, but directly organized, by special interest groups. The author of one study of such groups says that, although they knew of these links before they started their research, they never expected to uncover, as they did, a campaign so 'huge, well-funded and well-organised'.[19] Several of the large oil and coal companies have been directly involved, as well as a range of other corporations and political groups. Their concerns have not been to promote open and rational debate, but to exploit uncertainties surrounding the dangers posed by climate change to create the impression that the scientific evidence is far more suspect than it actually is.

Scepticism, to repeat, is essential to the scientific method, and there are some sceptics who are prepared to submit their work and their claims to the same rigorous process of examination by critics that they (rightly) demand of the mainstream scientific community. The trouble is that the majority are not, setting up a clear double standard. Attacks on science, or individual scientists, cannot only become quite vicious, but proceed in quite another dimension from that of science as such.

The internet has a problematic and complex role in all this. On the one hand, it is a driving force for openness and transparency. Climate scientists will have to get used to making their data, and the grounds for the conclusions they draw, available for public scrutiny. In principle, the cause of science is advanced by such a process. Yet the internet also creates a world where anyone can be an 'expert', without having to master the canons of professional expertise – and can command a large following, as well as influencing public opinion.

It is worth drawing a distinction between those climate change sceptics who are in the business of ensuring the scrupulousness of science and policy-making based upon it, and those who merit the name of deniers. Martin McKee identifies six tactics which deniers use:

1 Portray a consensus as a conspiracy, alleging that agreement between scientists comes not from evidence, but from collusion and manipulation.
2 Deploy pseudo-experts to support this contention – people with sufficient credentials to create a façade of plausibility, even if they may have no real credentials in the field in question.

3 Pick and deploy evidence selectively, concentrating on whatever seems to support the case being made, ignoring or rubbishing other findings. Continue trotting out your own 'evidence', even after it has been discredited.

4 Set completely different or even impossible standards for your opponents from those you yourself follow. If the opponent comes up with the evidence demanded, move the goalposts.

5 Deliberately misrepresent the scientific consensus and then demolish the straw man that has been created.

6 Repackage scientific uncertainty as doubt. Falsely portray scientists as divided when they are not, insist that 'both sides' must be given equal play and make claims of censorship if 'dissenting' arguments are rejected.[20]

The radicals

Risk and uncertainty cut two ways. The sceptics say the risks are exaggerated, or even non-existent, but it is quite possible to make the opposite case. There are some who say we have underestimated both the extent and the imminence of the dangers posed by climate change. They argue that the IPCC is in fact something of a conservative organization, which is reserved in its judgements exactly because it has to cover a wide constituency of scientific opinion and because of its bureaucratic nature.

Fred Pearce, a writer for the *New Scientist*, says that the world's climate does not go in for gradual change, as the past history of climatic variation shows. The climate (as the sceptics also argue) has undergone all sorts of changes in the past, long before human beings appeared on the scene and well before the advent of modern industrial production. However, Pearce draws quite a different conclusion from this observation to that of the sceptics. Transitions from one climatic condition to another are often very abrupt, and climate change in our era, he argues, will probably be the same. We can make a distinction, he says, between Type 1 and Type 2 processes of climate change. Type 1 changes evolve slowly and follow the trajectories outlined in most of the scenarios of the IPCC. Type 2 change is radical and sharp – it comes about when a tipping point is reached, which triggers a sudden lurch from one type of system to another. Such change does not form part of the usual models for calculating climate change risk.[21]

The potential for Type 2 change today, Pearce says, is large. Some areas that were widely thought to be stable may in fact be dynamic and volatile – they include the ice sheets covering Greenland and Antarctica, the frozen peat bogs in Western Siberia, the Amazon rainforest and the weather pattern known as El Niño.

The IPCC has suggested that, should the world warm any more than 3°C, the Greenland ice pack could start to melt, a process which, once it gets under way, would be impossible to reverse. According to the IPCC this possibility is one for the distant future. Some specialists in glacial studies, however, as Pearce points out, warn that such a process could happen much faster. As warming proceeds, and in conjunction with certain natural processes, lakes form at the tops of the glaciers. These set up water flows which drain down crevasses in the ice and, at the same time, widen them so that, instead of water taking many years to reach the bottom of the glaciers, it can do so almost instantaneously. The result, it is argued, might be the fracturing of large areas of ice, with profoundly destabilizing consequences. Were such effects to become generalized, large-scale melting could take place in a matter even of a decade.

The vast area of peat bog stretching from Western Siberia through northern Scandinavia, Canada and Alaska is covered by solid and seemingly permanent frost, but it has begun to thaw, a phenomenon 'that makes even the soberest scientists afraid'.[22] The Arctic permafrost holds down very large amounts of decayed vegetation, packed with carbon. As the frost melts, the leaves, roots and mosses beneath it start to decay, and release not only CO_2, but also methane. Methane is many times more potent a greenhouse gas than CO_2. One of the problems is that, so far, there have been relatively few studies of just how far these processes are advancing, largely because of difficulties of access to Siberia on the part of non-Russian scientists. One estimate is that the release of methane occurring from the West Siberian peat bogs is already equivalent to more than the greenhouse gases emitted by the United States in a single year.

And then there is El Niño, linked to the so-called 'Southern Oscillation'.[23] The term refers to unusually warm ocean conditions that can develop in the Pacific Ocean along the Western coasts of Ecuador and Peru. 'El Niño' means 'boy child' in Spanish, referring to the infant Jesus Christ. The name came from the fact that the phenomenon normally develops during the Christmas season. It happens every three to five years and can have a major effect on global climatic conditions. As El Niño moves across the world, following a path along the equator, disruptive weather follows in its wake, causing storms and heavy rainfall in some areas and droughts in others. After some 12–18 months it usually abruptly goes into reverse, causing unusually cold ocean temperatures in the equatorial Pacific, which also have disruptive effects upon weather conditions (moving this way around, it is known as La Niña).

Little is known about the long-term history of El Niño, but in recent years it has occurred more often, and with increasingly severe consequences. As with so many other climatic changes, we do not know how far global warming is playing a part. El Niño may act to moderate warming, but – at least as likely – could serve to accentuate turbulent weather conditions.

James Hansen, of the NASA Goddard Institute for Space Studies, is one of the most influential authors to argue that the dangers from advancing temperatures have been underestimated. It is a theme he has pursued for more than 20 years. He says that the goal of confining global warming to 2°C, already very difficult to achieve, is not enough to prevent the dangerous consequences. The safe level of atmospheric carbon dioxide is 350ppm – below that which already exists.[24]

In his book *Storms of My Grandchildren* Hansen talks of 'our last chance to save humanity'.[25] The earth, he points out, is the only one of the three terrestrial planets that has the right balance of circumstances for life to exist. Venus is too hot, and Mars too cold. The latter planet has so little gas in its atmosphere that there is virtually no greenhouse effect. The atmosphere of Venus has so much CO_2 in it that the greenhouse effect produces warming of several hundred degrees Celsius. At one time Venus was probably cold enough to possess significant oceans. They vanished as the surface of the planet heated up, the greenhouse effect of the water vapour serving to heighten the process of warming. Over the progress of time, a 'runaway' greenhouse situation was created, with the water vapour eventually being lost to space.

Could a runaway greenhouse effect occur on earth as a result of humanly created global warming? Yes it could, Hansen says. Recognizing that we have to be wary of computer-generated climate models, he nevertheless says they can be very useful in terms of measuring risk. The models he examines indicate how sensitive the earth is to atmospheric change – and how vulnerable it is to a runaway greenhouse effect. Until recently, Hansen says, he didn't worry too much about such a possibility, but in the face of incoming evidence he has revised his earlier views. The reason is that mechanisms that were once thought likely to moderate warming will not have time to come into effect, given the speed with which it is now happening. As Hansen puts it: 'I've come to conclude that if we burn all reserves of oil, gas and coal, there is a substantial chance we will initiate the runaway greenhouse.' If we also burn the tar sands, he goes on to add, 'I believe the Venus syndrome is a dead certainty'[26] (tar sands can be used to extract oil on the large scale, but release far more emissions in so doing than orthodox oil production).

A long way before such a cataclysmic happening materializes, and potentially in the very near future, there will begin 'a chaotic climate transition' as one or more tipping points is passed. Disintegrating in sheets, beginning in West Antarctica, will exacerbate trends already present. The 'storms of our grandchildren' will progressively intensify: 'continued unfettered burning of . . . fossil fuels will cause the climate to pass tipping points, such that we hand our children and grandchildren a dynamic situation that is out of their control'.[27]

The British scientist James Lovelock is even more sombre. We have to understand, he says, that our existence as humanity depends on the living earth. Because of our burning of fossil fuels, the earth 'is ever more at risk of changing to a barren state in which few of us can survive'.[28] 'I am not a

willing Cassandra', he says, 'and in the past have been publicly sceptical about doom stories', but he now thinks that,
without major remedial action, climate change 'may all but
eliminate people from the earth'.[29] We should not be taken
in by the slowly rising temperature curve portrayed by the
IPCC. Global warming – or, as he prefers to call it, global
heating – he accepts with Pearce is non-linear and prone
to producing sudden and dramatic change in the earth's
ecosystems.

Far from driven by 'alarmism', as the sceptics like to say,
Lovelock agrees that the IPCC is essentially a conservative
organization, precisely because of its bureaucratic character. Good science, he says, is manipulated so as to reduce its
more dangerous and problematic implications. In contrast to
Hansen, but reaching similar conclusions, Lovelock argues
that we should mistrust models. We have plenty of evidence
from direct measures of the warming of the oceans, the rising
sea levels, the melting of the glaciers and of the Arctic ice-cap
to be perfectly clear that humanly created climate change is
accelerating.

Like the sceptics – but for completely different reasons
– Lovelock is disparaging of attempts to establish international agreements to reduce carbon emissions. None of the
technologies involved, with the partial exception of nuclear
power – of which Lovelock is a great advocate – comes even
close to being able to generate the energy on which our civilization depends. In all likelihood, Lovelock thinks, the advance
of climate change will devastate large parts of the world
and render them uninhabitable. The main reason will not be
the 'storms of our grandchildren', dramatic and devastating
though these will be. Rather, the damage will be done by prolonged drought.

The combination of climate change, increasing population levels and other changes that are undermining global
ecosystems will be lethal. Some parts of the world will
remain habitable, such as the northern regions of Canada,
Scandinavia and Siberia, and some islands, even in the tropics.
But these will become like 'continental oases' and 'lifeboats',
into which humanity will be compressed. We should do all
we can to reduce carbon emissions, but concentrate mainly

on adaptation, to prepare those areas of the world likely to be least damaged by climate change 'as the safe havens for a civilised humanity'.[30]

Conclusion

What are we to make of the contrasting assessments of the risks posed by climate change offered by the sceptics on the one hand and the radicals on the other? I believe that the overriding principle is that we should stay close to the science. As mentioned in the Introduction, there is a chance that the sceptics could be right – that climate change will be relatively harmless in its consequences, or will prove the result of natural causes. However, the scientific evidence that global warming is proceeding apace, and that it is caused by the accumulation of greenhouse gases in the atmosphere, is very substantial and detailed.

Since they are not climate scientists, the majority of sceptics do not publish in peer-reviewed journals. As I have mentioned, most do not submit their own views and claims to anything like the same degree of intensive scrutiny and assessment of the evidence as do the scientists whose findings they attack. Scepticism is indeed an essential quality of science, and when so much hangs on the findings of a scientific body, those findings must be scrutinized intensively and in a continuous way. Even a scientific consensus could be flawed. Yet the 'climate wars' have made virtually no impact at all on the evidence about climate change and its dangers, which remains as well founded and convincing as it did before the episode of the leaked emails and the discovery of the errors in the IPCC report.

I am not a scientist. It is up to the scientific community to assess the ideas of the radicals and decide how much weight to attach to them. The views of the radicals should count for more than those of the sceptics, since they themselves are practising scientists. As more detailed findings continue to come in, it should be possible to judge the validity of their major claims.

One should remember that global warming is no ordinary risk. It is an awesome prospect to acknowledge that, as collective humanity, we are on the verge of altering the world's climate, perhaps in a profound manner. Previous civilizations had an impact on their environment, but those civilizations were only regional, and that impact was trivial compared to what is happening today. No earlier civilization remotely intervened into nature to the degree to which we do every day, and on a global scale.

2

RUNNING OUT, RUNNING DOWN?

Oil, gas and coal, the three dominant energy sources in the world, are all fossil fuels, producing greenhouse gases on a large scale. The industrial revolution in its country of origin, Britain, was fuelled by coal – or, more accurately, by the scientific and technological discoveries which turned coal into a dynamic energy source. The changeover from burning wood – previously the prime energy source – was not easy, since it meant a transformation of habits. By the mid-seventeenth century, wood was running out as a source of fuel; but many initially detested the sooty coal that came to replace it and which, in the end, actually helped create a whole new way of life based on cities and machine production.

The turn to coal ushered in the world we now inhabit, in which the energy of the individual citizen or worker is of trivial importance compared to that produced from inanimate resources. As Richard Heinberg has observed in relation to the US:

> If we were to add together the power of all the fuel-fed machines that we rely on to light and heat our homes, transport us, and otherwise keep us in the style to which we have become accustomed, and then compare that total with the amount of power that can be generated by the human body, we would find that each American has the equivalent of over 150 'energy slaves' working for us twenty-four hours a day.[1]

Oil has never replaced coal, but it began to mount a challenge to coal's dominance from the turn of the twentieth
century onwards. For a while, in the early part of that century,
the US was the biggest oil producer in the world and for a long
period was largely self-sufficient in oil. During much of that
time, the US was an anti-imperial power, with quite a different
philosophy from the dominant imperial formation, the British
Empire; for instance, the US opposed the Franco-British intervention in Suez in 1957, partly on strategic grounds, but also
on moral ones. Of course, these roles were later reversed, as
the US came to see the Middle East as more and more vital to
its interests. Yet it is worth restating the obvious – the history
of oil is the history of imperialism, in one guise or another.

Britain's oil derived mostly from its colonies in the Middle
East, where it set the conditions of the relationship. The
Anglo-Iranian oil company (later to become BP, aka 'Bloody
Persians', 'British Petroleum' or, under the leadership of CEO
John Browne more recently, 'Beyond Petroleum') was set up
under a one-sided arrangement of 'concessions' – a system
adopted also by US corporations. The country that needed
the oil provided the expertise and technology to locate and
extract it; the one that owned the oil was paid in terms of the
volume extracted. The colonial or ex-colonial countries thus
became 'rentier' states – income flowed into them without cor-
responding processes of economic development. Even within
the oil industry itself, expertise was rarely shared with the
host nations. These phenomena are at the origins of the much-
discussed 'curse of oil' that afflicts so many oil-based states
around the world, and to which I will return in the concluding
chapter. The often vast wealth generated by the presence of
oil and other mineral resources either is transported abroad,
or ends up in the hands of local elites. It is not accidental that
oil and gas resources are so widely concentrated in countries
which are authoritarian and corrupt.

OPEC, the Organization of the Petroleum Exporting
Countries, was set up by the producing nations to act as a
counter-balance to the influence of the oil corporations. It
was followed over the years by the widespread and progressive takeover of oil assets by state-owned companies in those
nations. OPEC was founded in 1960 and for some while there

were no major shocks affecting energy prices or world supply. However, the leaders of OPEC were outraged by the support given by the US and other Western countries to Israel in the Arab-Israeli war of 1973. Oil exports to the US, Britain and some other states were blocked, while OPEC raised the price of oil by 70 per cent, precipitating economic recession in the industrial countries.

I mention these well-known episodes because they bring home how close the connections at some points between international politics and energy security are (and will continue to be); and also because they serve as a reminder that whether or not the oil will flow does not depend upon the assessment of resources alone, but on how those resources intersect with geopolitics.

French emissions of greenhouse gases are markedly lower today than they might otherwise have been because, following the oil crisis provoked by OPEC's actions, France took the decision to become more independent of world energy markets and invested heavily in nuclear power. Japan also took note and introduced policies to regulate energy use and promote energy conservation. Today it is among the most energy-efficient of the industrial countries and is in the vanguard of clean energy technology, for instance in the car industry. Its emissions are relatively high, however, because of its dependence upon coal for electricity production. Sweden instituted a range of energy-saving policies and started to reduce its oil dependency, a process that is still continuing. Far more waste is currently recycled in Japan and Sweden than in most other industrial countries. Having no indigenous resources of its own in the 1970s, Denmark took fright and initiated measures to transfer parts of its electricity production to renewable energy sources, particularly wind power. At the same time, Brazil made the decision to invest in biofuels and now has a higher proportion of motor transport running off them than any other country, although the environmental benefits are dubious because of the deforestation involved.

The US was also obliged to react. Its responses included considering plans to invade Saudi Arabia, but also, more realistically, introducing measures to conserve energy, in the shape of the Energy Policy Conservation Act.[2] It was a significant intervention, because it showed that the wasteful energy habits of US consumers could be curbed if the impetus was strong enough. The aim of one section of the Act was to double the energy efficiency of new cars within 10 years. The target wasn't reached, but major improvements were nevertheless achieved. However, as the sense of crisis receded, fuel consumption rose again, soon to become higher per mile travelled than it had been before.

Peak oil

The debate about the limits of the world's fossil fuel resources is of great consequence for climate change policy. In 1956 the American geologist Marion King Hubbert made the now famous prediction that indigenous oil production in the US would peak in 1970 – a prediction that was widely rejected early on, but which turned out to be valid, even though the actual level of oil production was still going up in 1970. Peak oil calculations depend upon assessments of what in the oil industry is known as the 'ultimate reserves' a given country or oilfield has. It does not refer to how much oil exists, but to how much can ever be extracted – usually a much smaller amount.[3]

The controversies surrounding peak oil are as intense as those concerned with global warming, and the two debates in fact closely resemble one another. There are those who believe that there is plenty of oil and gas to go round. They do not accept that we should be worried about future sources of supply. In their view there are sufficient resources to last for a long while, even given the rising levels of economic growth of the large developing countries and even given the growing world population. David Howell and Carol Nakhle, for example, argue that there is enough of the 'known, relatively easy-to-extract stuff' to last for at least another 40 years. More reserves, they continue, are certain to be found. Under the melting ice of the Arctic, 'billions of tonnes of oil and billions of cubic metres of gas lie waiting'. New oilfields are available for exploration in Alaska, off the coast of Africa and offshore in Brazil. Even in the much-explored Middle East, a possible further cornucopia awaits.[4]

Such authors are the functional equivalents of the climate change sceptics – they are saying, 'Crisis, what crisis?' Mainstream opinion is less sanguine, or at least has become so over the past few years, and is represented by the bulk of industry analysts and the official publications of the major oil countries. It holds that there may be enough oil (and even more gas) to continue to expand levels of production for some while. However, no one knows, almost by definition, how much there is in as yet unexplored fields or what the difficulties of recovering it may be. The International Energy Agency (IEA), set up to monitor oil production after the 1970s oil embargo, predicted in 2007 that there will be no peak in oil production before 2030.[5]

Others believe that the world is rapidly approaching peak oil and that the adjustments that will have to be made by the industrial and industrializing countries, perhaps in the quite near future, are of epic proportions. As one prominent writer expresses it, we are likely to confront 'the kind of dramatic, earth-shattering crisis that periodically threatens the very survival of civilization. More specifically, it is an energy crisis brought about by the conflict between the rising global demand for energy and our growing inability to increase energy production.'[6] These words come from the investment analyst Stephen Leeb, who in the early 2000s predicted that world oil prices would reach $100 a barrel, a claim regarded by many at the time as ridiculous. Before 2008, Leeb was one of very few individuals talking of the possibility of oil prices reaching $200 a barrel or more. By the middle of that year – prior to the financial crisis – talk of such a possibility became commonplace; at the same time, it was publicly endorsed by the investment bank Goldman Sachs. Oil prices had risen to $147 a barrel by July 2008, but by December, as recession started to bite, they fell back to $40 a barrel. In 2011, oil prices went to over $150 a barrel again, as a result of events in the Middle East.

Leeb is one among a clutch of writers who hold that orthodox claims that world oil supplies will not peak for another 20 or 30 years are fundamentally mistaken.[7] The disagreements between those who write about oil production centre upon

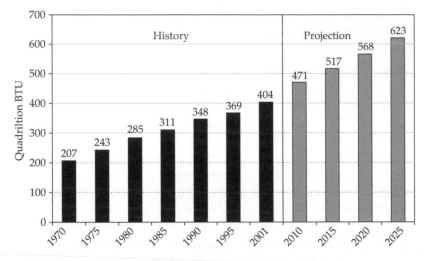

Figure 2.1 World primary energy consumption
British Thermal Unit (BTU) is a measure of energy use. It is defined as the amount of heat needed to raise the temperature of one pound of water by one degree from 60 to 61°F.

Source: Energy Information Administration

two main issues – how much recoverable oil there is in existing fields, and what the chances are of large new oil deposits being found. As in the climate change discussion, it will make a great difference to humanity's future who is right, or more nearly right.

The amount of new oil discovered each year has been declining for some while. According to David Strahan, discovery was at its highest point as long ago as 1965: 'These days, for every barrel we discover, we now consume at least three.'[8] Most of the world's biggest oilfields were identified long before that date. Of the 50 highest-producing oil countries, 18 have now passed their peak, even according to conservative estimates. If one includes the smaller producers, more than 60 oil-producing countries have done so too. Their production losses have so far been offset by growth in other areas and by improvements in extraction and processing technology.

Such authors reject the idea that big new oil and gas fields will be opened up under the Arctic or anywhere else, pointing to the extraction difficulties that will be involved. They argue that production in areas of the world outside the OPEC nations and Russia has remained static for years, in spite of successful finds in a range of countries. Russia's output growth of oil, although currently on the increase, looks likely to founder. The world will probably continue to have to look to OPEC and to the Middle East, with all its tensions and problems.

Saudi Arabia is one of the largest oil producers in the world, and has been a key state in the US's Middle Eastern policy for decades. Analysts disagree quite sharply about how large the oil reserves of the kingdom actually are. Many regard the official statements on the part of the Saudi government about the level of the reserves as either optimistic or simply false. In February 2011, Wikileaks, which has been making available many hitherto secret US diplomatic communications, published some such texts concerning Saudi oil. The texts in question urged Washington to take seriously a warning from a senior Saudi oil executive that the country's oil reserves may be overstated in official estimates by as much as 40 per cent. He said that the Saudis had exaggerated their recoverable reserves in order to sustain foreign investment, and for fear of the consequences for oil prices if the truth were made public. If he was correct, Saudi oil could peak in 2012 or shortly thereafter. Following the leaks, the executive in question denied the views attributed to him, but worries remain about whether the Saudis regularly overstate their known reserves.

The quest for new sources of oil has led to drilling not only in more and more remote places but at greater and greater depths under the sea, from floating platforms. The Deepwater Horizon platform in the Gulf of Mexico, owned by BP, was a technological wonder. Early drilling platforms were built to stand on the sea bed. However, as the drilling moved to deeper and deeper locations, the oil companies introduced 'semi-submersible' rigs, which float on the surface.

In April 2010 the rig exploded. Eleven crew members were killed and a huge volume of oil gushed into the Gulf. Government scientists estimated that over the lengthy period before the spill was finally plugged, 62,000 barrels-worth of oil were flowing per day into the ocean early on, and 53,000 barrels per day just before the closure. The authors of a study of the events argue that the episode was 'not just a tragedy, but also a challenge . . . to move to confront the reality of using ever-increasing quantities of scarce precious petroleum', and to move towards a future that will not be shackled to 'our dependence on the fast-disappearing remnants of the time when dinosaurs last roamed the earth, a good hundred million years ago'.[9]

The Deepwater Horizon rig was drilling in an area where the water was nearly a mile deep, and where the oil reservoir was a further two and a half miles below the sea-flow. To have to resort to such extreme endeavours to produce oil surely reeks of desperation, however much our current dependence on oil is prolonged by such endeavours. The US government blamed BP and its collaborators for inadequate management of Deepwater Horizon, and, looked at narrowly, it was right to do so. Yet the US is a country where no government has been willing or able to curb the country's thirst for energy.

Supposing the theorists of peak oil are right, can natural gas step into the place of oil to some degree? After all, gas produces lower emissions than either oil or coal, and can be used for at least some of the purposes to which oil is put – for instance, cars can be converted to run on compressed natural gas without too much difficulty. It is often said that world supplies of gas far outstrip those of oil; some say there is enough to last the world for some 70–80 years from now, even given growing demand. David Victor and colleagues have suggested that there will be a worldwide move towards this energy resource.[10] By 2050, they argue, gas could supplant oil to become the most important energy source in the world. According to them, there is enough gas available to last for a century at today's rates of consumption. Yet, as in almost every aspect of energy security, controversy exists here too. There is a large distance indeed between the most optimistic estimate of recoverable gas reserves (20,000 trillion cubic feet) and the lowest (8,000 trillion cubic feet). The availability of natural gas has been transformed by techniques of extracting it from shale. The impact of the technology looks to be considerable. It has attracted interest and widespread investment in the United States in particular, but also in Europe, Asia and Australia. About 6 per cent of US natural gas production now comes from shale. Some experts predict that natural gas will supply 50 per cent of the energy requirements of the US by 2020, in part because of abundant reserves of shale gas. As a transition technology, natural gas could possibly play a significant part in reducing emissions from power stations, by reducing dependence on coal. How far the actual process of extracting the gas generates unacceptably high carbon emissions remains a matter of some controversy, and will need some careful monitoring. Supporters argue its carbon footprint will be the same as orthodox natural gas, because it is more widely available locally, and will not have to be transported across very large distances. Critics say its impact on emissions is considerably greater than normal gas production.

In February 2011 a Chinese state energy company, PetroChina, paid $5.4 billion for a shale gas acquisition in Canada. The deal will allow the Chinese to derive natural gas in large quantities from the reserves, but also to acquire the know-how the country needs to exploit shale gas in China. The rationale for the bid explicitly recognizes the need for China to break away from its reliance upon coal, with its noxious consequences for carbon emissions.

It is normally assumed that, in contrast to oil and gas, one thing we can be sure of is that the world has vast supplies of coal at its disposal. By and large, such is the case; however, some are now saying that world coal supplies might be more limited than has hitherto been supposed.[11] There may have been over-reporting of coal reserves. Energy Watch, a German energy consultancy, has looked at the reserves listed by coal-producing countries and found that they have stayed the same even though those countries continued to mine extensively. For example, although China has mined 20 per cent of its coal since 1992, its listed reserves remain unchanged. Countries that have revised their figures have done so in a sharply downward direction, suggesting that improved techniques of assessment have produced more sober estimates than those made previously. Energy Watch has calculated that coal supplies may peak far earlier than is conventionally thought, perhaps as soon as 2025. Majority opinion, to repeat, is against such a conclusion. Indeed, one of the main worries about the world possibly running out of oil is that there could be an upswing in the use of coal.

Sweating the assets

Electricity generation is a major source of energy consumption and of the generation of greenhouse gases. To see what has happened in this area, we have to look first of all at the institutions and practices set up at the time when energy was cheap, because the thinking behind them now looks remarkably shallow. In the period following the Second World War, energy was the *locus classicus* of the state planning that was everywhere in vogue. Coal-mining was widely nationalized, while miners in numerous countries enjoyed an almost mythic status, partly because of the dangers of their jobs, but also because of the centrality of their work to the economy.

Partly as a hangover from the war years, security of energy supply was a core concern, to which government control was the response. The widespread turn to nuclear power in the 1950s and 1960s was also guided everywhere by the state. Many believed that this source would eventually provide energy in abundance; instead, it proved obstinately expensive and, in the public mind at least, hazardous. Apart from in one or two countries – as mentioned earlier, particularly France – the nuclear option was largely suspended. In many countries, nuclear power stations built decades ago are still in use, although they are now approaching the end of their lives.

The state took a back seat during the subsequent period of market deregulation from the 1980s onwards. From the late 1970s there was a more or less universal turn towards open competition in energy provision. Announcing the UK government's position in 1982, Secretary of State for Energy Nigel Lawson declared:

> I do *not* see the government's task as being to try to plan the future shape of energy production and consumption. It is not

even primarily to try to balance UK demand and supply for energy. Our task is rather to set a framework which will ensure that the market operates in the energy sector with a minimum of distortion.[12]

Most other industrial countries followed suit, to a greater or lesser degree, as did the energy policy of the European Union. Privatization and the liberalization of energy markets became the orthodoxy, even if resisted in some quarters. In effect, there was no energy policy as such, apart from opening up sectors to competition so that markets could do their work in encouraging efficiency and finding appropriate prices for energy goods. Security of supply barely appeared on the radar as prices dropped, while electricity and oil remained plentiful.

However, these measures were to become self-undermining. Since there was excess capacity, and hence no worries about supply, energy companies became focused on paring back operating costs, with pre-existing investment effectively written off. Little new investment was made in the upgrading of plant, save in certain sectors of the oil industry. The situation – especially in countries where privatization had advanced furthest – as Dieter Helm puts it, in a Marxisant way, 'contained the seeds of its own destruction'.[13] In a whole swathe of countries in recent times there have been large-scale interruptions to power supply, exposing vulnerabilities that derive in part from under-investment and in part from market failures.

Since the early 2000s, what Helm calls a new energy paradigm has emerged. It is marked by rises in the price of oil and gas well beyond what seasoned observers had once thought possible. But it also involves a return to the protection of national energy supplies, modernization of plant, investment for the future, a consciousness of the finitude of oil and gas resources, recognition of the key importance of foreign policy to energy security – and an awareness of the need to integrate energy policy with the struggle to limit climate change. Political considerations have come once more to intrude deeply into energy markets because of their concentration in the hands of states which use them as instruments of domestic and foreign policy.

The US is heavily dependent upon Middle Eastern oil producers, as are Europe and Japan, although all are now scrambling to diversify their sources of supply. Russia's attempt to return as a great power is based upon its fossil fuel resources and the high prices they currently command. China's very rapid rate of economic growth has led the country to take far more of an international role than it had done previously, as it makes its presence felt in the Middle East, Africa and Latin America in pursuit of oil, gas and minerals.

The EU countries import a great deal of gas from Russia and a substantial proportion of their oil too. The implications on both sides for climate change policy are considerable. Russia is maximizing its income from oil and gas without the modernization that could have come about had the country permitted the introduction of outside investment and encouraged effective management. Gazprom, Russia's largest state-owned company, is notoriously inefficient and poorly managed. Domestic and industrial consumers in Russia get their energy at heavily subsidized prices, a policy that is changing only slowly, but which does nothing to promote energy conservation.

The Russian leadership developed a confrontational approach to the EU, with consequences that also spill over into the area of climate change. It firmly rejected EU approaches to find a meeting point: 'We intend to retain state control over the gas transport system and over Gazprom. We will not split Gazprom up. And the European Commission should not have any illusions. In the gas sector, they will have to deal with the state.'[14] On the other hand, Russia has found it quite easy to do individual deals with EU member–states and thereby undercut European unity. A notable example is the Nord Stream pipeline project, which brings together Gazprom and two of Germany's biggest energy companies. By February 2011 two sections of the pipeline, running through the Baltic Sea, had been built. The pipeline passes through the territories of Finland, Sweden and Denmark as well as Russia and Germany.

The very idea of the project runs contrary to the spirit of European solidarity. Since energy security and responding to climate change are so closely linked, an EU that cannot speak with one voice on the first could find its ability to make progress with the second compromised – a serious matter, since, in terms of concerns to combat global warming, it aspires to be the world leader.

The struggle for resources

Only the US is ahead of China in terms of oil and gas consumption. In 2010 China accounted for about 40 per cent of the worldwide growth in demand for oil. Its level of demand will rise by about 6 per cent a year over the next decade if its rates of growth are sustained and its energy policies remain the same. In casting around for oil, China is pursuing an expansionist foreign policy – following, it could be said, in the footsteps of Britain and the US. China does not work through oil corporations as Western countries tend to do, but its objectives are much the same. It essentially buys oilfields in different countries for its own use, setting the terms of sale locally. Countries where China has done such deals range from Venezuela to Indonesia, Iraq, Oman, Yemen and Sudan.

It has also made substantial inroads into the Middle East, to the chagrin of the US. Saudi Arabia has become the largest oil supplier to China, and the Chinese have been allowed to explore for gas within the country. China has forged a close relationship with Iran and is importing increasing amounts of gas and oil from that state. American oil companies are prohibited from doing business with Iran as a result of an Act of Congress, so cannot get a look in. In the meantime, along with Russia, China for some while blocked the imposition of sanctions on Iran, which most other nations in the international community support in their attempt to stop the country from acquiring nuclear weapons and the rocket systems able to deliver them. 'Both sides behave as if an oil shortage is looming, and that it's "us or them".'[15] American observers have claimed that, although China has now accepted imposing sanctions on Iran, it does not implement or enforce its trade controls properly. Indeed, some 15 per cent of its oil is imported from Iran, which is China's second largest provider.

India has not yet adopted such a high foreign policy profile as China in respect of oil, but it will need much more fuel as its economy advances and as consumer tastes change. In China, there has been a steep rise in car use over the past decade, with no heed at all being paid to environmental considerations. Much the same is set to happen in India. The Tata Nano car was unveiled in that country in January 2008. Costing 100,000 rupees (£1,300), it is by far the cheapest new car in the world; millions of Indians, even those on a relatively modest income, will, for the first time, be able to buy a car. The Tata Nano has a 33bhp petrol engine, which, because of being so small, is reasonably fuel-efficient. Yet the sheer numbers likely to appear on the roads will certainly result in large-scale environmental consequences.

Outside India, there are also plans to market the car in Latin America, South-East Asia and Africa. The chief scientist of the IPCC, Rajendra Pachauri, himself an Indian, said he is 'having nightmares about it'. The response from the industrialist Ratan Tata sums up perfectly some of the dilemmas surrounding both energy security and climate change: 'We need to think of our masses. Should they be denied the right to an individual form of transport?'[16]

Commentators on energy security have started to speak of 'Chindia' to refer to the combined impact of Chinese and Indian economic growth on world oil and energy markets. For most of the time since the Second World War the rise in demand for oil has been only about half that of overall economic growth. Since 2000, however, that proportion has increased to 65 per cent.[17] At the moment, measured on a per capita basis, Chindia consumes one-seventh of the total for the industrial countries. If Chindia joins the high-income group of countries within the next 20 years, as seems likely, growth in worldwide energy demand will dramatically accelerate.

In the areas of both climate change and energy security, the main divergence between the more sanguine and the apocalyptic writers is time – how much time remains before large changes will have to be made to the ways in which we live. Even if the effects of climate change are progressive rather than abrupt, and will mainly affect subsequent generations rather than ourselves, the lesson should still be to prepare early, and to start now. Exactly the same is true of energy security, even if those who say that oil and gas have several decades to run turn out to be right.

The situation in the Middle East looks to be changing dramatically. The geopolitical bargain whereby the US kept a strategic hold over parts of the region is breaking down. That bargain was the key to the stability of oil supplies to the US, and to some extent the global economy in general. It underpinned the US's profligate use of energy. Successive generations of American presidents promised to reduce the US's dependency on imported oil, but none succeeded.

Will the dwindling of US influence in the Middle East cause the country to look in a much more serious way at its indiscriminate use of energy? At the time of writing, the answer to that question is imponderable, but the consequences of the transformations affecting the Middle East will certainly stretch well beyond that area itself.

The United States in particular, and to some degree the other developed countries, have become used to 'cheap' energy, delivered in some degree by the influence of the US in the region, and by the strategic alliances it deployed there. A sharp dimunition in such influence may give a jolt to complacency about supplies of oil and gas and produce a wave of investment in alternative technologies – as happened 30 years before. However, it may also prompt more conservative attitudes, such as a continuing love affair with coal.

In the following chapter I return directly to climate change, beginning by looking at the impact of the green movement on environmental thinking. Issues to do with energy, however, intrude at most points throughout the remainder of the book, since there is no chance of mitigating climate change without radically reducing our fossil fuel dependency.

3

THE GREENS AND AFTER

Now that climate change discussions have moved into the mainstream, it isn't surprising that they reflect a variety of different perspectives. Those in the green movement tend to argue thus: 'This is our topic, since we were speaking about pollution of the environment well before anyone else.' And indeed, the green movement – or certain currents of thinking within it – has been the main source of philosophical reflection relevant to climate change objectives. Green concepts and imagery permeate the writings of even the most sober scientific writers on climate change.

However, others are pressing their claims. Environmental economists dismiss most green thinking as woolly. For them, a proper approach must be hard-edged and phrased in terms of the costs and benefits of different strategies, with markets having the upper hand. They also tend to look towards carbon markets as likely to contribute most to enabling us to cope with global warming.

For writers on the left, climate change offers the opportunity to renew the case against markets that has for so long been associated with left-of-centre traditions. After all, Nicholas Stern, the author of a major review on climate change, has remarked that global warming 'is the greatest market failure the world has seen'.[1] Although Stern himself doesn't draw any such conclusion, the quote is food and drink to those who would like to see the role of markets shrink and that of the state expand. As a political issue, responding to global warming also appeals to some on the left in a different way – it offers the chance to recover the radicalism that disappeared with the dissolution of revolutionary socialism. It might be seen as a means of renewing the critique of capitalism, regarded by them as the source of the troubles we face. The red–green coalitions that have been proposed by different authors, and that have existed in some real-life political contexts, have their origins in this type of reasoning.

Bandwagon effect in respect of global warming is noticeable on a strategic as well as on a more abstract plane. Thus, those who want to revive the European Union and give it more legitimacy and sense of direction find in climate change a way of doing so. Europhiles see the issue as a way of demonstrating to their own sceptics what a crucial role the EU can play in influencing global issues.

I hope I have managed to avoid bandwagon effect. Plainly, it is important to be careful about using global warming as a way of surreptitiously legitimating other concerns. There is nevertheless a left/right tinge to current climate change debates: those who want to respond to climate change through widespread social reform mostly tend towards the political left; most of the authors who doubt that climate change is caused by human agency, on the other hand, are on the right. Yet it is vital that climate change policy as far as possible transcends such divisions and survives changes of government within democratic systems. I shall discuss this issue in more detail in chapter 5.

The greens

Strictly speaking, of course, there is no green movement – rather, there is a diverse range of positions, perspectives and recipes for action. I do not pretend to cover all of these, but instead will concentrate upon a number of key themes.

Like socialism, green thinking is a creation of the industrial revolution. Factories and rapidly growing cities transformed and, in many areas, came to dominate the landscape, while the 'green and pleasant land' retreated into the background. New-found wealth was brought to many, but in the eyes of critics the price paid was far too high. The 'hatred of modern civilization', which William Morris spoke of as 'the leading passion of my life', found widespread echo in the arts and in the thinking of the early conservationists. Is it all, he wondered in a remarkable anticipation of today's social critics, 'to end in a counting house on top of a cinder heap?'[2]

Ralph Waldo Emerson's *Nature* appeared in 1836. Emerson protested volubly (although to no immediate effect) against the logging which was devastating the forests. In modern industry, he argued, nature appears as an object pressed into the service of the production of commodities. We should seek to recover the unmediated relationship to nature that our ancestors enjoyed, and which is the source of aesthetic experience and morality.[3] The theme was taken up by Henry Thoreau who, in celebrated fashion, put it into practice by living alone in the woods for two years, depending wholly on his own labour to do so. 'That man is the richest whose pleasures are the cheapest', he wrote, adding prophetically: 'what is the use of a house if you haven't got a tolerable planet to put it on?'[4] Walden Pond in Massachusetts, where Thoreau spent his two years in isolation, is considered by many to be the birthplace of the conservation movement.

The Sierra Club, founded in the US in 1892, and influenced by the ideas of Emerson and Thoreau, is widely recognized to be the world's first significant environmental organization, devoted in the first instance to protecting wilderness areas. It has a history of activism, dating back to protests against the damming of rivers in the early years of the twentieth century. Today, fighting global warming has become its main activity; it seeks to combat the 'reckless energy policy' of the US.

The modern green movement had its origins in Germany in the 1970s. The term 'green' in its political sense was coined in Germany, where the Green Party was also the first to achieve a measure of electoral success. The greens have since developed into a global movement: their first worldwide gathering was held just before the UN conference in Rio in 1992. The Global Green Network has party representatives from some 80 different countries. Amid the diversity of views represented by green parties, there are some common threads that hold them all together. The Network lists a charter of principles 'defining what it means to be Green in the new millennium'. It involves the four principles first set out by the German greens two decades ago – 'ecological wisdom' (ecological harmony or equilibrium), social justice, participatory democracy and nonviolence, with two others added: sustainability and respect for diversity.

Influenced by earlier social protests in the 1960s and early 1970s (for example, against the Vietnam War), the greens emerged as a movement that in some part set itself against parliamentary politics, and feared too great an involvement with the state. This is why it tends to emphasize grassroots democracy and localism. Greens oppose established institutions of power, whether in the shape of big government or big business. They also contest 'productivism' in economics – a stress upon economic growth as a prime economic value. Growth that lowers the quality of life, or, in particular, which damages the biosphere, is 'uneconomic' growth. Orthodox economics is 'grey' – human life and nature both figure as 'factors of production' alongside other commodities. Most greens have tended to mistrust capitalism and markets, and view the large corporations with considerable hostility.

Greens often describe themselves not as anti-science, but as anti-'scientism' – against untrammelled faith in science and, especially, technology. A key aspect of green thinking in relation to technology is the precautionary principle – one of the main concepts, in fact, that the greens have contributed to the wider political discourse. It connects readily with the early thinking of Morris, Emerson and Thoreau. The precautionary principle is not easy to state – indeed, I shall argue below that it is actually incoherent. However, it has quite often been taken to mean that technologies should be rejected, unless it can be proven that they will not cause harm either to human beings or to the biosphere. The precautionary principle lies behind the objections that almost all greens have had to nuclear power. The greens had a strong influence on the decision of Germany and Sweden to phase out nuclear power stations, for example.

A somewhat bewildering variety of philosophical standpoints has been associated with the greens. The Australian philosopher Robert Goodin has sought to impose some order upon this diversity. He argues that green political thinking depends upon two basic strands – a green theory of value and a green theory of agency. The first tells us what greens value and why; the second, how they do (or should) go about pursuing them.

In economics, value is assessed in terms either of prices or of welfare, the second of these defined narrowly as material benefit. In the green theory of value, by contrast, what makes something valuable is that it has been created by natural processes rather than by human beings. We can understand this position by answering a question posed by another philosopher, Martin Krieger: 'What's wrong with plastic trees?'[5] In the late 1960s, the city authorities in Los Angeles, finding that real trees planted by the freeways died because of air pollution, planted plastic ones instead. They were surprised when these were pulled down by irate citizens. Goodin suggests that even if artificial trees could be made in such a way as to be indistinguishable from the real thing, we would still (rightly) tend to reject them – much as we would a forgery of a picture. We value nature, because it is larger than ourselves and because it sets our own lives in a much more encompassing context.

Unlike the 'deep ecologists', who try to derive values from nature itself, Goodin accepts that objects in nature can only have value through us – when we speak of values there is inescapably a human element involved, since there must be someone to hold these values. Such values are at the same time relational: they presuppose and depend on a world larger than ourselves. A landscape doesn't have to be wholly untouched by a human hand for us to value it in this manner. Thus the English fields and hedgerows are human modifications of nature – they house (or used to) a way of life in which people broadly live in harmony with nature. This situation is different from circumstances where we seek to impose our own order on nature in a tyrannical fashion. Goodin gives the example of Los Angeles, in fact, where, he argues, nature has been obliterated.[6] Sustainability, a basic green concern, can be inferred from such an emphasis; so can concern with the interests of future generations. Many greens have argued against further economic growth on the grounds that it is too damaging – they would like to see a 'no-growth society'.

Values do not realize themselves. They have to be connected to a 'how' that explains the means whereby they can be realized. Greens, as mentioned, have a distrust of power and the state – the desire for participatory democracy is found in the manifestos of virtually all green parties. Goodin searches for a logical connection between green values and the typical green political framework – advocacy of participatory democracy, distrust of large-scale power, and nonviolence – and finds none. This is an important conclusion, for reasons I shall mention later. He also argues – I think correctly – that a green theory of value should have priority, in cases of clash, over the green theory of agency. As he points out, such an emphasis runs counter to the intuitions of most greens, who believe that direct personal action should have priority over orthodox politics, and see this belief at the core of what it means to be green.

Although Goodin does not discuss the issue in an extensive way, one should point out that the relationship between the greens and the question of global warming is problematic. Global warming is not simply an extension of more traditional forms of industrial pollution; it is qualitatively different. Scientists, and scientists alone, have directed our attention to it, since it is not visible in the way London smogs were, or smoke-stack pollution is. We are also wholly dependent on the research and monitoring work of scientists to track the progress of warming and map its consequences.

Some concepts which play a major role in current environmental thinking, such as the aforementioned precautionary principle, come from the green movement broadly defined. Other notions sound as though they have green origins, but in fact do not, such as 'ecological footprint', a phrase first introduced by William Rees in the early 1990s.[7] One might think it refers to a footprint in the sand, but it actually has high-tech origins – it came from the comment of a computer technician, who spoke admiringly of the small space his new computer took up on his desk.

A lot more order needs to be brought into this jumble of ideas and concepts. I see no problem in accepting that there are green values which are relevant for significant aspects of political life. However, such values are not necessarily the same as those connected to controlling climate change, and may indeed run counter to them. For example, a key green value is that of 'staying close to nature' – or, more briefly put, conservation. It is a value that has a certain aesthetic quality to it. It is very possibly important to the good life, but it has no direct relevance to climate change. Clashes can easily occur between conservationist values and policies relevant to global warming – for example, conservationists might resist the building of a nuclear power station, or a wind farm, in a given area of the countryside.

The desire to protect animal species from extinction might also be a worthy one, but its only connection to climate change is if extinction threatens the ecosystems that help reduce emissions. For these reasons, although being 'green' has become synonymous with acting against global warming, I don't use the term. Of course, green values or policies could be and are relevant to wider political concerns. In other words, actions that are politically attractive because they serve widely held green values could also serve the goal of limiting climate change. It is quite right to say that economic growth shouldn't be valued in and of itself, especially as a society becomes more affluent.

The green movement will lose (or has already lost) its identity as environmental politics become part of the mainstream. Although green groups and parties holding these ideas will of course remain, the absorption of the greens into the mainstream means discarding those aspects of green theories of agency that have nothing intrinsically to do with green values. These include the theses that participatory democracy is the only kind of democracy that counts; that the best kind of society we can aim for is a radically decentralized one (decentralization may quite often be a valuable political goal, and even relevant to green objectives, but only alongside other forms of political organization); and the commitment to nonviolence (plainly an important goal in most contexts, but arguably not a universal one, and in any case one that has no intrinsic connection with climate change objectives as such).

We must also disavow any remaining forms of mystical reverence for nature, including the more limited versions which shift the centre of values away from human beings to the earth itself[8] – tackling global warming has nothing to do with saving the earth, which will survive whatever we do. Living in harmony with the earth, respecting the earth, respecting nature – these ideas fall into the same category.

The green movement leaves behind it some central dilemmas. In what sense, if any, does coping with climate change and energy security mean that economic growth, in its usual sense, is inevitably compromised? Can and should political life in the industrial countries, and perhaps elsewhere too, be reshaped so that well-being replaces affluence as a core aspiration of development? We also have to ask how useful the concepts are that have come, at least in some part, from the green movement. They include especially the precautionary principle, sustainability and the principle that 'the polluter pays'.

Managing risk: the precautionary principle

The precautionary principle (PP) has been used well beyond the green movement to handle risk in the context of climate change and other environmental areas. The notion has been incorporated into numerous official documents concerned with global warming. It was built into the 1992 Rio Declaration and has been applied widely since, including in the programmes of the European Commission. Its core meaning can be summarized as the aphorism 'better safe than sorry', although it is invariably clothed in more technical garb. Like other aspects of everyday wisdom, 'better safe than sorry' is a theorem that dissolves into ambiguity when subjected to scrutiny. Moreover, there is no reason why 'better safe than sorry' should be prioritized over its opposite: 'he who hesitates is lost'. All popular maxims, in fact, have their opposite, which explains their lack of explanatory or predictive capacity. We tend to apply them retrospectively depending on what the outcomes of a course of action prove to be.

The PP concentrates only on one side of risk: the possibility of harm. The reason why it has become so prominent is bound up with its origins in the green movement and the attitude of that movement towards nature. Conservationism easily slides over into the view that we should beware of interfering with natural processes as a matter of principle. Risk, however, has two sides. The opposite of precaution is boldness and innovation – taking the plunge. Taking risks adds edge to our lives, but, much more importantly, is intrinsic to a whole diversity of fruitful and constructive tasks.[9] Risk-taking is essential to new thinking in all spheres, to scientific progress and to wealth-creation. We have no hope of responding to climate change unless we are prepared to take bold decisions. It is the biggest example ever of he who hesitates is lost.

The American legal scholar Cass Sunstein has produced a devastating critique of the precautionary principle. He notes how divergent are the situations it has been taken to cover. The definition of the PP most often offered is 'that regulators should take steps to protect against potential harms, even if causal chains are unclear and even if we do not know that those harms will come to fruition'.[10] Yet thus formulated, the PP can be invoked in quite contradictory ways. It could be used to endorse interventionist action to prevent a given state of affairs from arising, as in the case of taking action against global warming – or, as Sunstein points out, the invasion of Iraq. More often, however, the PP is invoked to justify exactly the opposite – inaction on the grounds of being better safe than sorry. Such is the case, for example, when groups oppose the introduction of GM crops, in the belief that it is better to maintain the status quo than to make risky interventions into nature.

Since it can be used to justify completely opposed courses of action, it isn't surprising that there is little consistency in definitions offered of the PP. Sunstein traces some 20 different such definitions, in fact, remarking that 'they are not compatible with one another'.[11] They range from 'weak' to 'strong'. A weak definition is one such as the following: that 'a lack of decisive harm should not be grounds for refusing to regulate, in relation to a specific hazard'. Strong definitions are those such as 'action should be taken to correct a problem as soon as there is evidence that harm may occur'. Sunstein shows that both types of definition are worthless as guides to action. Weak versions of the PP do no more than state a truism. Governments could not possibly demand certainty in risk situations before taking regulatory action.

However, stronger versions, if they were applied strictly, would paralyse all action. Take the example of GM crops. The risks to human health and local ecologies are not known with any precision. A strong version of the PP requires that they be banned completely, on the basis that this way we avoid any risks they are likely to pose. However, prohibiting their use creates significant risks too, including the possibility, for example, of rising levels of starvation and malnutrition. The strong definition of the PP would entail that we avoid these risks too. Hence the strong definition is logically incoherent; it goes against both the cultivation and the non-cultivation of GM crops. The PP in its strong form, Sunstein shows, tends to lead to extreme conclusions, as a means of concealing its incoherence. It tends to focus only on worst-case possibilities, producing either a paralysing focus on the status quo, or endorsements of extreme reactions.

Precautions against some risks almost always create others. This observation is important to my arguments about climate change, since there is always a balance of risks (and, crucially, opportunities) whenever a given course of action is considered. We cannot therefore justify a 'bias for nature' – leaving nature intact – as an argument relevant to dealing with global warming. We will need to push the boundaries of the end of nature further, rather than (as green thinkers want) pull back from them.

How can it be that the PP is self-contradictory, yet is so widely accepted as a framework for policy? The reasons, Sunstein says, lie in the social perception of risk. We tend to focus on some risks to the exclusion of others, and use rules of thumb that are quite often very misleading in judging risks. Sunstein lists a number of such rules of thumb or 'heuristics', including:

1 The 'availability heuristic'. We may pick on certain risks simply because they are in the news, ignoring other

relevant threats. For instance, Sunstein says, at the moment there is a distinct tendency to overplay the risks posed by terrorism.

2 'Probability neglect'. We tend to focus on worst-case scenarios, even if they are very improbable. This tendency is noticeable among some of the writers on climate change, as noted earlier.

3 'Loss aversion'. People tend to have a bias in favour of the status quo because they are more concerned about losses than about future gains, a well-established finding in behavioural economics. This tendency is related to future discounting, as discussed in the Introduction.

4 A belief in the 'benevolence of nature' that makes risks created by humans particularly suspect.

5 'System neglect'. This tendency prevents people from seeing the risks created by their own attempts at risk avoidance.

If one adds to these points the exploitation of risks by special interest groups, it is easy to see how biased risk assessments arise. Since people usually concentrate only on some risks, filtering out others, and since they tend to concentrate on worst-case scenarios, strong versions of the PP result. They offer no proper policy guidelines, however, because of their self-contradictory starting-point.

I draw several conclusions from Sunstein's analysis. The first is that we have to operate in terms not of the precautionary principle, but of another PP – the 'percentage principle'. In assessing risks, no matter how catastrophic, some form of cost-benefit analysis of possible forms of action is nearly always involved. That is, we have to assess risks and opportunities in terms of costs incurred in relation to benefits obtained. Risks which shade over significantly into uncertainties, like those involved in global warming, however, inevitably mean that there will be an element of guesswork, perhaps a large element, in whatever we do (or do not do).

Second, cost-benefit analysis in democratic settings presumes public debate, since choice among risks is involved. For instance, nuclear power can help reduce emissions, but it creates other risks, such as those involved in the disposal of radioactive waste. Debate, however, will not necessarily lead to agreement, and policy-makers will in the end have to make the leap one way or the other.

Third, all risk assessment is contextual. It depends upon values, which inevitably shape the threats considered most salient at any point, given that no course of action is ever risk-free. Consider the introduction of a new medical drug. From a regulatory point of view, it is certainly sensible to test it thoroughly before it is used on a wide scale. However, those suffering from a condition that the drug could help may well decide to take it before full testing has taken place. In such a case, 'he who hesitates is lost' trumps 'better safe than sorry', because sufferers have little to lose by not taking the drug.

The issues just discussed are relevant to all areas of risk and public policy. They are important to the arguments of this book, since how people assess and respond to risk in general is a key part of the politics of global warming. However, they are also relevant in an immediate way to strategies for mitigating climate change and also to problems of adaptation.

'Sustainable development'

The year 1972 was important in the history of environmental thinking, since it was the date at which a landmark study appeared: the Club of Rome's *Limits to Growth*. The work argued that our civilization is exhausting the resources upon which its continued existence depends.[12] It sold in its millions and, although it was subjected to numerous criticisms, its overall emphasis is now widely accepted. In the same year, a major UN conference on the 'Human Environment' highlighted the importance of reconciling economic development with the more efficient use of resources. The term 'sustainable development' was introduced in the 1987 report of the World Commission on Environment and Development – now usually referred to as the Brundtland Report, since it was chaired by the Norwegian ex-Prime Minister, Gro Harlem Brundtland.[13] Like *Limits to Growth*, it focused on the possibility that modern industry is using up its source materials at an alarming rate, which cannot be maintained for much longer without major change.

The Brundtland Report recognized that economic growth is necessary in order to bring greater prosperity to the developing world. However, development overall has to become sustainable. The Commission defined sustainable development as 'development that meets the needs of the present without compromising the ability of future generations to meet their own needs'.[14] The 1992 UN Rio Earth Summit endorsed a declaration setting out 27 principles of sustainable development and recommended that every country produce a national strategy to achieve these ends. A few years later the Treaty of Amsterdam embraced sustainable development as integral to the aims of the EU, and a comprehensive Sustainable Development Strategy was established in 2001.

The introduction of the notion has had a valuable effect. At least to some degree it has helped bring together two previously discrepant communities – on the one hand, greens and others who were 'anti-growth' and, on the other, pro-market authors. As Richard North has observed, it 'has exposed green extremists as being indifferent to human realities [the plight of the poorer countries] and hard-nosed industrialists as obsessing about the short-term. And it has provided some solid middle ground from which former hotheads, dreamers and radicals can hone workable policy.'[15] The meeting-point came through world poverty. Greens and conservationists could argue that a no-growth policy made sense in the industrial states. However, they also support global social justice, whose realization means that poorer countries must be given the opportunity to become richer – that is, to develop economically.

The term gained such popularity that it is now deployed almost everywhere and has figured in thousands of books, articles and speeches. Yet it has had its detractors from the beginning and their voices have become ever more strident. What accounts for its popularity, they argue, is precisely its anodyne quality – an intrinsic vagueness, coupled with a have-your-cake-and-eat-it quality. The two prime terms, 'sustainability' and 'development' – as many have observed

– have somewhat contradictory meanings.[16] 'Sustainability' implies continuity and balance, while 'development' implies dynamism and change. Thus environmentalists are drawn to the 'sustainability' angle, while governments and businesses (in practice, anyway) place the focus on 'development', usually meaning by this term GDP (Gross Domestic Product) growth.

One response to the elusive nature of the concept has simply been to avoid defining it and instead to substitute a cluster of goals in its place. In *Implementing Sustainable Development*, for example, William Lafferty and James Meadowcroft argue: 'Sustainable development indicates an interdependent concern with: promoting human welfare; satisfying basic needs; protecting the environment; considering the fate of future generations; achieving equity between rich and poor; and participating on a broad basis in decision-making.'[17] Such an all-encompassing list, however, surely empties the notion of any core meaning. It is an example of 'the way that sustainable development has become an all-embracing concept to the extent that it has no clear analytical bite at all'.[18]

'Sustainable development' is more of a slogan than an analytical concept, and I shall avoid using it in this book. Rather, I will consider its two components separately. 'Sustainability' is a useful notion, although itself a little slippery to define, since it concerns an indefinite future. We don't know what technological innovations will occur down the line, and hence assessments of the limits of the earth's resources usually operate under a question-mark. Sustainability in its simplest meaning implies that, in tackling environmental problems, we are looking for lasting solutions, not short-term fixes. We have to think over the medium and the long term and develop strategies that stretch over those timescales. There is an obligation to consider how present-day policies are likely to affect the lives of those as yet unborn.

It can be given substance in various ways. For example, the World Economic Forum has elaborated an Environmental Sustainability Index, which has been applied to more than 100 countries.[19] Environmental sustainability is defined in terms of five elements:

1 The condition of ecological systems such as air, soil and water.
2 The stresses to which those systems are subject, including their levels of pollution.
3 The impact of such stresses upon human society, as measured in terms of factors such as the availability of food and exposure to disease.
4 The social and institutional capacity of a society to cope with environmental hazards.
5 The capacity to create stewardship of global public goods, especially the atmosphere.

We should also look again at the idea of 'development'. 'Development', on its own, has two somewhat different meanings. It can simply mean economic growth, as measured by GDP, in which case it applies in principle to all countries. However, it can also refer more narrowly to the economic processes that take people out of poverty. This is the sense in which we contrast the 'developing' countries with the 'developed' ones. In the first sense of the term, of course, 'development' never stops.

In both senses, 'development' means the accumulation of wealth, normally measured in terms of GDP, such that a society becomes progressively richer. It implies that this wealth is generated in some large part by the economic transformation of the society in question, as a self-perpetuating process. We wouldn't say that a society is developing economically if, for example, it were simply getting income from selling off its mineral resources. We speak of 'developed' as opposed to 'developing' countries for a reason – namely, that growth is much less important to the former than to the latter. 'Developed' countries may continue to expand their economies, but the need for growth is much less pressing – they have reached some sort of equilibrium, albeit a dynamic one.

For the poorer countries there is a *development imperative*. It is not only that they have the right to become richer, but that such a process has direct implications for sustainability. Poverty is closely associated with population expansion, one of the root causes of the pressure that is now threatening resources. There will continue to be two separate trajectories of 'development' in the world, at least until the poorer countries reach a certain standard of wealth. Just what this 'certain level of wealth' should be is a massively important question, which has to be negotiated politically. Wherever possible, such as through technology transfer, reductions in emissions – at least relative to past practices in the developed countries – should be sought. The state of play in terms of the dangers involved in climate change, together with a peak in the production of oil and gas, will determine in large part how far 'development' today can mimic the trajectories followed by the existing industrial countries. We have already reached a point where the outcome of those trajectories is under immense pressure. Nevertheless, a certain 'licence to pollute' has to be acknowledged.

'Contraction and convergence' – whereby developed countries reduce their emissions first, and radically, with poorer countries following suit as they become richer – is a necessary point of connection between the two types of development. There are different versions of this idea around, but the underlying principle is simple.[20] The developed countries must aim to make large cuts in their greenhouse gas emissions, starting now. Developing nations can increase their emissions for a period in order to permit growth, after which they must begin to reduce them. The two groups of countries will then progressively converge.

Over-development

We can legitimately talk of *over-development* as a possibility in the affluent societies. The continued expansion of the economy may well bring benefits, but at the same time the problems of affluence tend to pile up.[21] The implication is not that economic growth has to stop, but that it should not be pursued irrespective of its wider consequences. For these countries it is essential to create more effective measures of welfare than GDP. GDP is normally defined as the total market value of all final goods and services produced in an economy in a given year. The formula includes personal consumption expenditures, gross private domestic investment, government purchases and net exports. It was not invented as an indicator of welfare, but has almost everywhere come to be used that way.

Using GDP as a measure of growth has distinct advantages, not least those of simplicity and ease of calculation. However, its inadequacies as an index of economic welfare are well known. It is essentially an indicator of the size of an economy and a measure of market transactions. Activities that are environmentally damaging can appear to be wealth-generating in GDP measures, as can many other harmful ones. GDP makes no distinction between industrial growth that acts to increase emissions and that which does not. Nor does it factor in economic inequality – GDP can continue to rise even though only a small minority of the population is making any gains.

The critique of GDP as a measure of welfare now dates back many years. Broader measures of welfare have to be introduced to get a true measure of how societies are faring as a result of economic growth. One such measure is the Genuine Progress Indicator (GPI), which was initiated in 1995. It starts with similar personal consumption measures to GDP, but adjusts for factors such as income distribution, the value of household and volunteer work, crime and pollution. As John Talberth and Clifford Cobb, who were responsible for producing the GPI, observe, in the developed societies 'GPI started declining around 1975, while GDP keeps increasing'. They comment scathingly on the reactions of economic analysts to hurricanes Katrina and Rita in the US. Whereas most analysts wrote about how well the economy reacted to the disasters, with growth rates unaffected, Talberth and Cobb wrote:

> In one fell swoop, these headlines dismissed the inequitable and catastrophic toll associated with 1,836 preventable deaths, over 850,000 housing units damaged, destroyed, or left uninhabitable, disruption of 600,000 jobs, permanent inundation of 118 square miles of marshland, destruction of 1.3 million acres of forest, and contamination caused by millions of gallons of floodwaters tainted by sewage, oil, heavy metals, pesticides, and other toxins as irrelevant to the US economy.[22]

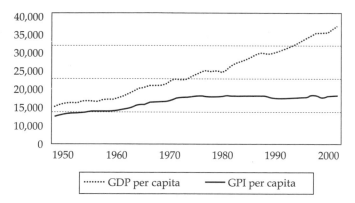

Figure 3.1 Real GDP and GPI per capita in the United States

Source: The Genuine Progress Indicator, 2006, p. 19, fig. 3

Another measure is the Index of Sustainable Economic Welfare (ISEW). It uses both national and local data to identify trends. A study looking at the period between 1975 and 1990 showed that, although GDP continued to rise, the ISEW went down by a quarter in the US. Over the same period, the ISEW in the UK declined by a full 50 per cent.[23] In common with other industrial countries, both societies showed record ISEW growth over the post-war period until the 1970s – the threshold point, it appears, for over-development.

A third index, the Sustainable Society Index (SSI), was set up in 2006.[24] This makes use of a wider range of environmental measures than the others, including resource depletion affecting wetlands, forests, farmland and non-renewable raw materials, together with the level of carbon emissions and other potential causes of environmental damage, such as the ozone-depleting materials. Also incorporated are indices such as income distribution, level of volunteering and dependence on foreign assets. The results show similar conclusions to those of the ISEW: as measured by the SSI, growth in most industrial countries has been stagnant since the 1970s.

Why are political leaders in most countries so reluctant to use such measures in a prominent way? There is an obvious answer – they show economic development in a far harsher light than GDP does. A government that seems to have a good record of economic success is suddenly shown to have presided over a decline in welfare. Yet we have to bite the bullet. Every country, but especially the developed ones, should introduce alternative measures of, and frameworks for, welfare alongside narrow economic measures, and they should be made public.

Polluter pays

As a concept, 'the polluter pays' is more easily dealt with than the others. It means that those who cause pollution – with carbon emissions at the top of the list – should be charged in ratio to the harm they cause. This is the logic behind climate change taxes and carbon markets; and it is also the origin of the principle that countries which have contributed most to greenhouse gases in the past should make the largest cuts today.

In practice, the notion can be difficult to pin down. Where does responsibility for pollution start and stop? The idea of 'extended polluter responsibility' has been coined in order to try to clarify this question. Those who cause emissions through manufacturing, for example, should bear the responsibility for the goods they produce throughout their life cycle, including their eventual disposal. Making such calculations is rarely easy in practice, however, simply because of the complexities involved. We cannot know, for example, which polluters are most culpable in the case of floods that have been influenced by global warming. Hence the costs of such damage have to be covered either by insurance companies or by the public authorities, or by a combination of the two.

Moreover, harmful consequences may take some time to unfold, or, in the case of new technologies, be difficult to assess. As in most areas of climate change policy, inventive solutions will be required. One way of dealing with these situations, for example, is through assurance bonds, which are a way of getting the polluter to bear insurance costs that might arise later. Funds are put up by the company or industry to insure against possible adverse environmental impact. The bond is recoverable, with interest, after it is demonstrated with reasonable confidence that the process in question is benign. If damage occurs the bond is used for environmental ends. The idea is that an incentive is provided for the potential polluter to reduce CO_2 emissions as far as possible.

Although 'the polluter pays' principle has its practical limits, it is nevertheless a guiding thread in bringing climate change into the sphere of orthodox politics. It is a principle of justice which not only stands behind that of the differential responsibility of developed and developing countries for responding to climate change, but offers the means of building such responsibility into law. The fact that it provides incentives to modify behaviour is also highly important.

Ungreen themes

Many in the green movement have been hostile, on the grounds of the precautionary principle, to innovations that would seem to undermine or transgress natural processes. On this basis they have opposed bioengineering and GM crops. Given the overriding importance of limiting climate change – as well as coping with wider areas of sustainability – here, just like in our assessment of global warming itself, trust in science should be the guiding thread. In a world where we face fundamental new risks, avoidance of risk perversely can be far more risky than an embrace of the new.

The growth in world population up to 2050 will place enormous strain on global resources. At the opening of the twentieth century, there were only just over 1 billion people in the world. Today there are almost 7 billion and that number will continue to rise. It may stabilize at fewer than 8 billion, or may rise to more than 9 billion. In terms of food production, this situation contributes 'a major threat that requires a strategic reappraisal of how the world is fed'.[25] Competition for land, water and energy will accelerate. The British government's *Foresight* report, from which this quotation comes, identifies five major challenges for the future:

- balancing future demand and supply in a sustainable way – and ensuring that food supplies are affordable;
- ensuring that there are stable prices for food, protecting the most vulnerable from rapid shifts that might occur;
- achieving global access to food and ending hunger among the 'bottom billion' – the poorest fifth of the world's population (see below, pp. 213–17);
- a radical overhaul of food production systems to ensure that agriculture contributes significantly to the reduction of carbon emissions;
- maintaining, or enhancing, biodiversity while feeding the world.

In looking for ways to respond to these huge problems, the report drew upon contributions from some 400 leading experts from low-, middle- and high-income countries around the world.

Climate change is likely to interact with the world food system in two main ways. Increased demand for food must be met against a backdrop of the mixture of drought and greater rainfall, together with more extreme weather generally. Moreover, the demand of feeding a growing population must be achieved while simultaneously producing a steep decline in carbon emissions. The chance of coping with these exigencies through bringing new land into cultivation is minimal – unless there are dramatic advances of some kind that would allow cultivation on previously barren or inhospitable land. Under existing conditions, far from bringing new land under agricultural production, the main task is actually the reverse. Deforestation is one of the main sources of increased greenhouse gas emissions. The urgency of the need to protect the tropical rainforests is often stressed, but the same also applies to forests in more temperate parts of the world, including Europe. From a climate change point of view, reforestation should quite often take precedence over opening up more land to agriculture.

So far, so green, but when we confront the urgency of intensifying production from a finite landscape – while simultaneously reducing emissions – it is impossible to see how such an end could be achieved without encouraging advances in biotechnology, including the use of GM crops. The issue is not simply one of radically improved productivity, but of keeping abreast of evolving threats, including the emergence of new pests and the spread of plant diseases to areas where they were not previously known. New varieties of crops will be needed that are resistant to flooding, drought and the increased salt content of water as climate change advances. Much the same goes for waste reduction. The amount of waste involved in the global food chain is gigantic. A good deal can be coped with – in principle – by orthodox recycling; but disposal of some kinds of waste could be facilitated by the introduction of novel forms of chemical or biological agent that could break down that waste.

No strategy of any kind is risk-free, as I have stressed earlier, but there are fewer risks at this point involved in GM crops than there are in seeking to rely only on pre-established agricultural processes. Moreover, those risks to a large degree can be monitored through scientific scrutiny under controlled conditions. It would be quite wrong to treat GM crops as a magic bullet – they form one part of a wider front of advance in biotechnology. Market regulation is clearly called for, and should converge with other forms of regulation of monopoly in the wake of the financial crisis. A relatively small number of corporations tend to dominate the world food chain. Governance of the food system should for many reasons seek to ensure diversity.[26]

Reconciling expansion of the world food supply with diminishing emissions is even more difficult than may appear at first sight. Agriculture and the rearing of livestock release a high proportion of methane – a greenhouse gas more lethal in climate change terms than CO_2. The overall impact of food production, even where it is largely concentrated within the developed countries, is high. It has been calculated that over 30 per cent of the greenhouse gas emissions of the EU are directly the outcome of food production. Production and application of nitrogen fertilizers contribute most; in second place are the production of livestock and their digestive processes.

Using quite conventional agriculture, emissions can be reduced to some degree without loss of productivity – for example, through improvements in the use of water and fertilizers. However, further advances in agricultural technology will be needed if increased efficiency is to be reconciled with a substantial and progressive decline in emissions. As with all areas of innovation, how far such advances can be achieved is an open question. Areas to concentrate on include genetic modification of plants that can reduce the need for fertilizers, improve nitrogen use and create improvements in fodder of farm animals.

One should never consider technology in isolation from wider social and economic processes. Government has a major role to play here, alongside private companies and other groups. Advances in technical capacity, for instance, are of little or no use if they do not percolate down to farmers, and if the farmers do not have the knowledge and skills to apply them. Farmers probably quite often tend to be conservative in their outlook, but they can also be agents of change. Communications technology can be deployed to help create activist groups which can in turn communicate their ideas to others.

These points apply to the spread of biofuels. Most of the biofuels being cultivated at the moment take food out of people's mouths – in other words, they occupy land that could otherwise be used for agricultural production. Bioengineering will be needed if this situation is to be transformed. A range of strategies are in play in laboratories around the world. The cultivation of algae forms one promising line of approach. Attempts are being made to alter the genetic makeup of algae in order to be able to produce them in a diversity of environments. Some forms of algae can produce up to 60 per cent of their dry weight in the form of oil, which can then be turned into biodiesel. Efforts are under way to drive this percentage higher.

Genetically modified algae can produce up to 300 times more oil per unit of land than conventional biofuels, such as sugarcane, palms or soybeans. Moreover, such forms of algae can be harvested in a very short time-frame, up to 10 days from planting. Their rate of growth can be as much as 30 times that of orthodox biofuel crops. Algae can also in principle be cultivated on the large scale in the oceans, an idea also being explored around the world. In spite of these advantages, because of the time taken on full research and development, and safety testing, none of these approaches seems close to commercial realization. (For more on biofuels, see below, pp. 127–8.)

The politics of climate change: concepts

To summarize the above discussion: we should discard the precautionary principle and the concept of sustainable development. The first should be replaced by more sophisticated modes of risk analysis, as discussed at many points in this book. The second is something of an oxymoron, and it seems most sensible to disentangle the two component terms again. In the case of 'development', we should focus on the contrast between the developed and developing societies. Insofar as the rich countries are concerned, the problems created by affluence have to be put alongside the benefits of economic growth. I shall argue that dealing with these problems proves to be of direct relevance to the politics of climate change.

Below, I propose a list of concepts that I shall deploy in the remaining chapters. They mostly concern how to analyse and promote climate change policy in the context of political institutions. From the preceding discussion, I take the notions of 'sustainability' and 'the polluter pays'. The other concepts are:

1 The *ensuring state*. I talk about the state a lot in this book, both in the sense of the institutions of government and in the sense of the nation-state, but I don't want readers to get the wrong idea. I don't mean to go back to the old idea of the state as a top-down agency. The state today has to be an 'enabling state': its prime role is to help energize a diversity of groups to reach solutions to collective problems, many such groups operating in a bottom-up fashion. However, the concept of the enabling state isn't strong enough to capture the state's role, which also has to be to deliver outcomes. Nowhere is this principle clearer than

in the case of responding to climate change. The ensuring state is a stronger notion. It means that the state is responsible for monitoring public goals and for trying to make sure they are realized in a visible and acceptable fashion.

2 *Political convergence.* This idea refers to the degree to which policies relevant to limiting climate change overlap positively with other areas of public policy, such that each can be used to gain traction over the other. Political convergence is likely to be crucial to how far we can effectively respond to global warming; being abstract, and concerning mostly future dangers, global warming tends all too easily to give way to more everyday concerns in people's minds. Some of the most important areas of political convergence are energy security and energy planning, technological innovation, lifestyle politics and the downside of affluence, as just discussed. The largest and most promising convergence is between climate change policy and an orientation to welfare going well beyond GDP. For instance, the car is supposed to confer freedom and mobility, but can lead to the opposite – being stuck in traffic jams. Reducing congestion by upgrading public transport and other measures responds to this issue, and is also a positive gain for reducing CO_2 emissions.

3 *Economic convergence.* This notion refers to the overlap between low-carbon technologies, forms of business practice and lifestyles with economic competitiveness. Again, it will have a fundamental impact upon our efforts to contain global warming. Economic convergence has some similarities to what has been called 'ecological modernization' – the idea that environmentally progressive policies often coincide with what is good for the economy and for wider political goals. Ecological modernization has been defined as 'a partnership in which governments, businesses, moderate environmentalists, and scientists cooperate in the restructuring of the capitalist political economy along more environmentally defensible lines'.[27] At the time when it was first mooted, in the mid-1980s, the concept of ecological modernization marked an important step forward in the environmental literature, and a major deviation from green orthodoxy. The authors

who introduced it distanced themselves from the pessimism of the 'limits to development' literature, and also from those in the green movement who set themselves against modernity and, to some extent, against science and technology more generally.[28] The basic thesis was that environmental issues (not just climate change) could best be dealt with by being normalized – by drawing them into the existing framework of social economic institutions, rather than contesting those institutions as many greens chose to do. A strong emphasis was placed on the role of science and technology in generating solutions to environmental difficulties, including in coping with the problem of diminishing world resources. However, 'modernization' also included reforming governmental institutions and markets with environmental goals in mind; and it attributed an important role to civil society groups in keeping both the state and business on the right track. I have no quarrel with any of these emphases and am therefore in general a supporter of the ecological modernization approach. Valid criticisms have been made of it, however, at least in its original formulations. It seemed as though we could have the best of all worlds. Yet while I am strongly in favour of a win–win approach to climate change policy, we must at the same time recognize the compromises that have to be made and the difficult decisions that have to be negotiated. It is also a mistake, as I have said, to assume that growth is an unalloyed benefit, especially in the more developed countries.

4 *Foregrounding.* Given its potentially cataclysmic implications, we need global warming to be a front-of-the-mind issue; however, both in the political sphere and in the minds of citizens, it all too readily becomes a back-of-the-mind one. Foregrounding refers to the use of the various political devices that can be deployed to keep global warming at the core of the political agenda.

5 *Climate change positives.* It won't be possible to mobilize effectively against global warming simply on the basis of the avoidance of future dangers – that is, in a wholly negative way. We will need some more positive goals to aim for. I believe these can come mainly from areas

of political and economic convergence. Climate change
policy involves thinking in the long term, and it involves
an emphasis on the 'durable' rather than the ephemeral.
I shall try to show that these concerns overlap significantly with well-being, rather than with sheer economic
growth.

6 *Political transcendence*. Responding to climate change must
   not be seen as a left–right issue. Climate change has to be a
   question that largely transcends party politics, and about
   which there is an overall framework of agreement that will
   endure across changes of government. I have never agreed
   with the idea that the political centre – where the parties
   converge – is the antithesis of radicalism. Sometimes
   overall political agreement is the condition of radical
   policy-making, and coping with climate change certainly
   falls into that category.

7 *The percentage principle*. This concept marks the recognition
   that no course of action (or inaction) is without risks; and
   that, consequently, there is always a balance of risks and
   opportunities to be considered in any policy context.

8 *The development imperative*. Poorer countries must have
   the right to develop economically, even if this process
   involves a significant growth in greenhouse gas emissions.

9 *Over-development*. In the rich countries, affluence itself
   produces a range of quite profound social problems.
   Economic growth correlates with measures of welfare
   only up to a certain level; after that point, the connection
   becomes more problematic. Addressing problems of over-
   development forms a major area of political convergence
   with policies relevant to controlling climate change.

10 *Proactive adaptation*. Given that climate change will happen
   whatever we do from now onwards, a politics of adaptation will have to be worked out alongside that of climate
   change mitigation. We must as far as possible prepare
   beforehand in a pre-emptive fashion, basing what we do
   upon risk assessment, with policies evolving as scientific
   information shifts and matures.

In the next chapter, deploying some of these concepts, I
shall consider where the developed countries have got to in

their attempts to begin a switch to a low-carbon economy. I shall look to some extent across the board, but take the UK as a key example, since its experience is in some ways typical of the problems that all will have to face.

4

THE TRACK RECORD SO FAR

Some environmentalists argue that liberal democratic societies are not equipped to cope with ecological problems, especially climate change, given the far-reaching character of the social and economic reforms that will be needed. Is it really possible to formulate policies for the long term in such societies, given the concentration of most citizens on the immediate issues of their lives?[1] In *The Climate Change Challenge and the Failure of Democracy*, David Shearman and Joseph Wayne Smith argue that the answer is 'no'. Democratic states, they say, are too dominated by sectional interests and by a hapless materialism to be able to create policies substantial enough to meet the scale of the challenge we face. We should accept that confronting our environmental dilemmas will require a more authoritarian approach from government: 'For us, freedom is not the most fundamental value and is merely one value among others. Survival strikes us as a much more basic value.'[2]

The difficulties facing liberal democratic states as they confront climate change are indeed many. Yet one should not use them to reach a counsel of despair. After all, it is these countries that have helped create the conditions under which environmental issues have come to the fore.[3] Totalitarian states have generally had poor or disastrous environmental records. So also have most of those that have undergone processes of 'authoritarian modernization', such as China, Russia or South Korea.

Several factors explain the difference. Democratic countries not only permit but positively encourage the open development of science, the very basis of our awareness of the problems of global warming and also of most other forms of environmental threat. They provide for the possibility of the mobilization of social movements, environmental pressure groups and NGOs. By contrast, non-democratic states usually maintain a high degree of control over civil society organizations, involving registration of members and supervision of their activities, with the right to close them down if they are deemed a challenge to the world-view of the authorities. Non-democratic societies have proved themselves able to stimulate technological advances in the military sphere, by concentrating their resources there; but they have lagged far behind the democratic countries in most other areas of technological development.

Taking a wide set of indices of environmental criteria, the best performers are all democratic countries. As ranked by the Environmental Performance Index developed by Yale and Columbia Universities, the top five countries in the world are Sweden, Norway, Finland, Switzerland and, interestingly, a developing society, Costa Rica.[4] Costa Rica is a middle-income country, but one that has long-standing democratic traditions – a notable exception in this respect among Central American states.

Sweden, Germany and Denmark

It is worth having a look at the policy records of the countries which have been most successful in controlling their carbon emissions. I shall concentrate more on them than the laggards, of whom there are all too many, in order to form some idea of best practice. To do so, we have to begin well before the Kyoto baseline year of 1990. I shall start with Sweden, which, according to most criteria, is the outright leader in environmental performance, and will move on from there to consider some of the other states mentioned above.

Sweden

Sweden took major steps to improve its level of energy efficiency following the OPEC oil embargo of 1973. Shortly afterwards, because of worries about oil dependency, several major regions in the country announced programmes for reducing domestic and commercial energy use through improvements in insulation and generation of local block heating – programmes that have been refined and improved over the years.[5] The country also turned to nuclear and hydroelectric power. Since the early 1980s the use of oil has fallen by nearly 50 per cent. In 1970 fossil fuel imports corresponded to 80 per cent of the total energy supply of the country; today the figure is only 35 per cent.

Sweden has an ambitious programme to become the world's first oil-free economy by 2020 and has been in the forefront of states pressing for international regulation of emissions. It plans to cut its own emissions from transport by the extensive use of biofuels, derived from its vast forest areas. Biofuels have been used in transport in the country for some while (for the story of how this happened, see below, pp. 127–8), and biomass, mainly from wood pulp, has been used increasingly since the mid-1970s. The green movement has been influential in Sweden and a referendum was held in 1980 which led to a decision to phase out nuclear power. In spite of protests from green groups, the government allowed the development of six new reactors before the resolution actually came into force, and for the two decades after that date nuclear power more than doubled its share of energy production.[6]

In February 2009, the centre-right government announced it was putting new investment into nuclear plants as part of an ambitious new climate programme. The three opposition parties were against the proposal, which was endorsed in parliament by a narrow majority. In the wake of the radiation leaks at the Fukushima nuclear plant in Japan early in 2011, there were demonstrations against nuclear power in several Swedish cities. (For more details on the happenings at Fukushima, see below, pp. 133–4). The government, however is pushing ahead with its plans.

Sweden is one of six EU member–states to have a carbon tax, which – together with nuclear power – helped cut emissions from industry and energy production by about a third between 1970 and 1990. When the tax was introduced, in order to neutralize the overall fiscal effect, income taxes were cut by half. Sweden's greenhouse gas emissions were 9 per cent lower in 2006, prior to the recession, than they were in 1990. Over that period the economy grew by 44 per cent.

Sweden has adopted 16 environmental quality objectives, representing goals to be achieved by 2020. There are 72 interim targets to be met. Progress towards the objectives is monitored by the Environmental Objectives Council. Reducing carbon emissions brooks large among these, but they also cover other aspects, such as air quality, the soil, the forests and the Baltic Sea, which is a site of very heavy pollution.

Germany

Germany was the original home of the greens and has proved to be an environmental leader, especially among the bigger countries. Since the mid-1980s there has been substantial agreement among Germany's political parties about the need to lower greenhouse gas emissions. A report published by a parliamentary commission in 1984, *Protection of the Earth's Atmosphere*, set the tone for subsequent discussion, arguing for substantial reductions.[7]

The proportion of electricity generated from renewable sources grew from 6.3 per cent in 2000 to more than 14 per cent in 2011, and Germany is now the world's biggest user of wind power, boasting some 20,000 wind turbines – wind generates about 6 per cent of the country's total energy use. The country is also the world's largest producer of photovoltaic solar power and has the fastest growing market in terms of domestic installations. The Waldpolenz Solar Park is the most extensive solar power installation in the world. The plant deploys thin-film technology and supplies about 40,000 megawatts of electricity a year. Almost 80 per cent of all European solar energy production capacity is in Germany.

These achievements have been strongly influenced by the introduction of feed-in tariffs for renewable energy in the 1990s pioneered by industrialist Hermann Scheer. Anyone who attaches a renewable energy source to his or her property can have it connected to the grid at a subsidized rate fixed for 20 years. More than 300,000 private home-owners and small businesses have been incorporated into the scheme.

Yet Germany faces significant problems in further building upon its successes. At the moment, the country is heavily reliant upon coal for energy production. Coal-fired power plants supply about half of Germany's electricity, with nuclear energy making up 27 per cent. In September 2010 the German government issued an 'Energy Concept' document that set out energy strategies to 2050. Its aim is for renewable sources to supply 60 per cent of primary energy supply by that year. Achieving such a target would demand a quite fundamental change in the country's energy system, because of the dominance of coal and the continuing use of lignite – 'brown coal'. As of 2010 there were 22 coal or lignite power plants either under construction or in the detailed planning stage in Germany. The government is therefore pinning a lot of its hopes on carbon capture and storage (CCS).

Like Sweden, the country was in the past committed to phasing out its nuclear power stations – in both cases mainly because of the influence of the green movement. In 2000 the then-Chancellor Gerhard Schröder announced that the country's 19 plants would be shut down after a life-span of 32 years. According to such a schedule, Germany's last nuclear plant would close in 2020. The legislation was enacted as the Nuclear Exit Law, and two plants were turned off – one in 2003 and one in 2005.

In August 2007, a climate plan – the 'Meseberg programme' – was published by the government. It then was promoted by the Social Democratic Party within the governing coalition, and called for a reduction in Germany's greenhouse gas emissions by 40 per cent over 1990 levels by 2020.[8] Energy efficiency, a further extension of renewable energy sources and the cleaning up of coal and gas power stations were the basis of the plan. Nuclear energy did not figure, but without it, critics argued, the figures do not stack up. In their 'Energy Concept', the authorities included an extension of the operating life of the country's nuclear power stations. The plants were to be run for 8–14 years longer than was originally decided. The last nuclear plant was supposed to close in 2034.

More recently, policy changed again, with a return to a more positive attitude to nuclear. In 2008 Schröder's successor, Angela Merkel, from the centre-right, shifted the government position to oppose the phase-out of the nuclear industry. These plans in turn were reversed following the episode at the Fukushima nuclear plant. All the country's reactors are now due to be shut down by 2022.

Denmark

Denmark is also an interesting case, because of its forceful programme for expanding renewable sources of energy and because of the ambiguous results that have followed.[9] At the time of the OPEC oil embargo in the late 1970s the country was heavily dependent upon oil, all of which had to be imported. The government of the time determined that this level of dependency should be reduced, and its successors continued similar policies. Taxes on natural gas and petrol were introduced to stimulate energy efficiency. Oilfields in the North Sea belonging to Denmark also started production at this time. In the early 1990s the country introduced a system of subsidies to facilitate the expansion of wind power. At that point renewables accounted for some 5 per cent of its electricity.

The fluctuating nature of wind energy was compensated for by importing hydroelectricity from Sweden and Norway, and by the use of small-scale combined heat and power stations which run on biomass of various kinds and which can be switched on and off quickly. By 2009 the proportion of electricity generated by wind power had jumped to well over 25 per cent and contributed 18 per cent of electricity use. Over the period from 1997 to 2003, under the aegis of a social democratic government (which fell in 2001) an average of 325 megawatts of wind-power capacity was installed each year. Under the successor right-of-centre government, that figure dropped to only 3 megawatts a year. Three projected new wind farms were cancelled, and in 2007 more wind-power capacity was dismantled than was put up. The country has the notable achievement of having kept energy consumption stable during a lengthy period of economic growth. However, over the past few years CO_2 emissions have risen once again.

As of 2011, Denmark derives about 80 per cent of power from fossil fuels. A committee appointed by the government has reported upon how a zero-carbon economy could be achieved by 2050.[10] The programme envisages a wholesale movement towards electricity, powered from renewable sources. As much as 70 per cent of energy consumption could be met by electricity, compared to the current figure of 20 per cent.

Spain and Portugal

The experience of Spain and Portugal deserves special mention. In Sweden, Germany and Denmark, it took quite a while to develop low-carbon energy sources. Spain and Portugal have shown that rapid energy transformation can be achieved. Spain moved from having 2 per cent of its energy delivered by renewables to 12.5 per cent in little over a decade – with some of its autonomous regions, where the new installations were clustered, greatly exceeding this percentage. More than 11 per cent of Spain's electricity comes from wind power. In total, 20 per cent of the country's electricity now comes from renewable sources. Some of the autonomous regions are aiming at 100 per cent renewable electricity generation in a few years' time.

Although it is a much smaller country, Portugal has managed to act even more quickly. In 2004 the country's leaders decided to reduce its dependence on imported fuels. At that point 17 per cent of Portugal's electricity came from renewable energy sources. By the end of 2009, that proportion had risen to 42 per cent. In both cases these achievements were made with the support of tax incentives and by a partial restructuring of the energy system. The Portuguese government privatized and restructured former state-owned energy companies; at the same time, it took back the grid into public control. The changes in the two countries have not been unproblematic. Consumers saw a rise in the cost of energy. Both were seriously affected by the financial crisis and have vulnerable economies, which in turn has had consequences for their investment plans. On the other hand, renewables form one of the relatively few areas where their companies are internationally competitive.

There is a further important lesson to be learned from the cases of Spain and Portugal. A country that has a high proportion of renewables does not necessarily see an overall reduction in its greenhouse gas emissions, since so much depends on what happens in the rest of the economy. As of 2008, when the recession took hold, Spain's CO_2 emissions were a massive 43 per cent higher than in 1990. Those of Portugal were 30 per cent higher.[11] The reason is the importance of the construction industry to their economic development, together with other high carbon-emitting activities.

These are at most thumbnail sketches. Rather than looking at such initiatives from around the world in depth, I shall take the United Kingdom as a type case. Each country will tread a somewhat different path, but some core problems are generic.

The case of the UK

The fact that Britain is on track to meet its Kyoto commitments comes in some part from Prime Minister Margaret Thatcher's decision to privatize the large state energy monopolies. She was determined to face down the power of the unions, especially in coal-mining. The switch from coal-fired to gas-fired power stations was driven by these aims, but also by the fact that gas was seen as the cheapest available source of energy. The closure of the coal mines coincided with the availability of natural gas supplies from the North Sea. Coal production declined from 84 million tons in 1988 to 35 million tons in 1995, and has since fallen by a further half.

According to current government estimates, about 20 per cent of the UK's performance in terms of controlling emissions of CO_2 can be put down to the 'dash for gas', although its contribution to reducing other greenhouse gases is considerably higher. Improvements in energy efficiency (in some part driven by privatization) contributed about 40 per cent. A much smaller proportion can be attributed to environmental policy, such as the Climate Change Levy set up in April 2001, and voluntary energy agreements (in which companies pay a reduced rate of the levy in exchange for meeting more rigorous energy efficiency targets over a 10-year period).

A Climate Change Bill was introduced in the UK in 2008. It marked a new level of ambition for the Labour government in power at that time, which previously had only a modest record on environmental issues in general, and on combating global warming in particular. The bill introduced statutory targets for emissions reductions. According to its original version, greenhouse gas emissions were to be reduced by at least 60 per cent by 2050 over a 1990 baseline. This proportion has since been raised to 80 per cent. A report on progress has to be published every five years and reviewed by Parliament, as well as the ongoing results of an adaptation programme. A carbon budget will be established to cover each five-year period. Late in 2008 the bill was endorsed by Parliament and became the Climate Change Act.

A Committee on Climate Change has been set up to advise the government of the day on the level of the carbon budgets and on the optimal path towards emission reduction targets. The legislation includes provision for 'banking' and 'borrowing' between carbon budget periods. Banking is the capacity to carry over unused quotas from one budget period to a future one; borrowing allows the government to count future anticipated reductions against the current five-year period, such borrowing to be limited to 1 per cent of the following carbon budget. Banking is supposed to provide an incentive to 'overperform' during a given period, or at least remove disincentives that might kick in if a given budget were achieved early. It is accepted that there are costs involved in reducing carbon output and that energy prices will increase (and, therefore, so will other prices). The European Emissions Trading Scheme (ETS) (see below, pp. 198–200) is already having this effect in the UK, because power generators are able to pass extra costs on to consumers. However, it is suggested that the cost will not be large for individual households, and it might even act as an incentive to reduce energy use.

Recognizing how closely climate change and energy change policy are intertwined, the government introduced an Energy Bill at about the same time as the Climate Change Bill. It was passed as the Energy Act in November 2008. At that time the government also created a new ministry, the Department for Energy and Climate Change. North Sea oil and gas have supplied most of the UK's energy needs since the 1980s, but stocks are declining. Most of Britain's nuclear and some of its coal-fired power stations will reach the end of their lives by around 2020 – fully one-third of the country's electricity-generation system will need to have been replaced by this point.

The UK is committed to meet the target set for the country by the EU by 2020, which is that 15 per cent of its energy (including electricity, transport fuels and heating) must come from renewable sources by that time.[12] To achieve this, about 40 per cent of its electricity will have to come from renewable sources – an increase of 800 per cent over present-day levels. The Labour government of the time accepted that nuclear power has to be part of the mix, and included in the Energy Act were plans to build a new generation of nuclear plants.

The introduction of the two pieces of legislation shows a determination to confront the twin problems of climate change and energy security; the bills received a high degree of cross-party support in their passage through Parliament. Although some climate change sceptics used the opportunity to air their views during the debates, it turned out that the main clauses in the Acts were strengthened rather than weakened.

In December 2008, the Climate Change Committee published its first report on how the country should go about reaching its emissions reductions targets. The report included recommendations covering the first three budgets defining the path to emissions reductions to be followed up to 2022. Wind, solar, tidal and nuclear power, together with carbon capture and storage of 'clean coal', were the principal technologies listed as needing expansion. Home and office insulation together with increased vehicle efficiency also brooked large.

The Committee followed up with a further authoritative report in 2009.[13] In tracing out pathways towards the country's long-term emissions reductions targets, the report argued that a 'step-change' was needed from current practices and policies. The recession made it easier to meet the next carbon reduction budget, but deep structural changes are needed. A pathway to 'deep decarbonization of the power sector' by 2030, the Committee concluded, was demanding but feasible.

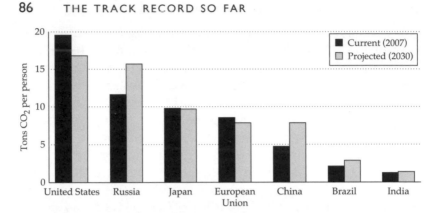

Figure 4.1 Per capita CO_2 emissions for select major emitters, 2007 and 2030 (projected)

Source: World Resources Institute: http://www.wri.org/chart/ capita-co2-emissions-select-major-emitters-2007-and-2030-projected

In May 2010 a coalition government of Conservatives and Liberal Democrats came to power. The new government retained, and vowed to further develop, the framework that its predecessor had left. The prime minister, David Cameron, promised to lead 'the greenest government ever'. Although the Liberal Democrats had been hostile to nuclear power, as part of the coalition they agreed to the building of new nuclear power stations, as long as they were not subsidized with public money. A new Energy Bill was introduced in 2011, with the objectives of increasing energy efficiency and promoting investment in low-carbon technologies. Other measures were promised, including placing a floor price on carbon.

On the face of things, the UK has the most robust framework for reducing carbon emissions in the world, supported by a cross-party consensus. Because the country has lessened its dependence on coal, it is in some ways in a more favourable position than, for instance, Germany. Yet as with every other country with ambitious aspirations to reduce emissions, the practical difficulties are formidable. As far as renewable energy is concerned, Britain at the moment lags far behind. Among the 27 EU countries, in such terms it is near the bottom of the league.

Looking at where the countries discussed above stand drives home how far there is to go in order to make significant progress towards major emissions reductions. The nations discussed are among the best performers in the world and even their progress is relatively limited. Germanwatch and Climate Action Network produce an annual ranking comparing 59 countries in terms of the effectiveness of their climate change policies. Sweden is top of the list, but the organizers of the ranking say that no country in the world is so far on a path compatible with keeping temperature rise below 2°C. An interesting feature of the ranking is that Brazil was placed second, largely because of progress made in reducing deforestation. (For more on Brazil's climate change policies, see below, pp. 225–6.) The index of the 10 largest emitters of CO_2 is alarming because some countries one might expect to take the lead rank very low down. The United States and Canada place very poorly, with the US in 53rd position and Canada last, at position 59.[14]

Climate change policy and the US

It is worth commenting at this point on climate change policy in the United States. The US may or may not be a fading power in global terms, but its importance in respect of climate change is enormous. With 4 per cent of the world's population, the United States consumes 25 per cent of global energy each year and generates over 20 per cent of the world's carbon emissions. Yet far from being in the forefront in seeking to reduce its emissions, it has been a laggard in climate change policy, especially at a federal level. Of course, the US is far larger and more diverse than those countries discussed earlier in the chapter, and on a regional and state level the picture is more complicated.

The Clinton administration played a part in negotiating the Kyoto agreements (see below, pp. 186–8). However, it was not possible to persuade Congress to ratify US participation. Carbon markets originated in the US, but neither the Clinton administration nor any subsequent one has managed to get a national scheme endorsed – or any other significant climate change legislation.

In 2002 George W. Bush set the goal of reducing the greenhouse gas intensity of the country by 18 per cent over the period 2002–12. This policy amounted to a 4 per cent reduction in total emissions over a business-as-usual trend and was in line with the decarbonizing trend already present in the US economy. The Bush administration did introduce some tax incentives for renewables, nuclear power and CCS, as well as energy conservation; and in 2007 Bush signed an Act aimed at improving the fuel efficiency of cars. However, these measures were largely driven by energy security considerations, not by a concern with climate change.

Because of the unwillingness or inability of successive US presidents to enact significant climate change legislation, the most important domestic initiatives emanated from the Congress. John McCain and Joseph Lieberman championed a Climate Stewardship Act in 2003, which was defeated in the Senate. It was followed by the Lieberman-Warner Bill introduced in 2007. The initiative provoked a deep schism between the Democrats, who mostly supported the legislation, and the Republicans, who were solidly against. It was also defeated.

When he was elected in 2008, President Obama spoke forcefully of the need for far-reaching climate change legislation, both on a national and international level. He supported the American Clean Energy and Security Act of 2009 (also known as the Waxman-Markey Bill, after its authors, Henry Waxman and Edward Markey). The bill set out a cap and trade system (see below, pp. 198–202) and would have introduced subsidies for nuclear power, CCS and other technologies. It was criticized by many environmentalists for not being radical enough; and by the political right on the grounds that it would be expensive and would cost the US economy jobs.

The bill was passed by the House of Representatives with a measure of cross-party support, but was abandoned in the Senate. In November 2010, in the congressional elections, the Democrats lost control of the House and with it any chance of getting climate change legislation enacted at a federal level for the time being.

In his State of the Union Address of January 2011, President Obama gave considerable space to clean energy. The US, he asserted, needs to invest in research and development in low-carbon technologies on a level not seen since the space race. He envisaged 'clean energy breakthroughs', 'that will translate into clean energy jobs'.[15] In so doing, he appealed for a renewal of bipartisan support, on the grounds that the drive for clean energy could renew the American sense of purpose. He also spoke of asking Congress to 'eliminate the billions in taxpayer dollars we currently give to oil companies'. However, in his speech he did not once mention global warming, let alone a policy package that would help to contain it.

At present, the US, the country with the greatest responsibility to develop a far-reaching climate change policy, has done nothing at all on a national level. It is almost alone among industrial states in this respect. How can this be? There would seem to be three reasons. First, the separation of powers in the American constitution, which requires the President to negotiate with Congress on almost all matters of domestic policy. Second, the ability of well-funded lobbies to have an enormous influence upon individual members of Congress. Running for office normally means spending large amounts of money, which quite often places candidates in the hands of corporations or well-funded interest groups. The fossil fuel and other extractive industries are highly organized, with access to influence through their support of congressmen and women.

Third, and partly as a consequence of the first and second points, is the fact that climate change has become so polarized politically. President Obama concentrated his energies on getting his Health Care Reform Bill through Congress. Although successful, the process increased the gulf between Democrats and Republicans. The Republican right views anything to do with expanding the powers of government with suspicion. Healthcare, intervention in the economy and efforts to combat climate change: all fall into that category as far as many Republican leaders and voters are concerned.

In no other country is opinion about climate change so acutely divided as in the US today. A poll taken by the Pew

Foundation late in 2010 showed that only 16 per cent of Republican voters agreed that climate change is real, caused by human activity and dangerous, compared to over 50 per cent of Democratic voters.[16] (See below, figure 5.1, p. 106.)

In some regions, states and cities in the US, the situation contrasts quite dramatically with that on the federal level – although the large majority of initiatives have been led by Democrat-dominated state or local leaderships. A recent study looked at climate action plans developed in 16 different states, and extrapolated the findings to the national level.[17] If the actions in question were implemented in all US states, American carbon emissions would fall to 27 per cent below 1990 levels by 2020. Of course, as things stand it is extremely unlikely that such an extrapolation could become a reality.

At the time of writing, yet another cap and trade bill is before the Congress, initiated by John Kerry and Joe Lieberman. The driving force of the initiative is once again primarily clean energy. The terms of the bill are quite modest – far short of what would be needed seriously to reverse the high level of emissions per person displayed by the US.

Lessons to be drawn

Some points of general interest emerge from the material discussed in this chapter:

1 With the partial exception of Germany and Denmark, countries that are at the top of the league in terms of reducing emissions are there because of a preoccupation with energy security rather than climate change. In this sense, they have arrived where they are largely by accident. This category includes one of the large emerging economies, Brazil, which early on introduced ethanol as fuel for vehicles – partly because sugar, from which it is made, was very cheap at the time, and a little later because of the oil crisis. Although it took a long time in some countries to create a significant renewables sector, it is now in principle possible

to move much more quickly. The reasons are that there is past experience to draw upon, for example, in introducing relevant tax breaks; and that the technologies involved have advanced.

2 The left–right dimension can significantly affect the continuity of energy and climate change policies. Thus far, effective policies have mostly been driven by left-of-centre regimes. The Scandinavian countries, for example, are in a prime position largely because they have had long periods of left-of-centre government. Germany provides a better model for the future, since there has been something of a consensus among the parties about environmental measures. The same is true of the UK. The case of the United States shows how paralysing it can be for climate change policy when the issue becomes seriously politically polarized.

3 Carbon taxes do work – although, as I shall discuss at a later point, they are rarely straightforward to implement. Putting a price on carbon is an essential component of climate change policy. Carbon taxes have the great advantage over other strategies in that they are universal and binding, although ways have to be found to reconcile them with issues of social justice, since the poor are very often the hardest hit. It is essential for the state to subsidize renewable technologies if they are to make an impact, and revenue from carbon taxes can be used to achieve this. One reason is the need to preserve a stable basis for investment, even as oil and other fossil fuel prices fluctuate. Subsidies can also be used to provide positive motivation for the take-up of possibilities on offer. The feed-in tariffs made available in Germany and in some other countries provide a model which can and should be copied elsewhere.

4 As far as limiting their emissions are concerned, most countries, even the leading ones, remain heavily contradictory. Germany is a case in point, with its continued strong reliance upon coal. Climate change policy has to be holistic. Policies that are potentially valuable may have little impact if pursued in isolation. Examples are investment in clean (low-carbon) technology, the pursuit of energy efficiency and the quest for greater energy security. Each can contribute greatly to reducing carbon emissions.

Each can be part of the 'positives' that help secure business and public support for policies that reduce emissions. Yet if taken in isolation they will not necessarily reduce emissions within a given national economy or wider economic sector. It is entirely possible to have a society, as the example of Spain and Portugal shows, in which there is quite a high proportion of renewables in the energy mix, but where carbon emissions continue to climb, perhaps even steeply.

Energy efficiency is important to combating climate change if part of a wide-ranging policy package. If not, it can in fact directly increase emissions, since the savings made may be simply spent on other carbon-producing activities. Japan is an example of a society that has a high level of energy efficiency, but growing greenhouse gas emissions. Finally, most countries want greater energy security, except those amply provided with natural resources. Energy security can be a driving motivation for reducing emissions, but only if carefully directed to that end. Thus a country that responds to worries about energy security by turning back to coal would exacerbate global warming rather than help reduce it. Coal is the most lethal fossil fuel in terms of emissions.

5 Despite objections – and the widespread worries caused by the happenings at Fukushima in 2011 – nuclear power likely to have to form part of the energy mix, at least in some states, if carbon emissions are to be reduced. The worries that many people have about the use of nuclear energy are real and significant. Yet we have to bear in mind the percentage principle. The risks involved when a country has little chance of reaching its emissions reduction targets without nuclear energy as part of the mix must be taken seriously too.

6 The inertia built into current ways of doing things is very large, both in energy systems and in the ways of life which they underpin. Not a single country in the world is as yet on track to reduce its emissions to a level compatible with limiting global warming to a 2°C increase.

7 Although I have not discussed the issue in this chapter in a direct way, we should bear in mind that the past 20 years

have been a period during which manufacturing continued to decline in Western countries. They have become
dependent upon manufactured goods produced in China
and the other developing countries. The levels of emissions
produced by the developed countries would be considerably higher than they currently are without this 'transfer of
emissions' eastwards.

5

A RETURN TO PLANNING?

Key arguments of this book are that the industrial nations must take the lead in addressing climate change and that the chances of success will depend a great deal upon *government* and *the state*. Whatever can be done through the state will in turn depend upon generating widespread political support from citizens, within the context of democratic rights and freedoms. I don't want to deny that reaching international agreements is essential, or that many other agencies, including NGOs and businesses, will play a fundamental role. However, for better or worse, the state retains many of the powers that have to be invoked if a serious impact on global warming is to be made.

What should the role of the state, as ensuring state, be? Its main function must be to act as a catalyst, as a facilitator, but certainly, as far as climate change and energy security are concerned, it has also to strive for guarantees. These are areas where solutions simply have to be found, and where there are timetables involved. If your living room is a mess, you can wait until you have time to clear it up. We can't do the same with emissions, as they pile up in the atmosphere and oil starts to run out.

These are some of the tasks in which the state has to be prime actor:

1 *The state must help us to think ahead*. It is the responsibility of political leaders to introduce policies for the long

term. For this shift in orientation to come about, there has to be return to planning, in some guise or another. In case it isn't self-evident, thinking long term is not the same as setting targets for some distant date in the future and then sitting back and relaxing. 'Rigorous' targets set two or three or more decades down the line might make government ministers feel good, but really there has to be an all-out concentration upon *means*. In the Soviet Union, five-, ten- and twenty-year targets were announced with a great deal of huffing and puffing. The results normally fell well short of expectations and new plans would then be instituted. Empty promises for the future won't do in the case of climate change, since the emissions in the atmosphere continue to mount. Planning, of course, isn't the sole prerogative of the state. Governments should encourage a shift towards long-term thinking among companies, third-sector groups and individual citizens.

2 *Climate change and energy risks must be managed in the context of other risks faced by contemporary societies.* Risk and opportunity are the two poles around which a great deal of social and economic policy now revolves. We face a future in which the past history of industrialism, as it were, is rapidly catching up with us, and major adjustments have to be made. However, the risks associated with climate change intersect with a variety of others, locally, nationally and internationally.

3 *The state must promote political and economic convergence, as the main driving forces of climate change and energy policy.* Both can and should be targets for the short and the longer term, and should form the foundation of forward planning. In the long term, a whole diversity of areas has to be considered, including preparing for the large-scale social and economic restructuring that a low-carbon economy inevitably will involve.

4 *The state must make interventions into markets to institutionalize 'the polluter pays' principle*, thereby ensuring that markets work in favour of climate change policy, rather than against it. In almost all developed countries at the moment environmental costs remain largely externalized. I am dubious about how effective carbon markets as such

will be, but there is a great deal that can be done to introduce full cost pricing, and therefore to allow market forces to become centred upon promoting environmental benefits. Government should act to reduce 'negative externalities' – situations in which environmental costs are not brought into the marketplace – in order that markets can work to environmental ends.

5 *The state must act to counter business interests which seek to block climate change initiatives.* Large-scale change is needed here, and at first blush this seems a tall order indeed. For business, especially big business, has a dominant role in contemporary societies. It is able to influence governments, even sometimes hold them to ransom and also influence consumers through advertising and other means. When governments threaten regulation, businesses can simply announce that they will up sticks and move elsewhere – the so-called problem of 'leakage'. Yet couldn't all this be turned around and the power of business become deployed to climate change objectives? I believe it is possible, even in the short term, as long as governments act together with enlightened corporate leaders. Here again we see the key importance of economic convergence. Joint action can emerge from a confluence of interests; it doesn't have to come from a sudden burst of altruism on the part of business firms.

6 *The state must keep climate change at the top of the political agenda.* For most people, most of the time, global warming is not a worry that intrudes deeply into the routines of daily life. It can drift off the agenda as other concerns come to the fore, or as elections approach. There should be an agreement among competing political parties that climate change and energy policy will be sustained in spite of other differences and conflicts that exist. In addition, climate change should feature in the curriculum of all schools.

7 *An appropriate economic and fiscal framework must be developed for moving towards a low-carbon economy.* Subsidies are needed if new technologies are to thrive, since, in the beginning, they will be unable to compete with fossil fuels. I shall argue below that a holistic approach is needed to carbon taxation – it will not do just to think in terms of a handful of

specific tax measures. The overall tax system needs continuous auditing in terms of its generic impact upon economic
behaviour and lifestyles.

8 *The state must prepare to adapt to the consequences of climate
change*, which will now be felt in any case. Thinking ahead
in this area is crucial – as in the case of mitigation, we can't
just wait around to see what develops. We must try to anticipate exactly how and where the effects of global warming
will be felt and act pre-emptively to counter or minimize
them.

9 *Local, regional, national and international aspects of climate
change policy must be integrated*. Without robust national
programmes, international agreements will not work.
Conversely, however, international collaboration of one
sort or another is a necessary condition for coping with
climate change.

Is this all asking too much, given the fact that governments
often find themselves hemmed in by the pressure of events
of the day? The political theorist John Dryzek argues that the
combination of capitalist markets, vested interests and state
bureaucracy means that government will be 'thoroughly inept
when it comes to ecology' He adds that 'any redeeming fea-
tures are to be found only in the possibilities they open up for
their own transformation'.[1] The first comment is too dismiss-
ive, but I agree with the thrust of the second. Responding to
climate change will prompt and require innovation in government itself and in the relation between the state, markets and
civil society.

The above points provide the basis for this and the following
two chapters. In the current one, I shall discuss what a return
to planning might imply, what surveys show about public
attitudes towards climate change and how we might keep the
issue at the forefront of the political agenda. I will then move
on to consider how consistent policy might be maintained
between otherwise antagonistic political parties. In the following chapter I discuss technological innovation and what help
government might play in furthering it, plus how taxation can
play a role. In chapter 7 I move on to the ticklish but necessary
topic of the politics of adaptation.

Planning, then and now

Planning was in vogue for some two or three decades in Western countries after the Second World War and was, of course, the very basis of the economy in Soviet-type societies. Between 1928 and 1991, as many as 13 successive national plans were instituted in the USSR. Planning was not only in fashion, but was *de rigueur* in Western countries too for a lengthy period after the Second World War, before falling into disrepute. In 1949 the economist Evan Durbin wrote: 'We are all planners now. . . . The collapse of the popular faith in *laissez-faire* has proceeded with spectacular rapidity . . . all over the world since the War.'[2]

In the post-war period, 'planning' normally meant strong central direction by the state in the interests of overall economic prosperity and social justice. In the mixed economies of the West, it signalled the nationalization of industry, especially those industries seen as strategically important, such as the energy industries, communications and iron and steel. It also referred to the creation of 'planned communities', such as 'new towns' and garden cities.

The reasons why the world retreated from planning, especially in its more centralized versions, were various. In Soviet-style society it was associated with an authoritarian, oppressive state. Even in the West many came to resent the heavy-handed outlook of government planners – faceless bureaucrats who could intervene in communities without much thought for local concerns or sensitivities. Moreover, centralized planning of the economy, supposed to overcome the irrationalities of capitalism, proved quite unable to cope with the complexities of a developed economic system. Bets were placed by governments on industries which promptly then went on to fail. Critics such as Friedrich von Hayek were proved correct when they argued that only markets can cope with the enormous numbers of on-the-ground decisions about prices and products that have to be made every moment of the day in modern economies.[3]

When the counter-revolution set in, from the 1980s onwards, involving widespread privatization, coupled with minimal macroeconomic steering, the very word 'planning' came under a shadow and has, until recently, remained there. Yet whenever we think about the future in a systematic way, in the sense of attempting to shape or guide it, planning of some sort is inevitable. The post-war period was one of reconstruction, in which large-scale investments had to be made in order to recover from a situation of immense material damage.

Many forms of planning were in fact carried on 'below the radar' by states, even after the time at which the idea fell into disrepute. Governments have had to monitor demographic shifts, for instance, in order to plan ahead for future needs in education, health and pensions. They have had to do the same with roads and railways in terms of future projections of use. Contingency plans have to exist in case of possible disasters. Even as 'planned communities' fell out of fashion, so urban planning of one sort or another continued.

There has now to be a return to greater state interventionism, a conclusion that is reinforced by the failure of deregulation. That failure can be summed up as too much 'short-termism' and a corrosion of public institutions, coupled to a lack of controls for system risk. In terms of the economy, ways will have to be found to introduce regulation without crippling that sense of adventure and entrepreneurialism upon which a successful response to climate change will also depend. In a nutshell, overall macroeconomic steering, the main economic role of government for the past three or four decades, is no longer enough. There needs to be a greater emphasis on industrial policy. This point is obvious in the case of the fostering of low-carbon technologies, but surely must apply more broadly – although the issues involved stretch well beyond my specific concerns here. Supply-side mechanisms will continue to be vital areas for state investment, as in the case of education or the provision of infrastructure.

A return to planning will in no sense be a straightforward process. Planning has to be reconciled with democratic freedoms, some of which should be actively extended, rather than reduced, in relation to the demands of climate change. There will be a push and pull between the political centre, regions and localities, which will have to be resolved through democratic mechanisms. It will not be easy to decide where the balance should lie. National planning will demand that local concerns sometimes be overridden – but how and to what degree?

This issue arises, for example, with the creation of new towns. For planned communities are back in fashion – this time as eco-towns, now being built or envisaged in many countries. It is clear also that planning must stretch across the boundaries of nations. National plans can't be hatched without due consideration of what neighbouring countries are doing. Compared to other countries, EU states should have a distinct advantage in this respect, since coordinated planning should, in principle, be much easier.

In thinking about planning, it won't do to consider only the form it will take; we also have to decide about its content. Lessons can be learned from those who make a speciality of studying that nebulous entity, the future.[4] How do we plan for a future which is inherently uncertain and in order to limit risks which, since we have no prior experience of them, cannot be assessed with complete precision? How can the mistakes made by the previous generation of planners be avoided? Planning in the old days was based on forecasting, but the limitations of this method are by now well known. It works best for short-term planning and also in cases where present-day trends are to some degree set in stone. In the case of energy forecasting in Britain, for instance, we know that the existing generation of power stations will need replacing within a certain timescale.

We often want to predict the future in order to change it – and where our attempts to change it become part of that future. This situation holds in the case of climate change. One way of dealing with it is by *backcasting*: asking what changes have to be made in the present in order to arrive at alternative future states. A successful outcome is imagined in the future, and different scenarios are calculated as to how it might be reached. We are talking therefore of alternative and plural futures, where adjustments, even radical revisions, are made as time unfolds and then built into other scenarios. This approach is essentially that used by the IPCC. The distinct advantage over traditional forecasting is that it allows much greater space for unforeseen contingencies that might dramatically alter predictions made at any specific date.

The point of backcasting is not to reveal what the future will be, but to weigh up future options and policy goals. Backcasting is especially relevant for environmental and energy planning issues, since they fit the circumstances to which the approach is most relevant. These are that the context is complex, a major reorientation of current trends is demanded and a timescale of several decades or more is involved. There are many examples from around the world. A project was instituted in the Netherlands in the late 1990s, for example, to look for alternatives to meat production and consumption. Its key assumption was that by 2040 new protein foods should replace 40 per cent of current meat consumption. The foods would have to be at least as tasty as the most popular forms of meat, while, among other qualities, having superior health value. The project considered how tastes might change to promote acceptance of such foods. It concluded that new protein foods could be produced 10–30 times more efficiently than meat, as measured in terms of reducing emissions, while at the same time producing a health bonus.[5]

Backcasting sounds technocratic. In fact, it almost always involves a visionary element, since, by definition, it projects a future that is different from that seen from the present. Of course, forecasting will not disappear and will continue to be part of government planning. It is obvious that backcasting and forecasting are often complementary. Take, as an example, planning for the future of the water industry in Australia, a country suffering from droughts that are probably influenced by global warming and where water is becoming an ever more scarce resource.[6] Cynthia Mitchell and Stuart White argue that forecasting can identify policies that will produce results in the short term – it can help pluck the low-lying fruit. Backcasting is needed to think more radically about future possibilities. Forecasts about security of water supply in urban areas in Australia indicate major problems in guaranteeing adequate supply within a few years. Several policies that could quickly make a difference within the existing water system were identified, such as installing water-efficient shower heads and tap regulators, dual flush toilets, waterless urinals, taps operated by sensors and local water collection and recycling. In Queensland, where there have been prolonged periods of drought, reductions in customer demand of up to 30 per cent have been attained using such means.

Backcasting, however, has helped suggest more far-reaching innovations. Thus at the moment it is commonly assumed that water, sewage and storm-water systems should be considered and planned for separately. Thinking 'backwards' from a hypothetical situation of a total water cycle has produced quite a different perspective. What can be achieved has been demonstrated in a residential development in Melbourne, which generated a 70 per cent reduction in water demand. Another possibility is, instead of simply providing a water stream, to think of providing a service of a more general nature. Thus, in central Queensland about 80 per cent of raw water demand comes from industry, and some 80 per cent of it is for cooling. A high proportion of that demand could in fact be transferred to air cooling, reducing the need to use water.

The state has a history of drought alternating with periods of flooding. The latest episode of flooding, beginning in December 2010, was devastating in its impact. No one can say with certainty whether climate change influenced recent weather fluctuations, but it is possible that La Niña (see above, p. 28), which lies behind them, is becoming intensified as a result of global warming. In any case, temporary periods of 'far too much water' do nothing to alleviate the more chronic shortages to which the region is subject.

In thinking about planning, especially over the longer term, we find ourselves back with risk and uncertainty. 'Planning' sounds like a straightforward process, but this is far from the case – it is highly complex and contingent. One of the main reasons for this is the fact that predictions, forecasts and plans that are made become themselves part of the universe of events which they are about. In an important sense they have to do so, since the point is to shape the future; yet, at the same time, an inherent element of unpredictability is introduced and has to be coped with. Trying to alter public attitudes towards risk is a key part of planning policy, and it is to this topic that I now turn.

Changing lives

Looking at public attitudes in a number of industrial countries 12 years ago, a group of researchers concluded: 'Our interpretation of existing data is that, all things being equal, a majority of citizens in most countries will support national and international initiatives designed to cope with global warming as long as these initiatives do not demand a significant alteration of lifestyle.'[7] Broadly speaking, that assessment remains the case today, as subsequent comparative surveys show.

In a national survey carried out in the UK in 2008, 30 per cent of respondents said they were 'very concerned' about climate change, with a further 47 per cent saying they were 'fairly concerned'.[8] However, many expressed doubts about the status of the scientific findings on the issue: 60 per cent either 'strongly agreeñ̃d' or 'agreed' with the statement that 'many scientific experts still question if humans are contributing to climate change', demonstrating the influence of the sceptics, which is out of all proportion to their numbers in the scientific community. Only 7 per cent 'strongly disagreed' with the statement, and 42 per cent either 'strongly agreed' or 'agreed' that 'I sometimes think climate change might not be as bad as people say'. Almost 60 per cent thought the government is using the climate change agenda to raise taxes. A large majority (77 per cent) endorsed the statement that 'most people are not prepared to make big sacrifices' to help stop climate change.

In terms of ranking the problems facing the country, 33 per cent chose the economy as their main worry – even before the 2008 financial crisis. Only 7 per cent put global warming at the top of the list. Climate change tends to be seen as a risk the responsibility for which lies with 'the authorities'.[9]

In a similar survey repeated in 2010, much the same pattern emerged. A majority – 76 per cent – still said they were 'very' or 'fairly worried' about climate change. About a quarter put global warming as one of the top three issues facing Britain. However, the proportion expressing trust in independent scientists to provide correct information about climate change had fallen, suggesting that the episode of the leaked emails did make an impact on public opinion. Moreover, the proportion not trusting any source had grown.

In such surveys, a high proportion of people agree that 'We are too small to make a difference', and that 'We shouldn't take action until bigger countries do'. The responses echo a problem in climate change policy which crops up in many different contexts – that of *free-riding*. Free-riding can arise in any area of social or economic life in which collective outcomes hinge on decisions taken by individual actors. For example, suppose that the residents in a street vulnerable to crime get together to set up a neighbourhood watch scheme – each has to pay £100 to make the scheme work. Some might refuse to contribute, yet the system is set up anyway. These people are free-riding, since they benefit from the scheme for nothing.

Problems of free-riding exist everywhere in the area of climate change policy, from the level of ordinary citizens right up to the international arena. People who continue to drive gas-guzzling vehicles are free-riding off those who have switched to smaller cars. Countries that have done little or nothing to reduce their greenhouse gas emissions are free-riding off those that have been more active. Feelings about free-riders in the area of climate change are very strong. The result is the 'I won't unless you do' syndrome, which is widespread.

Polls show that most people have only a vague idea about the causes of climate change. Many believe, for example, that healing the ozone layer will help stop global warming. A survey taken in the Seattle area – one of the most advanced in terms of environmental consciousness – showed that 45 per cent of respondents thought that stopping the use of aerosol sprays would be very helpful in reducing global warming.[10] Many did not appreciate that greenhouse gases are not just another form of pollution; a significant proportion believed that they can be removed from the air as easily as the pollutants which cause acid rain. Most people had a clearer understanding of problems surrounding energy, and in focus groups their opinions were often framed more in terms of energy requirements than of climate change.

Surveys taken on a global level show that people in the developing countries are the most concerned about climate change. A cross-cultural study of nine developed and developing countries indicated that about 60 per cent of people interviewed about climate change in China, India, Mexico and Brazil felt a 'high level of concern', in contrast to figures of only 22 per cent in the UK and Germany.[11] Furthermore, in the poorer countries, around 47 per cent of respondents expressed high levels of personal commitment to responding to climate change, compared to just 19 per cent in the UK. Although the proportion was even lower in the US, respondents there were by far the most optimistic of any that the problem could be solved. This finding is in line with a further study, which showed that 71 per cent of Americans agreed that steps taken to reduce emissions will help the US economy 'become more competitive . . . in the long run'.[12]

Research produced in Britain by the Department for Environment, Food and Rural Affairs (DEFRA) divides up the public into seven clusters in terms of their appreciation of the threat of climate change and their willingness to respond on the level of their day-to-day lives.[13] One group, the 'positive greens', accept that they should do as much as they can to limit their impact on the environment. They made up 18 per cent of the sample of the population studied. Those comprising this group came mostly from affluent backgrounds – social classes A and B in census terminology.

A second group, the 'waste-watchers', follow a 'waste not want not' philosophy, relevant to environmental goals, but not especially inspired by them. Thrift is part of their lives, presumably most often simply because of lack of resources. They represented 12 per cent of the sample, and were concentrated mainly among older age groups. The third cluster, the 'concerned consumers', making up 14 per cent, say they 'already do more than a lot of people' and are not willing at the moment to do much more.

A fourth cluster, the 'sideline supporters', accept that climate change is a major problem. Yet they are not contemplating any particular changes to their lifestyles. They say, for example, 'I don't think much about how much water or electricity I use, and I forget to turn things off', yet do seem to feel minor pangs of guilt about their attitudes. They comprised 14 per cent of the sample. A fifth group, the 'cautious participants', do little

Is there solid evidence the earth is warming?	Rep %	Dem %	Ind %
Yes	38	79	56
Because of human activity	16	53	32
Because of natural patterns	18	18	17
Don't know (Vol.)	3	8	7
No	53	14	31
Mixed/Don't know (Vol.)	9	6	12
How serious a problem?			
Very serious	14	50	30
Somewhat serious	27	32	32
Not too serious	23	8	17
Not a problem	34	7	18
Is it a problem requiring immediate government action?*			
Yes	24	68	44
No	39	19	31
Do scientists agree the earth is getting warmer because of human activity?			
Yes	30	59	41
No	58	32	45

*Asked of those who say global warming is a very serious, somewhat serious or not too serious a problem.

Figure 5.1 Wide partisan differences exist in the US about global warming

Source: Pew Research Center for the People and the Press. *Little Change in Opinions about Global Warming: Increasing Partisan Divide on Energy Policies,* 27 October 2010; a project of the Pew Research Center

to help the environment, but would do more if others did – they form another 14 per cent.

The sixth cluster, labelled the 'stalled starters', say they don't know much about climate change, and, in any case, lack the means to take any steps to help with the issue – they are mostly from non-affluent backgrounds. Most can't afford a car, but would like to buy one if they could. Finally, the 'honestly disengaged' are either sceptical about, or indifferent towards, climate change. As one interviewee remarked: 'Maybe there'll be an environmental disaster, maybe not. Makes no difference to me, I'm just living life the way I want to.'

It follows, the DEFRA report argues, that policy concerned with securing more environmentally responsible behaviour should vary. The 'positive greens' have a high potential to do more, and are willing to do so – and, at least to some degree, so are the 'concerned consumers' and the 'sideline supporters'. In these instances, policy should be to 'enable and engage' – it should be aimed at providing the means for individuals to build on the attitudes they already hold. Examples include providing information about how to lower carbon consumption, encouraging community action, improving infrastructure and so on.

For the 'cautious participants' and the 'stalled starters', the report says, the emphasis should be not only on enabling and engaging, but, in addition and in particular, on 'exemplifying'. In the terms I used earlier, people in these groups are worried about free-riding. Community leadership and neighbourhood groups can play a part in reducing the impact of feelings of unfairness about free-riding. As for the 'sceptics', their attitudes will be harder to sustain if others move the centre of gravity of public opinion onwards. The problem, as far as public policy is concerned, is one of 'engagement' – how to get such groups to take climate change seriously at all.

DEFRA hosted a 'citizens' summit' to see how far a deliberative process might shift public attitudes towards global warming and foster lifestyle changes. It formed part of a wider public consultation process as part of the lead-up to the introduction of the Climate Change Bill. A representative group of citizens from different regions in the country took part in a series of workshops. Information packs were provided, and the participants were requested to try out taking steps to reduce their carbon consumption before the final meeting, the 'summit', took place.

As in wider surveys, the desire for the government to take the lead came through clearly. People feel strongly about the gap they see between what they can do as individuals and the global scope of the problem. At the end of the deliberative process, the proportion of participants who agreed with the statement 'I am well informed about climate change' more than doubled – 66 per cent at that point claimed to be well informed. The percentage agreeing that 'action needs to be taken urgently' rose from 65 per cent at the beginning to 82 per cent by the close. Before the workshops started, just over half of the participants agreed that the responsibility for countering climate change 'belongs to all of us'. That proportion increased to 83 per cent.

About 40 per cent of emissions in the UK come from domestic sources if one includes household travel. There are many areas of day-to-day conduct where changes in behaviour would help lower this total. DEFRA separates them into 'one-off purchasing decisions', 'habitual everyday lifestyle activities', 'occasional purchasing decisions' and 'habitual purchasing decisions'. Those in the first category include, for example, installing home insulation or buying a more energy-efficient car. The second consists of such factors as energy consumption in the home and the level of car usage. Occasional purchasing decisions include buying energy-efficient products such as low-energy light bulbs. The fourth category is made up of activities such as the purchase of food and household goods.

The list of day-to-day activities outlined by DEFRA as relevant to reducing emissions is long. Should we be concentrating upon a blanket strategy, focusing on all of them? Many would say so. A proliferation of how-to-do-it books exists on how to reduce one's carbon footprint, and, if the majority of the population were to follow them, the impact upon carbon consumption would be significant.

I am quite hostile to such endeavours, however, no matter how well intentioned they may be. They are based upon a quite unrealistic assumption – that everyone is willing and able to live like the small minority of 'positive greens' in DEFRA's sample. It is possible that they may even be counter-productive, by actively putting off the majority of citizens from other steps they may take. Giddens's paradox holds. For most of the time and for the majority of citizens, climate change is a back-of-the-mind issue, even if it is a source of worry. It will stay that way unless its consequences become visible and immediate. In the meantime, no strategy is likely to work which concentrates solely upon provoking fear and anxiety, or which is based not only on instructing people to cut down on this or that, but also on expecting them to monitor that process on a continuous basis.

A different approach is needed from that prevalent at the moment. It must place an emphasis on positives as much as on negatives, and on opportunities rather than on self-induced deprivations. I would set out its main principles as follows.

Incentives must take precedence over all other interventions, including those which are tax-based. 'No punishment for punishment's sake': in other words, punitive measures should either supply revenue spent directly for environmental purposes, or be linked in a visible way with behaviour change – and preferably both. The drivers of gas-guzzling vehicles, for example, should face heavy tax duties for the privilege, as heavy as is politically feasible, under 'the polluter pays' principle. Clear and self-evident options for behaviour change are available – switch to smaller cars or drive less.

The positives must dominate. This isn't as difficult as it might sound. Take the issue of making homes more energy-efficient. There are several countries in the world that have managed to make major progress in this respect. How have they done so? Not by trying to scare people, but by emphasizing the advantages of having homes that are snug, protected against the elements and which also save money. An example is what has been achieved in Sweden, which was done by placing a strong emphasis on what was called 'community, style and comfort'.

Low-carbon practices or inventions that initially have only limited appeal can be fundamentally important if they set trends, or if they are seen as in some way iconic.[14] Most initiatives, whether social, economic or technological, are, in the early stages, open only to a small elite. In California, for example, there are long waiting lists for the hydrogen-powered Lifecar, although the first models will be extremely expensive. However, investment in such a car will provide the opportunity to see whether the vehicle could have a wider market, and also gives it an avant-garde cachet. This is what happened with the Toyota Prius hybrid vehicle, nearly a million of which have been sold worldwide. It was a vanguard model in the sense that it stimulated other manufacturers to start producing low-emission vehicles, whether hybrid or not.

Most initiatives that have successfully reduced emissions so far have been driven by the motivation to increase energy efficiency, rather than the desire to limit climate change. This observation applies to whole countries as well as to regions, cities and the actions of individuals. People are able to grasp and respond to this perspective more easily than to climate change, with all its surrounding debates and complexities; it is not difficult to present energy efficiency in a positive light. What is at issue, as mentioned earlier, is energy efficiency in the economy as a whole, since efficiency gains in one context are of little or no value if savings made are spent on energy-consuming activities elsewhere. The fundamental problem at the moment is to make clean energy sources competitive with fossil fuel energy sources, whether through public pro-vision of subsidies or through technological advance. Utility companies in the US have been offering electricity generated from wind or solar sources to consumers since the late 1990s. Initially, take-up was very small, however, since the prices were not competitive. In early 2006 Xcel Energy in Colorado and Austin Energy in Texas offered tariffs below those of the regular energy sources. Austin Energy encouraged its custom-ers to sign up for 10-year energy contracts, and was able to prosper even when the price of electricity dropped.

The role of technology in promoting low-carbon lifestyles is bound to be considerable. Technological innovation rarely determines what people do, since we often react to it in ways in which its initiators did not suspect. Thus the telephone was invented in 1876 as a signalling device; no one imagined that it would become so intrinsic to our lives as a medium of talk and conversation.[15] Yet, at the same time, our lives can change dramatically through such interaction with technology. It is said that we are 'creatures of habit'. And it is often true, espe-cially if habits become addictive. Yet such is far from always the case – we can change our behaviour quite rapidly and dramatically, as has happened, and on a global level, with the arrival of the internet.

Government should be actively encouraging the creative economy and the creative society, even when these don't seem to have an immediate bearing upon climate change, since cre-ativity has to be the order of the day. Richard Florida, who has written extensively on the subject, argues persuasively that the creative sectors of the economy – where innovation, lateral thinking and enterprise can flourish – are increasingly becom-ing the driving force of the economy as a whole. Florida rejects the idea that creativity – the capacity to innovate, to question conventional wisdom – is limited to the few. Creativity is a 'limitless resource. . . . It's a trait that can't be handed down, and it can't be owned in the traditional sense.'[16] R&D investment is important, but in pioneering responses to climate change, we need to be bringing science, the universities and social entrepreneurs closer together.

Step changes or 'tipping points' aren't confined to the field of climate change science. They apply to social and economic life too – that was the context, in fact, in which the author who popularized the term, Malcolm Gladwell, originally discussed it.[17] We should be looking to create tipping points when it comes to the transition to low-carbon lifestyles. From small beginnings, much larger changes can occur when a certain threshold is reached.

Governments have an important role in 'editing choice', and, in pursuing that aim, they shouldn't be afraid to take on big business when it is necessary to do so. Corporations influence our choices in many direct and indirect ways – the state shouldn't be reluctant to take a leaf out of their book. For instance, supermarkets usually place sweets and chocolates close to the exit, where customers line up to pay for their purchases. The reason is that at that point they are open to impulse buying, having relaxed after making their main purchases. Given the advance of obesity, I see no reason why such a practice shouldn't be either prohibited or actively discouraged (although thus far it has not). How far we should go with choices that affect carbon consumption is a moot point. Some examples of choice editing appear to be completely unobjectionable. Thus, for example, we could propose that heating and air-conditioning should be organized such that everyone knows immediately how much he or she is spending at any given time. The effect would be even more powerful if we knew how our expenditure rated compared to that of our neighbours. A study showed that heavy users made bigger cuts in consumption if a smiling face was inscribed on bills below the average, with a frowning face on the bills of those having higher than average expenditure. Other examples are more complicated. I see no civil liberties issue in cases where our behaviour is already being significantly influenced, or manipulated, by companies, and where the object of government policy is to counter that influence.[18] An example would be when a firm heavily advertises a product or service known to have adverse environmental effects. Should governments go further? The Australian government, for example, has instituted a total ban on all light bulbs that aren't of the low-energy type. Is it justified in doing so? In my view it is, given that the energy gains are substantial, while the difference in other ways between the conventional and low-energy bulbs is negligible. In any case, it is up to governments to explore these boundaries in conjunction with the electorate.

Foregrounding

Combating climate change demands long-term policies: how are these to be kept at the forefront of political concern? What can be done to keep global warming firmly on the political agenda? Agenda-setting theory helps supply some of the answers.[19] It concerns how and why different policy questions figure prominently in the programmes of governments while others tend to recede into the background or even disappear altogether. How far a given set of problems receives public and policy attention does not just depend upon its objective importance, but upon a range of other factors too. In democratic countries, numerous areas of concern at any one time jostle for attention in the public sphere. Very often, transient issues outweigh more permanent and profound ones in terms of the attention they receive in the political arena.

Three aspects of the political agenda can be identified. First, there is the 'public agenda', which refers to issues felt to be most important by voters at any specific point in time. Second, the 'governmental agenda' is about the questions that are under debate in parliament and surrounding agencies. Finally, the 'decision agenda' refers to a more limited set of policies that are actually being enacted. Each of these dimensions is limited in terms of the numbers of issues that can be considered at any particular moment. Hence, there is competition between items that press for attention.

According to John Kingdon, the leading author in the field, who coined these terms, the political agenda at a given time is the result of the interaction of different 'streams' of concerns, which he labels problems, policies and politics. They sometimes converge, but also often flow on largely independently of one another, with their own rules and conventions, personnel and dynamics. What actually gets done depends upon the points at which they connect, which canny political players manage to exploit. There is much more chance that an issue will command the interest of policy-makers at such a point – a window of opportunity opens. Kingdon's now classic work, *Agendas, Alternatives and Public Policies*, starts with a resounding quote from Victor Hugo, 'Greater than the tread of mighty armies is an idea whose time has come.'[20] But how can we know when the time for an idea has come? Why do those in and around government, at any particular point, attend to some issues and not others?

The problem stream comes to the attention of policy-makers, Kingdon says, through indicators, focusing events and feedback. Indicators are measuring devices that reveal the scale of the problem in question. They allow a process to be monitored. Thus a continuing issue may actually become a 'problem' when a change is witnessed, as when unemployment or crime rates go up. Shifts in indicators may be enough to push an item onto the agenda, but issues are more likely to attract attention when propelled into the limelight as a result of dramatic events that bring them into focus. A focusing event may be anything that catches the headlines, such as a particularly violent crime.

Feedback concerns the responses of different groups, or the public at large, to particular policy programmes. It is almost always negative feedback that highlights a given problem – policies or practices that are working well don't get reported. Nor do they tend to spark the interest of the public, which is most often stimulated when things go wrong or are seen to be going wrong. How events and reactions to them become framed – for example, how far a given problem is seen as open to government intervention or not – is of great importance in determining actual outcomes.

Work in the policy stream tends to be continuous. It goes on without much day-to-day reference to what moods may grip the public, and is pursued by specialists and experts within policy communities. Such work generates many possible policy proposals, but only a few ever make it onto the concrete political agenda. They are quite often 'solutions' waiting for problems – that is to say, they provide avenues for political intervention when the need for it arises as driven by a specific focusing event or set of events. The availability of 'solutions' is very important. Problems which do not come with potential courses of remedial action attached are not likely to get onto the agenda. Rather, they are accepted as situations that have to be lived with, and normally do not rate highly among the worries expressed by the public.

Organized interest groups of one kind or another play a role in shaping public opinion and limiting or opening out space for governmental action. However, what Kingdon calls the 'national mood' has a major impact upon when, where and how the problem, policy and political streams converge. For instance, when the mood is 'anti-government', voters may simply tune out from whatever strategies the government of the day might propose.

Some windows of opportunity are predictable – annual budgets, for example, usually provide an opportunity for a new departure. Most, however, are not, and policy entrepreneurs must therefore be prepared to grasp the opportunity when it presents itself, or to mobilize to block it. Public enthusiasm for a given policy agenda rarely lasts long, even when an issue is of continuing and manifest importance. In fact, studies show, it most often turns to disillusionment or indifference when the problem is not one that admits of a simple solution. Cynicism, unwillingness to make sacrifices, the perception that the costs are too great, or simply boredom can supplant the initial burst of public concern and support. With a constant search for novelty, and a distaste for 'yesterday's news', the media undoubtedly play a substantial role in public shifts in attention.

The implications for climate change policy are clear and significant. Public support for such policy is not likely to be constant and can only form a general backdrop to effective policy action. I have argued that anxiety about future risk can't be used as the sole motivator of public opinion, and that conclusion is backed up by studies of other risks and how people respond to them. For instance, concern about terrorism tends to move up and down the list of major public concerns depending exactly upon the factors identified by Kingdon – for instance, whether or not there has been a focusing incident of some kind. Worries not linked in the public mind with clear modes of response quickly slip down people's ratings of what disturbs them most. Talk of impending catastrophe – whatever the risk in question – has little impact and indeed may induce an attitude of fatalism that blunts action. Fatalism in response to risk is a common reaction, visible in many who choose to pay no heed to health warnings about their lifestyle habits.

A cross-party concordat, as discussed below, would give a firm anchor for climate change as a continuing preoccupation of the 'policy stream'. A diversity of groups in civil society – also discussed below – will certainly continue to press to keep necessary reforms and innovations going. Yet public support will be needed and it cannot be only latent. Based on Kingdon's work, Sarah Pralle suggests a number of ways in which public interest and concern can be charged and recharged. Indicators, if they are straightforward and easy to grasp, could have an important role; and with the continued advance of climate science, they are certainly abundant. A few key indicators, especially where they can be linked to focusing events, should be highlighted. However, they shouldn't be of the doom and gloom variety, but linked to potentially positive outcomes – to efforts that groups and communities are making to lessen the threats.

Problems that relate to people's immediate experience are most likely to be taken seriously. Rightly or wrongly, hurricane Katrina and the 2003 European heat waves made the impact they did upon the consciousness of citizens in the developed countries because they were 'close to home'. Only a small proportion of people in the industrial countries currently agree with the statement, 'My life is directly affected by global warming and climate change.'[21] They are also far more likely, on average, to be taking concrete measures to reduce their own carbon consumption. Most important of all, policy entrepreneurs should always connect problems with potential remedies or solutions. However, those solutions themselves must have 'salience' – they have to supply the motivation to act. One hundred books on one hundred ways to reduce your carbon footprint will have less effect than just one that is geared to what people are positively motivated to do.

A political concordat

Many have bemoaned the convergence of parties towards the centre ground in contemporary politics, but in the environmental field at least this could be a major advantage. Equating being in the political centre with an absence of radicalism only applies in the case of traditional left–right issues. As I have argued earlier, if one doesn't think in this way, it is entirely possible to have a 'radicalism of the centre' – indeed, in terms of climate change and energy policy it is an essential concept.

What does a 'radicalism of the centre' mean? It means, first of all, gaining widespread public support for radical actions – that is, for the conjunction of innovation and long-term thinking which is the condition necessary for responding to climate change. It implies the reform of the state. Climate change and energy security are such serious issues, and they affect so many other aspects of the political field, that a concern with them has to be introduced across all branches of government. Most of the industrial states are coming to recognize this, although progress on the ground tends to be slow. Climate change is generally allocated to the environment ministry, which, in turn, is rarely one of the most powerful in influencing government. Such ministries are quite often separate from those dealing with transport and energy, health or overseas development. Power lies mostly where the money is: in the Treasury or finance ministry. Yet from now on, where the money is will be influenced enormously by climate change and energy questions, so it is in everyone's interest that these issues achieve the primacy of place they deserve.

It is normal and acceptable for political parties to claim that they, rather than their opponents, are the ones to turn to for firm action on global warming. Yet beyond a certain area, and beyond the rhetoric of immediate party politics, there has to be agreement that the issue is so important and all-encompassing that the usual party conflicts are largely suspended or muted.

The disastrous situation in American politics, discussed in the previous chapter, shows what happens where there is political polarization around climate change. Fortunately, the US here is very much the exception rather than the rule insofar as the vast majority of countries in the world are concerned.

How a cross-party consensus might be achieved was explored in a British context in a comprehensive report on the issue produced by an all-party group in Parliament. The group tried to reach a consensus about consensus and, to a significant degree, it succeeded in so doing. The objective was to investigate 'the potential of a cross-party consensus on climate change to try to look beyond the tendency of politics to dwell in the terrain of competition for short-term advantage'.[22] Is a consensus desirable and, if so, what form should it take?

A wide range of opinions was solicited for the inquiry. Some argued that a consensus would in fact be undesirable, since it would be likely to stifle debate and the critical examination to which all political proposals and policies should be subject. Moreover, they pointed out, a consensus could potentially lead to a loss of public attention and awareness for the issue. In addition, reaching shared agreement might mean opting for the lowest common denominator (much as has happened in the Kyoto and post-Kyoto negotiations).

However, while recognizing the force of these points, the large majority of contributors accepted that a consensus across the parties was not only possible, but necessary. There was more agreement about the need for a consensus on targets for emissions reductions than upon how they should best be reached. Yet many emphasized the importance of overall agreement about means as well as ends. Policies initiated by one government in areas such as fiscal measures or investment in R&D and technology would have to have a core of stability across changes of government.

Cross-party agreement has to be robust, since there will be a clear temptation for parties to sacrifice longer-term goals in pursuit of immediate political advantage, especially when unpopular decisions have to be taken. A consensus that focuses only on goals, even if it involves a general agreement on targets, is likely to be too weak to be effective. The chairman of the committee, Colin Challen, MP, expressed the point forcefully:

> Until a binding consensus is reached, there will always be the danger that any party proposing the really tough measures necessary to tackle the problem will face . . . the strong likelihood that another party will present the electorate with a 'get out of jail free card' for their own electoral advantage. . . . There seems little point in drawing together a consensus that is merely promoting motherhood and apple pie. It is clear that the purpose of the consensus is to overcome the severe tension between short-term electoral politics and long-term climate change goals, a tension which has to date resulted in the triumph of short-termism.[23]

The committee concluded that a consensus doesn't have to be 'all or nothing' in order to work. It should concentrate upon targets and upon a long-term policy framework that would offer a reasonable chance of meeting the targets. Examples already exist where a cross-party consensus has been formed and clear results have been produced – such as that which helped lead to a settlement in Northern Ireland.

A main recommendation was that an independent body be set up to monitor progress towards targets; and that the prime minister of the day should be held directly responsible for the cross-party consensus process. Such an agency was in fact later set up, in the shape of the Climate Change Committee, coupled with the introduction of legal obligations on the part of successive governments to make specific progress towards the targets (see above, pp. 84–6). Several other countries, such as the Netherlands, Denmark and Japan, have set up similar programmes to try to create and preserve cross-party agreements.

Although it is important that there should be consensus, it cannot be too minimalist. We should perhaps speak of a *concordat* rather than a consensus, because there should be a clear statement of principles that are publicly endorsed.

In accordance with the overall themes of this book, I would emphasize that it must cover means as well as ends, and it has to home in on the short term as well as the long term in order to be effective. Agreement on targets set for decades down the line will be of little help, however demanding those targets appear. Should such a consensus imply a 'suspension of hostilities' between the parties, as far as parliamentary debate about climate change is concerned? Yes, it should. Left-of-centre parties or coalitions have a particular responsibility to tone down their rhetoric, especially of the red–green variety, since it stakes a claim to the privileged position of leftist thinking – a claim which is false. Such restraint is all the more important given the fact that it is the right-of-centre parties which tend to be most reluctant to support climate change policy.

A stronger monitoring body should be established than the Climate Change Committee set up in Britain. It should not be merely advisory, but have the capacity to intervene in legislation by, for example, having clearly specified rights to take the government to the courts if it has gone back on its obligations. Its composition is likely to be crucial, and appointment to it should not simply be the prerogative of the government of the day. Its brief has to extend beyond climate change and there has to be clear coordination with whatever major agency is responsible for energy and energy planning.

It will be essential to stop such a body from becoming too bureaucratic and fixed in its practices. Hence there must be a method of ensuring a regular turnover in its composition, whether by having relatively short terms of service or by other means. It must be subject to regular parliamentary as well as wider public scrutiny.

Moreover, government must not only be an agent of change as far as combating global warming is concerned; it must be an exemplar too. Government and its officialdom shouldn't find themselves in the position of the doctor who carries on smoking while advising his patients not to do so. 'Do as I say, not as I do' is not good enough. For example, governments shouldn't only be in the business of setting targets; they should also be in the vanguard of showing concretely how to reach them.

State and society: business and the NGOs

An ensuring state must work with diverse groups and, of course, with the public, in order to deliver upon climate change goals. The classical liberal view of the rights and responsibilities of individuals, simply put, is that every individual should be free to pursue whatever lifestyle he or she chooses, so long as those choices do not harm others. However, the liberal state has not been accustomed to extending that principle to environmental goods, or to the avoidance of harm to future generations; both now have to become absolutely central.

The rights of future generations should be incorporated within standard democratic procedures. Environmentalists often bolster their arguments about climate change by asking rhetorically, 'What would we say to our children's children in 50 years' time when they ask how we could have allowed such damage to occur, knowing that it was almost certain to happen?' That question should not be an isolated one, however, but part of what we ask ourselves on a regular basis, as a normal feature of the democratic process. It has many implications. For instance, the debate about oil and gas is about when available supplies will be half gone, and therefore at what date they will be largely exhausted. Yet it could, and should, be asked how far we (the current generation) have the right more or less to destroy such a natural resource forever, whatever other sources of energy are developed in the future. The same question could, and should, also be asked about other mineral resources.

Environmental rights and responsibilities, incorporating due attention to the rights of subsequent generations, should be introduced directly to the existing framework of liberal democracy. In other words, they should be added to and integrated with such rights and responsibilities as the right to vote, to enjoy equality before the law, freedom of speech and assembly. Robyn Eckersley[24] suggests that environmental rights and responsibilities should include the following:

- as just mentioned, a responsibility on the part of government to include future generations and non-human species as moral referents;

- right-to-know legislation in relation to pollutants and toxic substances, which the state is mandated to provide, both on a regular basis and when asked by citizens' groups or communities;
- the provision of public forums where the environmental impact of new technology or development proposals can be assessed;
- third-party litigation rights to allow NGOs and concerned citizens to ensure that environmental standards are being upheld;
- thoroughgoing acceptance of 'the polluter pays' principle, with penalties for those who cause environmental harm;
- the obligation of citizens, businesses and groups in civil society to act as positive agents of environmental change, rather than simply preventing destructive acts.

Such a framework would help integrate the diversity of groups whose activities are relevant to climate change policy. NGOs and businesses are the most prominent types of such groups and have long defined themselves partly in relation to one another. In each case they are quite often global in scope and their leading organizations are household names. Industry is, by any reckoning, a major force in the environmental area; it accounts for more than a third of the energy consumed across the world, and of course is involved in its production too. The NGOs like to portray themselves as minnows pitting themselves against the industrial giants, but, in truth, their influence has become very large. The best-known NGOs enjoy far higher levels of public trust than do their business counterparts.[25]

NGOs have long regarded large corporations as the prime agents of the irresponsible squandering of resources. In some large degree they have had good reason for such a view. Particularly important, in terms of climate change, have been the fossil fuel lobbies, representing heavy industry, transportation, coal, oil and chemicals. Until recently, the lobbies and the large majority of their individual members have argued that action to reduce greenhouse gases would be a mistake. They have mostly taken a sceptical position, as is shown in surveys of their literature and that of the think-tanks they help fund. The American Petroleum Institute, an industry research organization, claimed as its main goal to make sure that 'climate change becomes a non-issue'.[26]

Industrial lobbies are especially well organized and powerful in the US, and undoubtedly played a major role in influencing the hostile attitudes of the Bush administration towards efforts to take action against global warming. During the first term of George W. Bush's presidency, John H. Sununu, a prominent climate change sceptic, was the White House Chief of Staff. The lobbies had easy access to him, and to Vice-President Dick Cheney; they managed to block or dismember legislation regarded as a threat to fossil fuel interests. When Sununu stepped down, a newspaper headline announced: 'Sununu resigns . . . coal lobby in mourning.'[27] Industry groups have been a major influence in Europe too. They lobbied fiercely and effectively against the original commission proposals for a universal carbon tax, arguing, as their counterparts in the US did, that it would undermine competitiveness.

However, one should guard against the easy demonizing of the industry lobbies, and of big business more generally, that pervades much of the environmental literature. Business leaders are not all cut from the same cloth, while the lobbies themselves (as is true too of environmental lobbies) are quite frequently divided. For instance, in the run-up to the Kyoto Summit, the major oil interests were hostile to the proposals put forward, but the gas and electricity companies were in favour. The connection between these groups and the climate change sceptics has been well documented (see above, pp. 24–5).

NGOs tend to cloak themselves in moral garb and are no doubt sincere in their desire to better the world. Yet they too are lobbying groups, like the new associations springing up that represent the renewable technology industries. As has often been pointed out by critics, NGOs are neither elected bodies nor subject to the market discipline that industrial bodies have to face. It is difficult to assess the level of their influence, since their activities tend to be less formalized than those of the industry lobbies.

The Climate Change Network is an organization of 365

NGOs from diverse countries and regions, and includes the well-known ones, such as Greenpeace, Friends of the Earth and the World Wildlife Fund. The network boasts a world membership of 20 million people, which is the basis of its claim to speak for large constituencies of concerned citizens. It follows a 'three-track' approach. One involves putting pressure on nations to set themselves rigorous targets, as agreed at the 2007 Bali Summit, to set up a new round of international agreements to limit climate change. The second, the 'greening track', is about helping developing countries to adopt renewable technologies. The third, the 'adaptation track', is concerned with helping the most vulnerable countries anticipate and prepare for unavoidable consequences of climate change.

NGOs are not only pressure groups, but also play a significant role in coordinating scientific information and bringing it to the notice of decision-makers and the public. The two workshops set up in the late 1980s which led to the emergence of the IPCC were organized by NGOs. NGOs have also been closely involved in the setting of climate change policy in many countries, where they have tried to prompt governments to act, and have then pushed for their actions to be far-reaching.

A new generation of business leaders – who quite often work directly with NGOs – is arising which not only acknowledges the perils of climate change, but is active in the vanguard of reaction to it. Businesses such as Wal-Mart, which for years were seen by environmentalists as public enemies, have swung behind the climate change agenda, and in much more than just a face-saving way. Wal-Mart has planned substantial reductions in its own emissions, in the short as well as the long term, and it has demanded that its suppliers measure and report their emissions too. Tesco has pledged to put 'carbon labels' on all its 80,000 product lines, so that consumers know what volume of greenhouse gases has gone into their production. The firm has set itself the goal of halving its emissions per case of goods delivered worldwide by 2012 against a baseline of 2006. Of course, there are many who doubt the authenticity of these commitments. The NGO Corporate Watch lists no fewer than 20 kinds of 'corporate crimes' of which Tesco is accused.

As far as the environmentalist claims of businesses are concerned, it is important to separate the wheat from the chaff.

The making of disingenuous or false claims to environmental credentials – 'greenwash' – has become a real problem. In front of me, I have two large ads from a daily newspaper. One is for one of the most thirsty SUVs on the road, which, in this case, is seen in a field rather than the city streets where most of its counterparts roam. The makers announce how proud they feel to be doing their bit for 'the environment' because they have made some improvements in the energy efficiency of their production processes. The second ad, even more absurdly, makes similar claims for a sports car that, when driven in town, travels fewer than 10 miles per gallon of fuel consumed.

In most countries, regulatory authorities do not have sufficient authority, or resources, to intervene in an official and effective way. The same standards, backed by law, should be imposed that apply in other areas, such as those governing racism. Attacking 'greenwash' is not a trivial or marginal pursuit. One reason, of course, is that it is necessary to ensure that companies take seriously their obligations to reduce their emissions. Perhaps even more important, though, is the fact that 'greenwash' is a way of wilfully misleading the public.

The standards that companies should meet can be fairly easily described. Their claims should apply across the whole of their carbon output, not just one selected part of it where some sort of improvement has been made. Assertions made should be backed up with concrete and measurable actions, set against a given baseline, or they should not be made at all. Corporations could call in third parties to audit their performance, and their results should be published, just as are those of their financial operations.

We must wait and see with Wal-Mart and other supermarket chains, but some corporations have in fact already delivered on their promises. Nike, for example, has reduced its carbon footprint by 75 per cent over a period of 10 years. The company has stated that it aims to achieve zero waste, zero toxicity and complete recyclability across its product range by 2020. It might not happen, but there seems no more reason to doubt the firm's seriousness of intent than the declarations made by countries about what they will achieve by that date. Of course, as in the case of the state, NGOs exist in order to put pressure on organizations whose activities don't match up to their proclaimed intent.

There are many corporations today, such as those mentioned above, that are transforming their attitudes just as radically as are states. They are doing so partly for business reasons and in order to respond to the coming of carbon markets and carbon taxes – but they are doing so also because the message of the need for change has struck home.

The chairman of Coca-Cola announced in 2007 that the guiding principle of the firm's activities in the future has to be: 'We should not cause more water to be removed from a watershed than we can replenish.'[28] The company has entered into a partnership with the World Wildlife Fund to pursue the cause of water conservation. The partnership has come about because both Coca-Cola and the WWF have recognized that a change of tack is required. WWF's chief operating officer, Marcia Marsh, observed: 'The simple fact is that we are failing relative to our wider goals. Despite our successes in raising public awareness and funding, species are disappearing at historic rates. Habitat continues to be destroyed. Working alone, NGOs are simply unable to reverse the tide of global change.'[29]

Coca-Cola carried out an extensive project on world freshwater supplies in 2002, at a point when most governments had not yet appreciated the scale of the problem of looming world water shortages. However, the company was a long way from having analysed the impact of its entire supply-chain, and the firm later agreed that the WWF will be able to report publicly its findings about the environmental consequences of the company's worldwide activities. The two organizations will work together to develop binding targets for improved water efficiency.

In *Green Inc*, Christine MacDonald takes the NGOs to task for the closeness of the ties they have forged with business, on the grounds that they are being corrupted.[30] And, indeed, NGOs, businesses and governments to some degree have differences of interest that neither could nor should be eradicated. All are to some extent interest groups, with agendas that do not by any means always conform to the public interest; yet it is hard to see that much progress will be made unless they can form active and effective partnerships. NGOs not only have moral credibility, but have accumulated a fund of environmental knowledge and expertise that companies normally lack. The role of businesses, small and large, is going to be absolutely crucial in responding to climate change, not least because they will have to supply a good deal of the funding and also pioneer new technologies.

Coca-Cola and the WWF are not alone; many similar partnerships are developing around the world.[31] Unilever is working with the Rainforest Alliance on the environmental effects of its Lipton tea business; IKEA is collaborating with Brazilian NGOs to work towards regulating logging in the Amazon rainforest. Alcoa, the aluminium-producing company, a target for attack by many NGOs in the past, is doing the same as part of a new-found commitment to reducing its environmental impact. A great deal of water is used in the production of aluminium. The production process is also a major source of greenhouse gas emissions, while also generating waste that has to go to land-fill. Since aluminium ore (bauxite) is found near to the land surface, it is often extracted by open-cast mining. In the smelting process, CO_2 and perfluorocarbons (PFCs) are produced. PFCs are among the most harmful of greenhouse gases, more so even than methane. Alcoa has set itself targets of a 70 per cent reduction in water discharge from its plants by 2010 and zero discharge by 2020. It has introduced similarly radical programmes for recycling and emissions – its goals are to achieve 25 per cent recycled aluminium content by 2010 and 50 per cent by 2020.[32] Recycling not only saves emissions directly but will help in another way too. Aluminium cans may use bauxite mined in Australia, be smelted in China, and pressed into cans and filled in the US or Europe. When cans are recycled, the whole process can be completed domestically, reducing emissions by as much as 75 per cent.

It is not only manufacturing companies that are undergoing such a change of attitudes, but those in other sectors too. In February 2007, Citigroup Bank issued a 'Position Statement on Climate Change' accepting that serious risks are posed by global warming.[33] The key questions now, it says, concern the rapidity and severity of the changes and the practical implications that flow from them. During the Bush years, the company argued that the US government must shift its position quite dramatically and assume a world leadership role in countering climate change. Citigroup committed itself to a 10 per cent reduction in its own greenhouse gas emissions by 2011 and pledges investment in alternative energy technology.

In the same year the corporation announced that it will direct $50 billion over the next 10 years towards climate change projects, through investment to support the activities of its clients and through its own operations. To date, it has invested $10 billion. Citibank already has a substantial portfolio of equity investments in solar, wind and hydroelectric power, as well as in low-carbon building projects. According to its originators, the firm's comprehensive programme 'is not a wish-list, but a realistic, achievable plan'.[34] How far that plan will survive the serious economic difficulties the bank got into during the recession remains to be seen.

States, businesses and NGOs are not the only agents involved in active policy to counter global warming. We must also recognize the importance of local and city-based initiatives. As emphasized earlier, 'the state' does not only refer to the national level, but to regional, city and local government too. In the global age, many influences come in below the level of the nation-state, impinging directly upon localities, which in turn can have an impact much greater than their size would suggest. Moreover, at all levels inspirational individuals can break the mould of conventional wisdom.

Sweden is the country furthest along the line towards overcoming its dependence on fossil fuels, and one man, Per Carstedt, can take a certain amount of the credit.[35] Carstedt is a Ford car dealer who spent a number of years in Brazil, the first country to develop ethanol on a large scale as a motor fuel. He went to the Rio Summit in 1992, and came away clear in his mind that humanity couldn't carry on for long on its current path. When he returned to Sweden, he started looking into how ethanol might be introduced into the country. Initially he made no headway at all. There was no technical know-how, no filling stations were interested in supplying ethanol and, it was said, the fuel wouldn't work in Sweden's cold climate anyway. Eventually, he located a small flexi-fuel programme at Ford in Detroit, and through this contact managed to import three ethanol cars into Sweden, showing that they could run perfectly well there. Later he imported some more, but neither Ford nor any other manufacturer he approached showed any interest, arguing that there was no market for them. Carstedt then spent several years travelling the country, building up support in a consortium of local governments, companies and individuals who would buy the vehicles.

There was still no ethanol in filling stations, but Carstedt finally managed to persuade one close to his home and another in Stockholm to put in an ethanol pump. He and his colleagues then toured other stations, trying to persuade them one by one to do the same, offering finance if necessary. By 2002 there were 40 stations offering ethanol, and from then on they rapidly multiplied. About 1,000 such stations had come into existence four years later, constituting 25 per cent of the overall number in the country. Some 15 per cent of vehicles in Sweden today run on biofuels.

Carstedt anticipated early on the backlash that has occurred against biofuels. What is needed, he argues, is investment to develop fuels that do not compete with food production. The research group with which he is currently involved is producing biofuels from cellulose, coming from wood chips or industrial waste, which will meet that requirement. A new bio-energy refinery using this technology has been built, and a far larger one is planned. The refinery produces a total energy efficiency of over 70 per cent, which is much higher than the level produced by orthodox forms of ethanol.

Why not go the whole hog and argue, as some environmentalists do, that climate change issues should be dealt with piecemeal and primarily from the bottom up? The reason why not, in fact, is easy to see. Unregulated markets have no long-term perspective, and, insofar as they create externalities, may actively undermine such a perspective. Much the same is true of the thousands of local initiatives that exist, even if many of them on their own are worthy or necessary.

TECHNOLOGIES AND TAXES

Ambitious attempts have been made to anticipate how the spread of renewable technologies will transform modern economies. Some speak of the coming of a new industrial revolution, which will be initiated by such technologies. The American political thinker Jeremy Rifkin argues that the great changes in world history have taken place when new sources of energy have emerged in tandem with developments in communications. Thus the convergence of coal-based power and the printing press gave rise to the first industrial revolution. Previous forms of communication would not have been able to handle the social and economic complexities introduced by the new forms of technology. The 'second industrial revolution' started in the late nineteenth century. It was marked by the invention of electric communication, beginning with the telegraph and branching out into the telephone, radio and television. These developments converged with the emergence of oil as a major form of power generation and as the dominant source of energy for transport.

We now stand on the verge of a 'third industrial revolution', Rifkin says, which will have as its backdrop the development of networked communication, represented by personal computers and the internet. The potential of these technologies lies in their convergence with renewable energy. We can envisage a global energy economy where millions of people produce renewable energy and share it with others through national and international power grids – as happens today with information. Just as personal computers have vastly more power than the early machines, which took up several rooms, so intelligent energy networks will become more powerful and ubiquitous than anything we know at the moment.

Rifkin has his favourite renewable energy source to help point the way ahead: hydrogen.[1] Hydrogen, he says, is the 'forever fuel', since it is the most ubiquitous element in the universe – and it produces no greenhouse gas emissions. Fuel cells using hydrogen are already being introduced into the market for home and industrial use. The top-down energy regime that exists today with big oil and gas will be replaced by decentralized energy production and use. It will be 'the first truly democratic energy regime in history'.[2]

Such ideas aren't particularly compelling. In the first place, they reflect a view in which history is driven in large part by technology, a partial notion at best. The dating and nature of the supposed second industrial revolution are vague – as can be seen by the fact that other authors who propose similar ideas come up with quite different versions of when it happened and what its content was. Some, for example, date it 40 or 50 years later than Rifkin does. No one knows as yet what role a specific energy source such as hydrogen might play. Moreover, technologies never operate on their own – they are always embedded in wider political, economic and social frameworks, which are likely to govern both how they develop and what their consequences are.

In addition, the 'next industrial revolution' hasn't as yet actually happened. The original industrial revolution did not occur in a conscious way. The next one, however, has to be created as a deliberate project to protect us against future dangers – a very different situation. We don't know how things will turn out. It could be, as Rifkin hopes, that energy and politics will march in line – decentralized network systems, rooted in local communities, will replace current forms of political and economic power. It is the vision that many in the green movement would like to see realized. I'm not sure such an outcome is either likely or desirable. Certainly, it is very possible that most households will help create energy, rather than just consume it – as is already the case, for example, with feed-in tariffs. However, we will also need coordinated energy management on a national as well as an international level.

Technological innovation has to be a core part of any successful climate change strategy and the same is true of energy policy. The state and government must have a significant role in making such innovation possible, since a regulatory framework, including incentives and other tax mechanisms, will be involved. What role should this be exactly? The issue overlaps with that of planning. For a while, it became conventional wisdom that markets cannot be second-guessed; nor can we predict with any precision where innovation will happen. Today the pendulum is swinging back again. Various technologies or non-fossil-fuel energy sources are touted as the answer to our need to reduce emissions; large amounts of investment are flowing into them. People are again placing bets on the future.

Technologies: where we stand

Hydrogen is only one of many fuel sources and technologies that figure on most people's lists as relevant to mitigating climate change. At the moment it is impossible to say which are likely to be most important. Nuclear and hydroelectric power are the most tried and tested technologies. The first has vociferous critics, and is not (currently) a renewable resource, while the second has intrinsic limitations depending upon the flow of water within a given country or region. The following technologies or proposed energy sources are also in play: purified coal (carbon capture and sequestration, or CCS), wind power, tidal or wave power, biofuels, solar power, geothermal energy, smart electricity grids, geo-engineering technologies – such as heat shields that would turn back a proportion of the sun's rays – and 'scrubbers' – devices that would suck CO_2 and other greenhouse gases out of the atmosphere.

Each of these, at least in principle, could overlap with the others in specific contexts; and most could contain or link up with sub-technologies, or with gadgets (such as plug-in cars running off electricity supplied from one or other clean energy source).

The literature on low-carbon technologies is a minefield of claims and counter-claims. All the technologies on offer have their enthusiasts, who like to assert that their chosen one is more advanced than most think. Each has its detractors and, to use a familiar term, its sceptics. Take hydrogen as a starting-point. Rifkin sees it as the ubiquitous energy source of the future. Others take quite an opposite view. Hydrogen, they point out, cannot be drawn upon from natural resources; it has to be made, either from other fuels, or from water by means of electricity. It is far more complicated to deal with as a source of energy supply than other gaseous fuels because it has to be stored at very high pressures. Even small leaks can be dangerous.[3] Of course, as in every other area, these and other problems presented by hydrogen could at some point be solved. At this stage, we don't know.

Nuclear power remains mired in controversy, but, as mentioned in chapter 4, it is difficult to see how it will not figure in a prominent way – not for all industrial countries, but certainly for some of them. In Britain, nuclear power generated 19 per cent of the country's electricity in 2006, compared to 36 per cent from gas and 38 per cent from coal. In 2007 this proportion dropped to 15 per cent and it will decline more as the ageing plants lose capacity. The differential was partly made up in 2007 by the import of 3 per cent of electricity demand from nuclear plants in France. Since the proportion of electricity generated from renewable sources is so small, it is difficult to see how the UK could possibly meet its EU 2020 target of 16 per cent from renewables if nuclear were allowed to lapse.

Many in the green movement remain opposed to the use of nuclear power, but some environmentalists who were previously hostile have since revised their views. One is Stewart Brand, the founder of the Whole Earth Catalogue in the 1970s. He says he is now pro-nuclear 'because coal is so awful'.[4] Brand calls for the rapid deployment of a new generation of nuclear power plants, in the US and elsewhere.

Risks and problems there are plenty. Yet, as I have stressed throughout this book, it is the balance of risks we have to consider and there are no risk-free options. A nuclear reactor emits virtually no CO_2, although emissions are involved in the building of nuclear power stations. The IPCC calculates that the total life-cycle level of emissions per unit of energy is some 40g CO_2 equivalent per kilowatt-hour, the same as that for renewable energy sources.[5] Supplies of uranium are plentiful and not concentrated in unstable countries. The biggest difficulties concern the connection between nuclear power and the building of nuclear weapons, the possibility of nuclear terrorism and the difficulty of disposing of the nuclear waste. No one could possibly be sanguine about how serious these questions are. The first is arguably more dangerous than the second or the third. Many countries that have nuclear power do not possess nuclear weapons. Yet some states, at the moment most notably Iran, almost certainly want to develop nuclear power in order to build a nuclear arsenal.

I do not want in any sense to downplay such risks; like many others, I am a reluctant convert to nuclear power, at least insofar as some of the industrial and developing countries are concerned. There simply is no substitute on the horizon at the moment and the risks of taking nuclear out of the mix are too great. Nuclear power stations can be engineered to be almost impervious to terrorist attack, at least in terms of such an episode causing a release of radiation. The reactors currently being built in Finland incorporate such safeguards. It is at least possible that the waste-disposal issue could be resolved at some point in the future. Some have argued that fourth-generation nuclear technology could burn almost all the energy available in the uranium ore, and also run on the depleted uranium left behind by conventional reactors. Pie in the sky? It may be, but almost all renewable sources of energy need comparable technological breakthroughs if they are to serve to replace oil, gas and coal.

In March 2011, in the wake of a massive earthquake, an explosion occurred at the Fukushima Daiichi No. 1 nuclear plant in Japan. The reactors at the station were subsequently flooded with water and boric acid to try to prevent a meltdown and a large-scale release of radiation. These efforts were not successful and a significant radiation leak did occur. The plant in question was over 40 years old and of antiquated design. Critics had long warned that plants of this design constructed anywhere near geological fault-lines should be closed down. At the time of writing, it is not clear what either the short- or the longer-term consequences will be for human health. In April 2011, the Japanese government raised the level of risk to the same as that experienced at Chernobyl in the Ukraine, in 1986. However, the radiation released at the Japanese plant was less than one-tenth of that at Chernobyl.

In the wake of the events in Japan, most countries with an existing nuclear industry, or plans to develop one, stated that they would reassess their programmes. The German leadership reversed its intention to extend the life of the country's nuclear plants (see below, pp. 80–1). Two of the country's oldest nuclear stations were closed temporarily until they were thoroughly tested. Switzerland was among several countries going back on proposals to replace its existing nuclear plants and build new ones. The Chinese leadership put on hold its plans to construct new nuclear plants, pending tests of the proposed designs. The happenings in Japan are certain to affect the expansion of nuclear power, whatever position governments take. The main reasons are that communities are likely to object if a proposed nuclear plant is sited in their area, while groups that were anti-nuclear from the beginning will renew their protests.

From the point of view of containing carbon emissions, these developments could be unfortunate. It is possible that countries could decide upon programmes of large-scale investment in renewable technologies to fill the gap left by nuclear. More likely is that they will turn back to, or continue their dependence on, coal, the most polluting of the fossil fuels in terms of carbon emissions, but for many states the most reliable and accessible.

Wind, wave, tidal and geothermal energy, together with biofuels, are all reasonably well developed. They are likely to play a part – albeit in most countries only a relatively small part – in the total energy mix. None is problem-free. Thus, wind power delivers energy in an erratic way, although it can be topped up from other sources to produce a more stable output. There is some concern that wind farms could interfere with the radar used in air-traffic control. In Britain, a number of proposed wind-power installations have been deferred because of such worries. Widespread enthusiasm for the use of biofuels has diminished as it has become clear that growing them can seriously affect world food production. They could have an important role to play in the future, but further technological advance is needed if they are to be employed on the large scale, as discussed in chapter 3.

Geothermal energy looks promising. At present, apart from some areas in Iceland, Japan and New Zealand where volcanically active rocks are near the surface, it is too far below the earth's crust to be accessible. However, technology has quite recently been introduced which could overcome the difficulty. It involves fracturing hot rocks and injecting water which heats up as it circulates through them.[6] A commercial plant has been set up in Landau, Germany, which already produces 22 gigawatt-hours of electricity annually. As with most other technologies, substantial government subsidies are needed to get the industry off the ground.

The technologies whose development will probably be most consequential, as far as we can see at the moment, are CCS and solar energy. CCS potentially is enormously important, because even if world reserves have been exaggerated, coal exists in some abundance; and also because of the fact that coal-fired power stations are very widespread and a major source of global warming. If most of these cannot be retro-fitted with carbon capture technology, then the battle to contain emissions will be seriously handicapped, or even simply lost.

Some environmentalists more or less write off 'clean coal' – CCS – altogether. For them, it's not a clean technology at all, because of the number of mine-related deaths and the fact that even de-carbonated coal contributes to illnesses such as asthma and heart disease.[7] Moreover, they worry that the promise of CCS is being used as a justification for building more coal-fired power stations, in spite of the fact that no one can be sure how effective or affordable the technology will turn out to be. Yet CCS has to stay very high up the agenda for the reasons given above. There are difficult problems to be faced. The CO_2 extracted from the coal has to be interred deep underground, with enough pressure such that it turns into a liquid. No one knows how far it will in fact stay buried. If the technology comes into widespread use, it may be difficult to find enough sites.

The other major problem is expense, which is partly caused by the need for storage, but mainly results from the costs of the process of carbon extraction. CCS is nowhere close to being competitive with orthodox coal production. Four major projects exist at the moment, in North Dakota in the US, in Algeria, in Germany and off the coast of Norway. They are all experimental and none is connected to an electricity grid. Each will require the storing of a million tonnes of CO_2 per year. The electricity system in the US alone produces 1.5 billion tonnes of CO_2 annually, which would mean finding 1,500 appropriate sites.[8] Crucial though it undoubtedly is, no one knows at the moment how far, and within what timescale, the problems of CCS can be overcome. In the meantime, untreated coal, which a few years ago seemed a fuel from yesteryear, is on its way back.

The picture is quite complex, as there are trends and countertrends. Coal remains, as the International Energy Agency (IEA) puts it, 'the backbone of global electricity generation'.[9] World consumption of coal continues to mount, up 2 per cent in 2010 over the year before. In the OECD countries, the proportion of the energy mix taken up by coal has dropped, and the building of new coal-fired power stations has slowed – largely because of opposition from environmentalist groups, but partly as a result of government policy. The drop in coal consumption in the industrial countries has been more than offset by large increases elsewhere, especially in China. China now consumes more coal than the US, Europe and Japan combined. Coal supplies 80 per cent of China's electricity, compared to 45 per cent in the US.

However, China has become a world leader in the production of coal plants that create substantially fewer emissions than older types. Power companies are obliged to close down at least one older-style plant for each new one they construct. The most efficient plants in China cut down emissions by 30 per cent over the older versions.

And so – on to solar energy, for many the best hope of all. The energy that comes in the form of sunlight every day is far greater than we would ever need to fuel our needs. Such energy can be generated effectively even in temperate climates, but at present it only works well when there are long sunny periods. Solar energy has a range of practical advantages. It can be deployed on the small or the large scale and, once installed, has high reliability and low maintenance costs, with a lifespan of 30 years or more. So far it only supplies about 1 per cent of the world's electricity. Solar power has been around since the 1970s, which could mean that the technology has got stuck; or it might mean that the long lead-up time will set the stage for major expansion.

Silicon semiconductors, which so radically altered the nature of computers, may be set to do the same for solar technology. The search is also on for non-silicon materials that are cheaper to produce. Solar technology takes various different forms, but the most advanced is photovoltaic, which turns sunlight into electric current; it can be directly connected to the grid. One of the main difficulties, which also arises with other intermittent energy sources, is how to store the electricity so as to have stocks in reserve. Various modes of storage exist at the moment, but none is of the capacity needed to use solar power on a large scale. For instance, the heat energy can be stored in containers in which stones are placed, which can conserve the energy temporarily; the same can be done with water. A pilot study, funded by the EU, is under way to study how solar energy might be converted into chemical fuels that can be stored for long periods of time and transported over long distances.

Finally in this lengthy list there is geo-engineering, although none of the projects of this sort being mooted at the moment is more than a gleam in the eye of their potential inventors. In its Fourth Assessment Report, the IPCC concluded that, at present, geo-engineering projects are 'largely speculative and with the risk of unknown side effects'. Most would agree, but in Britain the Royal Society nonetheless commissioned a report on them, on the grounds that we have to explore all possibilities in the struggle to limit climate change. The report concluded that 'no geoengineering method can provide an easy or readily acceptable alternative solution' to the prime need to reduce emissions of greenhouse gases.[10] Geo-engineering is likely to be technically possible, but the

Selected indicators	2007 ➡	2008 ➡	2009
Investment in new renewable capacity (annual)	104 ➡	130 ➡	150 billion USD
Renewables power capacity (including only small hydro)	210 ➡	250 ➡	305 GW
Renewables power capacity (including all hydro)	1,085 ➡	1,150 ➡	1,230 GW
Hydropower capacity (existing all sizes)	920 ➡	950 ➡	980 GW
Wind power capacity (existing)	94 ➡	121 ➡	159 GW
Solar PV capacity, grid-connected (existing)	7.6 ➡	13.5 ➡	21 GW
Solar PV capacity (annual)	3.7 ➡	6.9 ➡	10.7 GW
Solar hot water capacity (existing)	125 ➡	149 ➡	180 GWth
Ethanol production (annual)	53 ➡	69 ➡	76 billion liters
Biodiesel production (annual)	10 ➡	15 ➡	17 billion liters
Countries with policy targets	68 ➡	75 ➡	85
States/provinces/countries with feed-in policies	51 ➡	64 ➡	75
States/provinces/countries with RPS policies	50 ➡	55 ➡	56
States/provinces/countries with biofuels mandates	53 ➡	55 ➡	65

Top five countries	#1	#2	#3	#4	#5
Annual amounts for 2009					
New capacity investment	Germany	China	United States	Italy	Spain
Wind power added	China	United States	Spain	Germany	India
Solar PV added (grid-connected)	Germany	Italy	Japan	United States	Czech Republic
Solar hot water/heat added	China	Germany	Turkey	Brazil	India
Ethanol production	United States	Brazil	China	Canada	France
Biodiesel production	France/Germany		United States	Brazil	Argentina
Existing capacity as of end-2009					
Renewables power capacity (including only small hydro)	China	United States	Germany	Spain	India
Renewables power capacity (including all hydro)	China	United States	Canada	Brazil	Japan
Wind power	United States	China	Germany	Spain	India
Biomass power	United States	Brazil	Germany	China	Sweden
Geothermal power	United States	Philippines	Indonesia	Mexico	Italy
Solar PV (grid-connected)	Germany	Spain	Japan	United States	Italy
Solar hot water/heat	China	Turkey	Germany	Japan	Greece

Figure 6.1 Selected indicators and top five countries in terms of renewable energy sources

Source: REN21, 2010. Renewables 2010 Global Status Report (Paris: REN21 Secretariat)

technologies that would be needed are 'barely formed', while great uncertainties surround their potential effectiveness. Two categories of geo-engineering exist: those which would reflect a proportion of the sun's radiation back into space; and those that would remove greenhouse gases from the atmosphere.

The first could involve interventions such as placing shields or deflectors into space to reduce the amount of solar energy reaching the earth. The second would mean either removing greenhouse gases directly, or using the natural world to do so – for example, by seeding the oceans with substances that would cause them to absorb more CO_2. Some place faith in the possibility of constructing a technology that will extract CO_2 from the air and allow it to be stored.[11] Small-scale models of such 'scrubbers' exist. Just as in clean coal technology, the CO_2 would have to be sequestered – which, given the quantities involved, is a problem. It will be a mammoth task to develop the technology on the scale needed to make a meaningful impact. Yet its potential is large, since it is the only technology known at the moment that could actually reverse the causes of global warming.

The Royal Society notes that there are no major programmes of research on any of the methods considered, and proposes that such programmes be instituted, since, otherwise, discussions of geo-engineering will remain wholly speculative. International scientific organizations should coordinate a programme of research that would provide concrete evidence about what might be feasible.

As there are no guaranteed technological solutions, radically increasing energy efficiency has to be high on the agenda. The constructing of eco-homes and other environment-friendly buildings is likely to be very important for the future. The German *Passivhaus* has such high levels of insulation that it can be heated by the warmth of the human body alone, even in sub-zero temperatures. Dramatically heightened energy efficiency is the essence of Amory Lovins's notion of 'natural capitalism', which he defines as capitalism that includes a full economic valuation of the earth's ecosystems.[12] It involves ensuring that natural resources – not just energy, but also minerals, water and forests – stretch many times further than they do today. His ultimate aim is not just to reduce waste, but to eliminate it altogether. In closed production systems, every output would either be returned to the ecosystem as a nutrient or become an input for another manufacturing product. A further objective would be to move away from the usual notion of making goods for consumers to purchase; instead, they would rent them. At the end of a given period, the producing company would buy them back. Manufacturers would thereby have an interest in concentrating on the durability of their products;

when they are exchanged against new ones, they would be wholly recycled.

These ideas may sound unrealistic, but in some ways and contexts they are closer to being realized than most of the hoped-for technological innovations, since they have already been put into practice. For example, a large glass-clad office tower in Chicago needed a major renovation some years after it was built. The glazing was replaced by a new type that let in six times more daylight than the old units, while reducing the flow of heat and noise fourfold. The need for lighting, heating and air-conditioning was reduced by 75 per cent. Lovins claims that in the US there are some 100,000 office towers of a similar type that are due for renovation, where the same order of saving could be made.

In terms of the near future – the next 20 years – it seems certain that a diversity of energy sources will be required to reduce emissions and break dependence on oil, gas and coal. In a now well-known article published in *Science* magazine, two Princeton professors, Robert Socolow and Stephen Pacala, identified 15 energy 'wedges' that, combined with one another, could stabilize world emissions over the next 50 years.

They calculated that, given current patterns of economic development, emissions must be reduced by about seven gigatonnes to hold the increase in world temperatures at or below 2 per cent. Each wedge could reduce emissions by one gigatonne, so, all other things being equal, seven of the wedges out of the substantial number they identify would be enough to reach that end. The wedges include factors such as the successful deployment of CCS technology, nuclear power, increased fuel economy for vehicles, and improvements in building insulation.[13]

The role of government

The issue for governments is how best to encourage technological innovation without prejudging where the most relevant and profound innovations are likely to occur. Subsidies are needed to provide a platform, since virtually all new technologies are more costly than fossil fuels. Innovation, however, is obviously not all of a piece. In a classic study, Christopher Freeman distinguishes a number of different levels of innovation, each of which might have to be dealt with in a different way as far as industrial policy is concerned.[14]

There can be incremental improvements in a given technological context, based upon improved design and efficiency, as in the case of the evolution of jet engines. This situation can be distinguished from new inventions, which alter the nature of a product – as when those engines were invented in the first place. On a more comprehensive level, changes in a technological system can occur when innovations are made which affect that system as a whole – an example would be the impact the computer has had on office work. Finally, changes can be introduced whose effects are felt in almost all fields of social and economic life, as has happened with the coming of the internet. Those in the final category are, by definition, the most significant, but they are least predictable and hence the most difficult to encourage by active policy.

Analysis of the economics of innovation helps suggest where government might be effective in its interventions.[15] For instance, new processes or inventions may not become cost-effective until significant investment is made and experience developed as to how they might effectively be applied. An industry might wait around for someone to take a leap of faith, which might not happen, with the result that the industry (and consumers) remain locked into old technology. This point is one at which state-provided subsidies, in the form of challenge schemes, for example, could promote a breakthrough. Another major area is patenting, since companies will be reluctant to innovate unless they receive protection against their competitors simply taking over what they have pioneered. Government must look for an appropriate balance. If patents are too strong, innovation may in fact be discouraged, since other firms will find it difficult to build on the work of the originating company. Much the same applies on the international level, where safeguarding intellectual property is more difficult. Allowing poorer countries to bypass patents will be vital. Yet a similar dilemma to that operating nationally applies here too. If the international regime is too loose, it could militate against much-needed technological advances.

Of particular importance will be what happens in the power industry, especially given its history of widespread deregulation over the past three decades, as described in chapter 2. Power supplied through national grids is a public good, but in the 1970s and 1980s governments took the decision to turn much of it over to private firms – with the UK leading the way. Planners emphasized quantity first and foremost, having in mind issues of security, which were uppermost in policy-makers' minds; cost was a secondary consideration. Following privatization, these emphases were in effect reversed. Once the major companies had been privatized, prices were pushed down towards marginal costs, leading, in effect, to a writing-off of the sunk costs. Much-needed investment was put off or scrapped, and the concentration on extracting the maximum from existing assets meant there was little capacity to cope with external shocks. Moreover, electricity generation became caught up in the more extreme edges of financial speculation, with consequences seen most spectacularly in the case of Enron in the US. Enron's troubles came from the corrupt activities of its leadership, but these developed when the complex system of trading in deregulated energy markets, which Enron set up, failed, creating a 'regulatory black hole'.[16]

One of the results of the sweating of assets in power generation is the low level of R&D in the industry generally – a major problem now the emphasis has swung so heavily in favour of innovation. In earlier days, state-owned industries invested a good deal in R&D, drawing upon an indigenous manufacturing base that was much stronger than is now the case. The proportion of turnover spent on R&D varies in a major way between different industries. In the big pharmaceutical companies in the UK, as of 2007, R&D intensity was 15 per cent. A survey of power-generating firms found the average to be only 0.2 per cent. In-depth studies have shown that the decline in R&D corresponds closely with electricity reform.[17]

As elsewhere, the response cannot simply be a return to top-down measures on the part of the state or the regulators appointed by the state. Policies that encourage consumers to become active partners in the supply chain are very likely to be important in terms of innovation; among other advantages, they create markets for smaller firms to enter. Yet, as elsewhere, wholesale decentralization would not work. A system like an electricity grid has to have organized coordination mechanisms, especially if smart grids are to be introduced.

It is up to government to move towards a thorough clean-out of anti-environmental subsidies. In the energy market, major hidden – and not so hidden – subsidies exist, even more so if we emphasize that producers must face the full environmental cost of their decisions. The subsidy for fossil fuels has been estimated at $20–30 billion in the OECD countries, without counting externalities at all.[18] Unless some of that money is directly and explicitly turned towards new technologies, innovation is likely to be blocked. Indeed, without substantial government intervention there is virtually no chance of effective transformation in electricity production. National grids are geared towards a centralized system of power plants; since cost reductions with new technologies usually take years to come about, there is a gap that capital markets cannot fill.[19] Some of these factors also apply to transport, the fastest-growing source of emissions.

Against this backdrop, consider the example of the hypercar, first proposed by Amory and Hunter Lovins.[20] The hypercar aims to reduce fuel consumption by over 80 per cent and the emissions involved in making the vehicle by as much as 90 per cent compared to the most economical vehicles of similar capacity that exist at the moment. The machine would be made out of materials that reduce its weight to a fraction of the average vehicle today, without sacrificing its ability to withstand accidents. It would be modelled to reduce air resistance to a minimum and be powered by a hybrid-electric drive using hydrogen fuel cells. Trucks and cars made this way would be able to return from between 80 and 200 miles per gallon and they would be neither small nor sluggish.

The hypercar, the Lovinses argue, would transform other industries around it. It would displace one-eighth of the steel industry, saving that proportion of emissions. A wholesale move towards hypercars could save the equivalent of the total OPEC production of oil. It would also aid in introducing inexpensive fuel cells in other industries. In addition, hyper-cars would generate surplus electricity that could be fed back into the national grid.

At the moment, manufacturers are managing steadily to increase the overall economy of their vehicles, but nowhere near to the degree which is already in fact practicable. The main reason is the technological inertia bound up with an industry locked into existing markets and the surrounding structure of supply. Public policy is required to begin a transition to new networks and surrounding support systems. Such policy will have also to help ensure that the electricity consumed by low-emission vehicles itself comes from low-carbon sources.

How can government minimize the problem that the money spent funding best guesses for innovation might be wasted? One way is to support a range of technological possibilities, the equivalent of a portfolio approach in spreading market risk. Diversity in energy supply has additional benefits too, including provision of greater security should any one source become threatened. There is a downside, however, since there is a danger that subsidies and incentives may become spread too thinly to have their desired effects. Governments and businesses have to accept that some technologies may fail or prove to be a dead end, while others, perhaps even the most influential ones, may slip in from the side.

We should recognize also that it is not only large, established industries that can form lobbies which tend to act in favour of the status quo. The same can be true of smaller producers, especially where there is a clear mechanism of subsidy involved – the proponents of wind or solar power, for example, are likely to push their own cases forcefully. One responsibility of government is to make sure that state funding does not produce the equivalent of welfare dependency, where those who receive support come to treat it as a natural right and then resist change.

There are few technologies that do not have spill-over effects, so, in practice, government support of innovation has to be connected with broader concerns. Where spill-over effects are positive, they may need state support, or an appropriate regulatory framework, to have greatest effect.

Thus, materials developed in the motor industry may have direct application to building more energy-efficient homes and workplaces if technology transfer is actively rewarded. For these reasons, holistic thinking is going to be essential in promoting technological innovation. Any fundamental technological breakthrough is going to be felt throughout society, as happened in the case of the internet. Urban planning and land regulation must be flexible enough both to promote and to respond to transformations of this sort.

Eco-towns might help explore the advantages and difficulties of future changes that later become more generalized. It is evident that innovative forms of technology could create complex problems of urban and rural land planning. The days when power stations could be located in the centre of cities, as used to be the norm in the early twentieth century, are long gone. Even in remote areas there may be deeply felt opposition to the building of nuclear power stations, which is why countries contemplating nuclear renewal are proposing to build on existing sites. Many citizens also have aesthetic objections to wind-farms.

Wherever new initiatives are made, whether in technology itself or in areas where its impact is felt, areas of uncertainty are created. A technology that is unproven has no confirmed price and it is difficult to cost the consequences of its widespread adoption, given all the factors just discussed. Take for an example a problem of far-reaching importance – the development of new ways of storing electricity. As in the case of the hypercar, the starting-point is likely to be a shared vision of what could be achieved, involving industry, government and other agencies.[21]

Creating new ways of storing electricity is an issue that goes well beyond solar power and other intermittent renewable energy sources. It could have an enormous impact upon the power grid, on transportation and other areas. For instance, it would help directly with one of the problems of some leading renewable technologies: that they only provide intermittent supply. Various means of electricity storage are conventionally recognized, such as batteries, fly-wheels and compressed air.[22] A range of other possibilities exists, awaiting possible commercial development. These include flow batteries, lithium battery systems, supercapacitors and power conversion systems. *Smartgrids*, published by the European Commission, offers a vision of the future of Europe's electricity networks that includes anticipating more effective storage technologies.[23] It not only traces out the implications in a holistic way, but proposes how partnerships between governments and business can overcome early investment hurdles.

As already stated, some of these technologies will turn out to be going nowhere, as is the case in all other areas where governments offer subsidies or incentives – or where private firms invest without such support. Failures can be accompanied by lessons, since they may generate significant knowledge along the way, and closing down possibilities can, in principle, lead to better focused investment. However, exit strategies should be in place from the beginning, at least as far as the state is involved, or there is the chance that good money will follow bad. Anyone who studies the history of early post-war planning will recognize that this danger is very real.

Promoting job creation

Job creation through the spread of renewable technologies sounds like a prime form of economic convergence – and so, in principle, it is. 'Wind power has created thousands of new jobs', it is often said of a given country – for instance, Germany. Yet put that way the claim is too simplistic, since jobs in new technology areas may come at the expense of others in more traditional energy industries where some workers, as a consequence, become unemployed. Moreover, most new technologies reduce the need for labour power. Wind and wave power, for example, typically employ fewer workers per unit of energy produced than coal-mining. Industrial policy planned with climate change objectives in mind cannot be based upon an easy equation between economic convergence and job creation.

In the environmental literature, lifestyle change is normally identified with reducing waste and profligacy. These emphases are no doubt correct, but there is no reason why other avenues of taste and self-expression should not open up as new technologies develop. We live in a post-industrial society and that will not change whatever else happens. The transition to a low-carbon economy can be expected to create new jobs, but they are likely to come about as much through developments in lifestyle or taste as from changes in the energy industries as such. Who would have thought that, having put up with inferior coffee for years, US and British consumers were secretly longing for a better product and for numerous varieties of it? Well, presumably they weren't, but an opportunity was spotted, and initiated a trend. Much the same is likely to happen, along a variety of dimensions, as the world moves towards low-carbon technologies and lifestyles. Just where the space for such initiatives will exist, however, is essentially unpredictable.

The United Nations Environment Programme (UNEP) has published a comprehensive analysis of how environment-friendly jobs might be created.[24] In true UN style, it starts with a glossary of acronyms used in the text – no fewer than 182 of them (one of which is 'UNEP' itself). Such jobs are defined as work in agriculture, manufacturing, research and development and services 'that contribute substantially to preserving or restoring environmental quality'.

The report says that employment will be affected in four main ways by an increasing concern with environmental quality, including responding to climate change. First, some additional jobs will be created without substituting for others, such as where pollution control devices are added to existing equipment. Second, certain jobs that are lost as new technologies advance will be directly replaced, as for instance where landfill or waste incineration are replaced by recycling. Third, others will disappear without being replaced – as where the production of packaging materials for manufactured goods is simply discontinued. And finally, yet others will be transformed and redefined, either through technological change or as the tasks involved are altered – such as in the construction industry. The report has the virtue of emphasizing that some industries will have to go through difficult processes of restructuring and there will be winners and losers.

The role of public policy, the report rightly continues, will be vital. Subsidies for environmentally harmful industries will have to be phased out, alongside the introduction or improvement of those promoting energy-efficient practices. Carbon taxes should be used to transfer the tax burden away from labour and towards taxing the sources of environmental pollution. Direct regulation is needed in many areas, in the shape, for example, of building codes, energy-efficiency standards, or the control of land-use and the eco-labelling of products. Governments should commission in-depth modelling and econometric studies to assess the likely consequences of investments and controls.

The proportion of workers currently involved in renewable technology industries is tiny, but will inevitably expand greatly. At present, some two million workers worldwide are estimated to be directly employed in such industries. About half of these are working in biofuels, mostly in growing and collecting the plants used to produce them. Since there are major worries about the implications of first-generation biofuels for food scarcity, this proportion may actually decline, at least in the short term. As far as other renewable technologies go, almost all the employment generated thus far is concentrated in a handful of industrial countries.

The problems of planning noted earlier apply with some force to environmental job creation. Innovations in renewable technologies cannot be predicted except in a general way, while by definition the implications of possible breakthroughs are unknown. There are huge gaps in available data about the environmental consequences of existing work practices and ways of life, especially as far as the developing world is concerned. In all countries, should environment-friendly jobs dramatically increase, there are major implications for education and training, knock-on implications for the work–life balance, pensions and many other areas.

Well before the arrival of the current financial crisis, US authors Michael Shellenberger and Ted Nordhaus had proposed a 'New Apollo Project', aimed at freeing the United States from its dependence on oil and at the same time creating new jobs. In a swingeing critique of America's environmental movement, which they see as having been narrow-minded and negative, they argue for a strategy that will 'create something inspiring' and will 'remind people of the American dream'. Together with others, they have put together a coalition of groups, involving business, labour unions and community agencies, to push forward their proposals, which involve large-scale expenditure on the part of government to advance low-carbon technologies and thereby create 'millions of jobs'.[25]

In *The Green Economy*, Van Jones proposes that state-led investment in low-carbon energy and energy efficiency could be a means of involving the less well-off in the concerns about climate change.[26] Many of the jobs involved in the two areas, he says, are not high-tech, but are middle skill ones. A detailed programme, centred on stimulating economic recovery, has been set out by others at the Center for American Progress. This involves public-sector spending in six main areas: improving the energy efficiency of buildings; expanding public transport and freight; setting up smart electricity grids; building wind farms; building solar power installations; and developing next-generation biofuels.[27] According to its initiators, Robert Pollin and colleagues, the programme would help renew manufacturing and the construction industry and also be a major source of new jobs.

Unlike others who make such claims, Pollin et al. offer an analysis of the conditions under which job expansion can proceed without significant job loss elsewhere, at least in circumstances of recovery from recession. A $100 billion government investment programme, according to their analysis, could generate 1.7 (net) million new jobs. Like Van Jones, they stress that such investment will offer a substantial proportion of entry-level jobs as well as more skilled and technical ones.

I am in favour of such proposals, especially in an American context, since the US has so much ground to make up on most other industrial countries in terms both of emissions reduction and energy saving. However, care will have to be taken about how they are instituted and plenty of difficulties have to be resolved. If they are to work, training will have to be provided, at all levels, and on a substantial scale – this means up-front expenditure without any immediate payback. Investment in infrastructure will be crucial, and will have to be planned over a longer period than just at the time of economic recovery. Consistency of policy will be called for.

There is not much point investing in renewables on the large scale if the effects on such investment are negated by policy decisions taken elsewhere. In the US, for example, a lot will depend upon what attitude the government takes towards the failing car industry, which is now demanding state support.

Most important of all, policy initiated to aid short-term recovery will have to be directed towards what happens later. The world financial crisis was not just a routine cyclical movement of the economy. I would see it as a '1989 of deregulation' – a transition perhaps as fraught with implications as was the collapse of Soviet communism, and as likely to be as protracted and complex in its consequences and implications. I have no quarrel with the view that there has to be a profound restructuring of financial markets themselves and of banking.

However, as with most forms of peering into the future, it isn't at all clear at the moment just what actions will be taken. Moreover, we will have to be very careful not to revert to a traditional model of the state, or to throw away the benefits that complex market instruments offer, including derivatives and the hedging of risk. For instance, as is discussed later in the book, complex insurance mechanisms, which are all about risk transfer, will be essential to cope with adaptation to climate change. The state will never be able to provide more than a bare minimum of the cover that will be needed.

It is up to policy entrepreneurs to deploy the range of interventions against such an eventuality mentioned earlier in the chapter. Possibilities of job creation in conditions of recovery will, in my view, have to be much more broad-ranging than those mentioned in the sources discussed above; and the knock-on consequences of job-creation strategies will have to be thoroughly examined. It is at least possible that an economy with a high proportion of its energy mix coming from renewables could be much more stable than one that depends on external energy sources. The best way of keeping climate change policy in the forefront will be to deploy the strategy suggested throughout this book – work to keep it at the cutting edge of economic competitiveness, integrate it with wider political programmes and avoid empty moral posturing.

Carbon taxes

Taxation regimes will play a significant part in stimulating innovation and, to some extent, in controlling its direction. Taxation is one of the main levers of state policy, and will of course have a broader role too in the struggle to reduce emissions. In the debate between writers who favour carbon emissions markets and those who place most emphasis on carbon taxes, I incline towards the latter, although obviously the two can coexist.

In what follows, I shall argue that we should not focus only on carbon taxes as such, but upon the consequences of a given fiscal system as a whole for outputs that are relevant to climate change. We should recognize that existing taxes which have not been devised for environmental purposes may nevertheless in some part serve them – in that sense, they are carbon taxes. For instance, taxes invested in railways can serve to reduce emissions in spite of the fact that such a concern was not what prompted them originally.

The reverse also applies. Taxes may have adverse, although unintended, effects as far as environmental issues are concerned. Such effects might be fairly obvious, as in the case of airline fuel being exempt from taxes applied to other forms of transport. But they can be more diffuse as, for example, where the location of a supermarket is left open to market forces, with no thought given to environmental implications.

Directly motivated carbon taxes can be of two sorts: those whose revenue, part or all, is spent for environmental purposes; and those whose purpose it is to influence behaviour in ways compatible with climate change objectives. Taxes invested in developing renewable technologies, for example, fall into the first category. Those aimed at persuading people to drive more fuel-efficient cars, or reduce the mileage they drive every year, fall into the second. As with other taxes, they can serve as incentives or they can be punitive.

Carbon taxes should be transparent to citizens rather than presented in some other guise or under some other pretext, as happened with the fuel levies in the UK. They are likely to be most successful where they combine several of the qualities just noted – i.e., if they are explicitly designed as such; directed at changing behaviour, whether of agencies in society, such as business firms, or citizens as a whole; wherever possible are incentives rather than negative taxes, since incentives draw upon positive motivations; form part of an overall fiscal strategy; and where their environmental consequences are openly stated and visible.

From an economic point of view, the point of carbon taxes is to help eliminate externalities as far as the environment is concerned – to ensure that they are fully costed, including costs to future generations. As in so many other areas of climate change policy, the principle is easy to state, but quite often difficult to apply. For instance, the cost of food produced by large-scale agriculture using fertilizers and pesticides does not include the destructive impact these can have on the soil. Nor does it include the pollution coming from the shipping that carries them around the world. True prices are very difficult to assess, as in many other areas, given the complex nature of modern manufacturing processes.

Taxes on the use of resources should be as near to the point of production as possible, in order to apply to all relevant aspects of manufacturing processes. Such taxes should promote efficiency in energy use and innovation at the beginning of the production cycle, limiting the need for repair and recycling later. There should be trade-offs where carbon taxes are introduced *de novo*. In other words, citizens should be offered tax swaps, basically trading environmental taxes against reductions elsewhere. Sometimes, such a strategy can create a 'double dividend' – limiting pollution but at the same time producing other benefits elsewhere.

It is a well-established theorem that, as far as possible, we should tax the 'bads' (the sources of emissions) rather than the 'goods' (such as human labour, in the form of income tax). This notion fits neatly with 'the polluter pays' principle. However, once again the distinction is not as clear-cut as one might assume, since, through taxation, we also want actively (via incentives) to encourage 'goods' in respect of climate change – such as investment in renewable technologies. Taxing the 'bads' implies that these will be replaced more and more by 'goods', insofar as taxation produces social or economic changes; hence revenue from such sources will inevitably decline, even if taxation takes the form of incentives. Hence, once more we must bear in mind the overall tax system, since compensatory changes will need to be introduced elsewhere.

The pioneers of carbon taxes have been the Nordic countries. They were introduced in the early 1990s, so there has been some time to assess their level of success. The task is complicated, however, by the fact that taxes vary from country to country and all have evolved over time. In the early 1990s the Danes introduced taxes on electricity, energy consumption and fossil fuels. These were later complemented by a household CO_2 tax. In Finland, what is generally seen as the first CO_2 tax in the world was established in 1990 and applied across industry, transport and private households. Initially, the tax was relatively low, but it was later expanded. Sweden, Norway and Iceland have followed somewhat different paths again.

The level of ambition of such taxes, at least initially, was modest and, judged against that base-line, the results have been significant.[28] In Finland, without the CO_2 tax, emissions would probably have been 2–3 per cent higher by the year 2000 than they turned out to be; in Sweden, Norway and Iceland the figure was 3–4 per cent. The absolute level of emissions, however, increased across the 1990s in all these countries. Only in Denmark did the absolute volume of CO_2 emissions fall. The reason is that the Danes directed the tax revenue to environmental ends – it was used to subsidize energy-saving practices.

Given that these are the most advanced countries in respect of carbon taxes, it is obvious that there is a long way to go before such taxes make the contributions we (rightly) expect of them. Most current discussions remain at the level of what 'could be achieved' – that is, they are hypothetical. The possibilities of tax swaps, for example, have been explored in detail in various national contexts. Thus a study in the US analysed a swap in which a tax of $15 per metric ton of carbon would be balanced against a reduction in the federal payroll tax on the first $3,660 that workers earn.[29] Payroll tax in the US is a flat-rate tax up to a limit (in 2005) of $90,000 and is a regressive tax, hitting lower earners disproportionately. In fact, for more than 60 per cent of households it is the largest single federal tax they pay. A 'double dividend' comes into play, since taxes on labour supply can discourage workers from increasing their productivity, or even from entering the workforce at all.

Since the potentially regressive impact of carbon taxes is a worry to many, it is worth looking at some of the strategies that have been put forward to counter it. A research study carried out in the UK by the Rowntree Foundation studied four sectors where such taxes either have been established or are under active consideration.[30] These were in energy, water and transport use by households, together with the household generation of waste. The point was to see what ways could be devised to make such taxes at least neutral in terms of how they affect the less well-off.

The study confirmed that, if nothing else changed, in these areas environmental taxes would have a significant adverse impact upon poorer households. People on low incomes may already be inclined to stint on energy consumption, perhaps even to the detriment of their own health, especially where heating is concerned.

A reason why the UK has not followed the Nordic states and other countries in introducing household carbon or energy taxes is that fuel poverty in Britain reflects the peculiarly inadequate thermal characteristics of the country's housing stock. The Rowntree Foundation study mentioned above shows an enormous variation in energy use even among households within the same income band. Within each of 10 income bands used in the research, some households consumed as much as six times more energy than others. There were also large variations in emissions. The research showed that the poorest households pay significantly more per unit of energy than the most affluent ones. Hence, if a uniform carbon tax were imposed, it would be even more regressive than might appear at first sight.

Tax and benefits packages aimed at the poorer households can help reduce this effect. However, some among the fuel poor would become actively worse off, which would be likely to sink such proposals politically.

There is an approach that could work. It involves a combination of incentives and sanctions. By means of incentives, households would be persuaded to implement energy-efficient measures; a 'climate change surcharge' would be imposed on all households which, after a certain time, had not taken steps to carry out these measures. A nationwide energy audit would identify cost-effective measures that would need to be implemented by every household in order to avoid the climate change surcharge. The scheme would be put into practice over a given time period – say, 10 years – beginning with those living in the most affluent homes, as measured by existing property tax categories. Those in the highest tax bands would be obliged to carry out the work first, with others following in sequence and the poorest left to last. The latter group would be able to get low-cost loans, paid for from the surcharge levied on households that failed to get the necessary improvements done on time. For rented accommodation, the property-owners would pay.

The researchers argue that a minimum of 10 per cent of household CO_2 emissions would be saved over the 10-year period. While the cost to householders would be £6.4 billion, they would be saved a net sum of £19.4 billion. The average return to householders would be 23 per cent, with the poorest gaining more than the affluent, resulting in a sharp drop in fuel poverty. The report concludes that 'the fact that such a scheme currently seems not to be considered suggests the public and political will to mitigate climate change is not yet very powerful'.[31]

The report suggests that similar results can be achieved in other areas too – household water use, transport and waste management. As far as the first of these is concerned, the study argues that water metering under any scenario would have more positive results for poorer households than the current situation, where households pay a bill partly based on a standing charge and partly on the value of their properties. Taxes on fuel for cars are not regressive, since over 30 per cent of households do not own a car and most of such households are poor. Ways can be found of compensating low-income motorists for fuel duties, for example by abolishing licence duty for those groups. However, for purposes of political legitimacy, it would be crucial to spend the revenue on environmental purposes.

Finally, it would be possible to increase the level of waste recycling without adversely affecting the poor. At the moment, the poor pay more for waste collection in relative terms than do the more affluent. The researchers argue for a reduction in council taxes by the same amount for all households, and the addition of a weight-based charge for waste disposal. The charge would vary according to how far waste material was recyclable.

The Rowntree Study is important, because it goes some way to providing a carbon audit of the tax system, at least in the areas covered. It takes into account existing fiscal instruments and tries to spot the unintended consequences of reforms. All the proposed strategies are fairly complex, suggesting that it is difficult to reach the holy grail of reconciling carbon taxes with greater tax simplicity while still protecting the underprivileged. At present, it seems that no country has attempted a full-scale carbon tax audit, but such appraisals are surely necessary, since virtually all individual taxes will have knock-on consequences.

Do we need carbon taxes at all if and when oil and gas prices rise again? Won't they act like taxes anyway? Won't poorer people have to be given subsidies as the price of energy to the consumer rises? These questions do not admit of straightforward answers, for reasons given earlier. High prices will act as the equivalent of taxes, when compared to previous price levels, and undoubtedly will prompt changes in behaviour in the direction of greater frugality and efficiency in energy use, as well as adding a powerful stimulus to the development of new energy technologies.

The difference from carbon taxes, however, is that they create no stream of revenue to the state, but instead generate large new costs, and hence inflationary consequences, that somehow have to be absorbed; moreover, oil and gas prices are essentially unpredictable. And there is the danger that they will result in a return to the use of coal. So we will need carbon taxes anyway, but in which areas, and how far they take the form of incentives rather than punitive taxes, will certainly be very strongly influenced by whatever happens in world energy markets.

Carbon rationing

Carbon rationing has some fervent advocates and some equally vociferous opponents. Supporters like the idea because of its apparent simplicity, its universal character and its radical nature. Each member of the population would have an annual carbon allowance for energy use in respect of domestic consumption and travel, including air travel. The allowance would be the same for all adults, with a smaller quota for children. The scheme would be mandatory. Once more, the role of government would be crucial, for it would have not only to determine at what level the quotas would be fixed, but also to be responsible for monitoring its operation.

Each year, the allowance would be reduced by an amount, specified well in advance, tracking the trajectory of national targets for emissions reductions. Individuals who live low-carbon lifestyles could trade their surplus emissions at a market price to those who consume more. Organizations as well as individual citizens could in principle be included. The quotas would be divided into carbon units. Everyone would have a smart card containing their allowance for the year, which would be used every time domestic bills were paid or travel services used. Carbon rationing, it is argued, would do away with many of the more specific government pro-grammes designed to encourage energy conservation; people would be able to choose for themselves how best to meet the quota.

Three different versions have been proposed – involving what their originators call, variously, Tradable Energy Quotas, Domestic Tradable Quotas and Personal Carbon Allowances. The first of these was proposed by David Fleming.[32] It would cover organizations (including the government) as well as individuals. A cap would be set based upon national emis-sions reductions targets. A 20-year rolling budget would be set up at the start of the scheme. For the first five years the quotas would be binding and for the second five years they would be 'firm'; the final ten years would be a 'forecast', to allow individuals and companies to prepare over time. Of the overall ration, 40 per cent would be allocated to adult citizens free of charge; the other 60 per cent would be issued to 'primary dealers' who would sell on to organizations in a secondary market. The scheme would cover oil, gas, electricity and coal. Individuals could choose to sell their units as soon as they received them, and then buy back from the market as they made energy-relevant purchases. In other words, they could opt for a pay-as-you-go procedure. Those outside the system (such as overseas visitors) would have to use such a means.

Domestic tradable quotas are the currency units in a comparable scheme suggested by researchers at the Tyndall Centre.[33] The principal difference between the two is that the Tyndall scheme includes aviation. The third approach, proposed by Mayer Hillman and Tina Fawcett, involves the allocation of what they call Personal Carbon Allowances, which would cover individuals only.[34] It would apply to all household energy use and personal travel, including flying. Like the other two, it would involve yearly reductions in allocated quotas with early warning given.

The authors of a study of the feasibility of carbon rationing note that the state of the debate at the moment is a somewhat unhappy one. Those who propose such schemes see them as something of a panacea. Others oppose them as being impractical, expensive, open to widespread fraud and likely to favour the affluent over the poor. Both sides base their arguments upon largely untested assumptions about political feasibility, operational feasibility and cost. 'Practical understanding and analysis', argue the authors – Simon Roberts and Joshua Thumin – are being undermined by 'confrontational debate', in which they 'take second place to the preservation of increasingly entrenched positions'.[35]

As Roberts and Thumin point out, the introduction of carbon rationing will not immediately make it easier for people to alter their activities. It may well motivate them to act, but will not enable them to do so. Carbon rationing is not therefore a substitute for other policies needed to curb greenhouse gas emissions. Roberts and Thumin set out to provide what they say is lacking – a careful analysis of the pros and cons of the approach.

In brief, their conclusions are as follows. Would carbon rationing lead to large-scale fraud? Not necessarily, but to prevent it such a scheme would probably have to be linked to biometric ID cards – themselves highly controversial and likely to be very costly. Even then, it might be hard or impossible to prevent a widespread black market from developing. Would people be able to manage their budgets effectively, or would some founder in the attempt to do so? Research on ordinary household budgeting has shown that most people are good at living within their budgets and keeping track of their finances. However, a significant minority are not good at either. What would happen to them if they mismanaged their carbon budgets is not clear. Would they face fines, or possible imprisonment?

Would carbon rationing favour the affluent at the expense of the poor? Not in every way, because affluent people create more emissions than the poor, especially if aviation is included; they will therefore need to buy from poorer groups. However, just as the better-off have found ways of exploiting welfare systems to their advantage, much the same would be very likely to happen in the case of carbon credits.

Would the public be prepared to accept carbon rationing? According to Roberts and Thumin, we simply do not know – virtually no research seems to have been carried out to assess public response to the idea. Among proponents 'there is a widespread assumption that [a carbon rationing scheme] will trigger significant change in behaviour . . . but [there is] no evidence of this'.[36] It would not be possible to test carbon-rationing proposals through pilot studies. The main reason is that, in order to work, a scheme has to be compulsory.

Roberts and Thumin do not reach any hard and fast conclusions, but on the basis of their observations, my own view is that carbon rationing is impractical and unfeasible. Its apparent attractions are blunted once the idea is carefully scrutinized. I would reaffirm my case made earlier: we will not be able to bludgeon people into submission when it comes to responding to climate change.

The re-emergence of utopia

Let us return for a brief visit to Sweden. In the Western Harbour area of Malmö, a new housing development is under way. Buildings sporting massive glass panels sit alongside modest timber structures, all surrounded by parks and walkways. Parking space is limited to 0.7 cars per apartment, and the area is connected to the rest of the city by a dense public transport network. Electricity is provided by wind turbines, solar panels and thermal heating. Solar window shades not only help generate electricity, but also reduce direct sunlight, lowering the need for air-conditioning in the summer. The energy-saving dwellings cost no more to build than conventional homes, but use only a third of the energy required by the average domestic dwelling in the rest of Malmö. Waste separation units positioned close to each home, coupled to a system of vacuum waste chutes, provide for recycling.

It isn't clear at present how far such communities can be generalized, or what some of their drawbacks might be. They are an example of the opportunities created by the twin problems of climate change and energy security. Could they be the outliers for broader processes of social transformation? I believe so, because now is surely the time for us to try to come more to terms with what I have earlier called the problems of over-development – put another way, the downside of affluence.

Consider that emblem of modernity, the car. The fate of the car will have a profound impact upon our struggle to limit global warming. Cars and other motor vehicles account for 14 per cent of total world CO_2 emissions – more if one includes those produced during the course of their manufacture. More than a billion cars have been made since the earliest models were introduced. If car-ownership and use follow their current trajectory, in little over a decade there will be a billion cars on the roads at the same time.[37] In the US, car use plus car manufacture account for fully 60 per cent of the country's emissions; the US produces 45 per cent of all CO_2 emissions generated by cars worldwide. What is the definition of a 'pedestrian' in America? Answer: someone who has just parked his car.[38]

We don't know the extent to which, or how quickly, new forms of propulsion for vehicles, such as electricity from renewable sources, or hydrogen, can come into use on a large scale. Yet, whatever happens to fuel sources, we can already catch a glimpse of the possibility of 'life beyond the car'.

The attraction of cars has always been that they offer freedom, mobility and speed. Yet the proliferation of cars on the roads negates these very qualities. What meaning do they have when drivers are endlessly stuck in traffic jams? We say 'stuck in a traffic jam' as though it came from external sources – in fact, every individual driver *is* the traffic jam. Part of the logic of eco-towns is to break dependence on the motor-car, and numerous experiments are being tried within orthodox city environments. For instance, local authorities have introduced congestion charging and traffic calming, and have banned cars altogether from some areas, thereby encouraging people to put a positive value on walking or cycling.

As French economic historian Jean Gimpel has shown, technological 'progress' is sometimes achieved through reversals.[39] For instance, nylon was once touted as the material of the future for clothing. Yet the 'traditional' cloths of wool and cotton made a dramatic comeback. A possible future (brought about by planning) is certainly likely to be a return to localism, involving networks of small, self-reliant communities (the future that many greens envisage). James Kunstler has remarked that city life will be marked by 'a return to smaller scales of operation in virtually every respect of travel and transport'.[40]

Much more likely, and desirable, is that such a tendency will interact with its opposite – a further expansion of mobility, but where transport will change its nature.[41] There could be a return to cityscapes that existed before the invention of the car, but which could nevertheless be integrated with a world of high mobility. The driverless car is already here, with its robot driver proven as being more capable and safer than even the most skilled and careful human counterpart. In cars now on sale, high-tech devices already exist that help prevent collisions on fast-moving roads without the intervention of the driver.

A digital system of transport could follow, perhaps

combining driverless with driven cars, all composed of small, ultra-light vehicles. The transportation device would be a 'personal multimodal pod in which passengers can stay in comfort throughout a journey leaving all the hassle of switching between different transport modes and network levels to the pod'.[42] Smart cards would be used to pay and control access. Such a system would rewrite the relationship between the 'public' and the 'private'. Real-life travel could be integrated with virtual access within 'tele-immersion environments'.

Utopian? Well, yes, but also actually at some point quite probable. The division between 'private' vehicles – the car – and 'public' transport has already begun to break down. Thus car clubs, where members don't own the vehicles they drive, but have privileged access to them, have sprung up in numerous cities in the US and Europe. It is not difficult to see that such systems could be liberating, as well as add significantly to quality of life. One should also remember that the car is a lethal instrument. The freedom it confers, and the love it can inspire, comes at a terrible price – it has been estimated that some 40 million people have been killed on the roads since the car first made its appearance, greater than the number that died in the two world wars combined.

Whatever happens from now on, climate change is going to affect our lives and we will have to adapt to its consequences. Politics intrudes here just as much as everywhere else and how processes of adaptation will be managed is an issue of prime importance. Just as in the case of controlling emissions, the developed countries have responsibilities towards the rest of the world as far as adaptation is concerned, and in the following chapter I shall discuss what these are.

7

THE POLITICS OF ADAPTATION

Initially borrowed from evolutionary biology, the term 'adaptation' has come into widespread use in the climate change literature. In a way, it is a misleading term, because it implies reacting to the consequences of climate change once it has occurred. However, just like our efforts to limit the warming of the world's climate, adaptation as far as possible has to be anticipatory and preventative.

Adaptation has been described as the 'poor and derided cousin of emissions reduction'.[1] For some while, discussing adaptation was taboo among environmentalists, on the grounds that it would adversely affect efforts directed at combating climate change itself. Times have definitely changed, however. In the discussions at Cancun (see below, pp. 193–5), as much time was devoted to discussion of adaptation as to mitigation. An Adaptation Fund, set up by the UN some years before, has had some flesh put on its bare bones. The fund had been widely criticized for being too difficult for countries to qualify for and for being seriously underfinanced. In future, developing countries will have direct access to it and it will have significantly greater resources to dispense.

In some ways the issues surrounding adaptation are even more complex than those to do with mitigation. For in preparing to adapt before climatic changes have actually taken place, or when they are in their early stages, we have to specify what the effects of global warming will be, in the many contexts in which they will have an impact. Providing some concepts to help guide our efforts at adaptation is important, because such concepts can help give shape and direction to policy. Let me first underline the relevance of the distinction already made, between adaptation after the event and adaptation oriented to possible futures. I shall speak of *proactive adaptation* (PA) to refer to the second of these categories. Within the limits of our knowledge – and in any real-life context, of funding – PA should be the prime focus of our attention whenever we think about adaptation, although reactive adaptation will certainly be necessary.

PA is about diagnosing and responding to *vulnerabilities*. Vulnerability is once again all about risk – the risk of suffering damage to a valued activity, way of life or resource. Vulnerability is plainly an economic and social phenomenon, not just one concerned with the physical environment. We can't discuss vulnerability without also focusing on its opposite, *resilience*. Resilience can be defined as *adaptive capacity*, the capacity not only to cope in the face of external changes or shocks, but, wherever possible, to respond actively and positively to them. It can be a property of the physical environment, of an individual or of a group. In the first case it is about the capability of the built environment to withstand shocks of one kind or another. It could take the form, for example, of strengthening dykes, or building new ones, in advance of expected increases in vulnerability to flooding. In the second, it refers to qualities of character – the ability to make the best of adverse circumstances, or actively to triumph over them. Defined as a quality of a group, it concerns factors such as the capacity of members of a community to act together rather than to become divided and fragmented; and to be able to modify, or even transform, existing ways of life should it become necessary so to do. Smallholders who grow a variety of crops, for example, will be more resilient than those dependent upon a single cash crop.

Most of the concepts introduced earlier in this book are directly relevant to adaptation. In deciding what forms of resilience to invest in and cultivate, we always have to bear in mind a balance of risks. Adaptation sounds like a version of the precautionary principle, because (as PA) it is a pre-emptive doctrine – it is intervention taken to prevent or contain future risks. Yet, as in all risk situations, when deciding on a particular strategy, we have to weigh different risks and opportunities against each other. The percentage principle applies.

Political and economic convergence are as important to the politics of adaptation as they are to mitigation – they are likely to influence how far citizens accept whatever policies are proposed. The limitations of the politics of fear and anxiety are just as pronounced here as elsewhere. 'The polluter pays' principle is also just as relevant as in the case of mitigation, both within nations and among them. The richer countries must shoulder the lion's share of responsibility for adaptation, as far as the developing world is concerned, just as they have to do in limiting the progress of global warming. The developing countries are much more vulnerable to the effects of climate change than the industrial ones, partly because many are located in climatically volatile regions and partly because they haven't got the resources that the developed countries have to prepare.

As with mitigation, the state will have to play a lead role in policy formation and enactment. However, all the points made earlier in the book apply. To promote adaptation, governments must help stimulate innovation and creativity in the diverse worlds of business and civil society. Citizen involvement is necessary, with a distribution of rights and responsibilities across the different levels of governance. A major political problem is the fact that funding for adaptation projects will inevitably compete, to some degree, with investment needed for mitigation.

What a country needs to do in order to adapt will vary greatly depending on its existing climate patterns and geographical location. The US has one of the most volatile climates in the world; extreme weather events will become even more pronounced and frequent. In countries with more temperate climates, such as in Northern Europe, climate change may initially produce some positive effects. The edge will go off winter, while the other seasons will, by definition, be warmer, although with greater day-to-day temperature fluctuations than before. However, if global warming proceeds unchecked, the adverse effects will quickly overwhelm these temporary benefits.

In the UK, as the frequency and intensity of storms increase, large volumes of rain will fall quite suddenly, resulting in flash floods. Yet, at the same time, summer droughts will put pressure on water supplies. As temperatures rise, there will also be wider implications for health; existing ailments, such as skin cancer or cataracts, will increase, and subtropical diseases previously unknown in the country could also make an appearance.

The first premise of adaptation policy for any country is to do a detailed mapping of vulnerabilities, local and national. Adaptation could promote innovation in much the same way as mitigation strategies can do. At least some such changes could be valuable in and of themselves, whatever happens to the climate – for instance, actions to promote more efficient use of water, improved systems of weather prediction, or the introduction of crops hardy enough to thrive under adverse circumstances.[2] Adaptation brings us back to the issue of planning, since it involves thinking ahead in a systematic way. It should be understood not only as looking for vulnerabilities and blocking them off, but as investigating also what the knock-on consequences of mitigation strategies are likely to be.

In the rest of this chapter I shall look at issues of adaptation in Europe and then consider in some detail a case study from the UK – adaptation to risks of flooding. I will then switch gear to consider the formidable problems that adaptation poses in the developing world. The role of insurance is likely to be crucial in adaptation – although most current discussions seem to ignore it – and I shall consider it in some detail. The insurance industry has done a great deal of work on climate change, as well it might; yet that work does not seem, thus far, to have been integrated with the rest of the climate change literature.

Adaptation in the context of Europe

Europe is diverse climatically and geographically. Adaptation will rarely be straightforward because of the combination of that diversity with the inherent complexity of the effects of climate change. This observation is even more apposite if one accepts that 'Europe' doesn't end at the boundaries of the EU, but stretches over to central Asia. The average temperature in Europe defined in this way rose by a full 1 per cent over the course of the twentieth century, more than that for the world as a whole.[3] I shall concentrate here on effects that are either being felt now, or are almost certain to happen regardless of how far climate change is successfully controlled from here on in.

A warmer atmosphere contains a higher proportion of moisture, and means more rainfall, but new patterns of precipitation will vary from one region to another in their frequency and intensity. Rainfall and snowfall have increased in Northern Europe, while in the south droughts are becoming more common. There are several main areas of especial vulnerability as global warming takes hold. Not just Southern Europe, but the whole of the Mediterranean basin will suffer from the combined impact of high temperature increase and reduced rainfall in areas already facing water shortages.

The effects of rising temperatures are more marked at higher altitudes than lower down and will affect the Alps in particular, leading to melting of the snow and changing river flows. Coastal regions will suffer from more storms, and in some areas increased erosion. Floodplains holding large populations will be at greater risk of flash floods. In Scandinavia, much more rainfall is expected than in the past, most of which will actually take the form of rain rather than snow – major changes will occur in particular in climatic patterns in the Arctic Circle, where temperatures are rising more rapidly than anywhere else.

A very large range of activities will be influenced in some way by these changes. They will affect businesses of all shapes and descriptions. Agriculture, forestry, fishery and tourist industries will be in the front line. In parts of the subcontinent, where rainfall will decrease, water flow for thermal and nuclear power plants, as well as for hydroelectricity, might be affected.

Possible adaptation measures are many, as are the levels of governance at which they would take effect. Inexpensive measures could make a significant contribution – for example, improving water conservation, making changes in crop rotation, changing the dates at which seeds are sown and introducing crops that are able to survive periods of drought. Other sorts of strategies that could be contemplated are much more demanding and expensive. New early warning systems could be introduced, perhaps on a pan-European level, such as flood and forest fire warning systems. Whole communities could be relocated away from low-lying coastal areas and floodplains. Poorer groups will be most vulnerable and systematic policy innovation will be needed to ensure their protection.

Flexibility in most cases is the key to resilience, since it isn't normally possible to predict in detail what will have to be confronted and when. Wherever possible, mitigation and adaptation should be combined. For example, insulation for buildings could be provided in such a way as to make them sturdier.

The principles of no risk without opportunity and looking for climate change positives apply. For instance, tourism in some areas may decline – rising heat, coupled to water shortages, is likely to affect summer resorts in the south. Yet as a result of the same changes other coastal areas could be opened up as tourist destinations. New economic opportunities could be created as a result of technological innovation, such as in the case of building techniques, materials and products. The need to rethink health systems could be a driving force of new forms of preventative medicine or healthcare.

The EU precept of subsidiarity – that decisions should be taken and policies applied at the lowest appropriate level, and the closest to the citizen – should come fully into play. Many policies will be best forged and delivered primarily in local communities. Local knowledge will be important in how best to proceed. There are examples already to hand. For instance, in southern Spain, farmers have got together with local municipalities to create initiatives to save water through electronic management and distribution systems for the irrigation of crops.

At the same time, coordination necessarily will have to be pursued at an EU level. Climate change will have effects everywhere and these will not follow administrative boundaries.

This theorem applies to the EU itself, which must concern itself also with 'wider Europe' – the North African side of the Mediterranean, and the Caucasus region – since coordination across these areas will certainly be desirable. Some sectors within the EU are already closely integrated – such as those covering agriculture, water, biodiversity, fisheries and energy networks – and adaptation policies will have to be tailored to this fact.

The European Commission is developing a range of programmes designed to apply to widely shared problems. In 2008 it set out a framework to tackle the impact of global warming upon human and animal health. The programme will consider different aspects of the effects of climate change on mortality and morbidity, including likely changes in the means of transmission of certain infectious diseases. The Water Framework Directive provides the opportunity for an EU-wide programme for water management that could incorporate adaptation objectives.

The directive includes measures for the prediction and management of floods that apply across all member–states. There are EU Action Plans on the safeguarding and restoration of biodiversity; Forest Focus programmes, which are concerned with tree stocks and soil monitoring across the EU; a forthcoming Sustainable Consumption and Production Action Plan; an Integrated Coastal Zone Management Programme; a Disaster Risk Reduction Programme; and more. The European Social Fund will be drawn upon to help raise consciousness about issues of adaptation and oversee other initiatives.

The EU is also funding adaptation policies and programmes in developing countries and has already set up partnerships with many of them. The Commission has published proposals aimed at sharing Europe's experience in creating adaptation measures with the developing world. It is examining the possibility of building a Global Climate Change Alliance that will promote dialogue and cooperation between the EU and developing countries.

Lots of impressive-sounding programmes: will they add up to much? Many pro-Europeans hope that such initiatives, as with tackling climate change more generally, will help provide a new beginning for the EU, which of late has been foundering. The thesis that the containment of, and adaptation to, climate change for some purposes should be dealt with on a European rather than a purely national level is incontestable. Yet how effective the EU will be, as in climate change policy, will depend on how far it can bring its member–states into line.

Floods in the UK

As a type case of issues about adaptation within countries, I shall take the example of flooding, storms and coastal erosion in Britain. Flooding in the UK involves a diversity of hazards. The value of property in the London floodplain alone is some £160 billion. The Thames Barrier has proved effective protection so far, but is coming into use with increasing frequency. Most of the occasions it has had to be closed have been over the past 10 years. During the winter of 2001–2 it was closed a record 24 times, as a result of historic highs in the freshwater levels of the river. Of the total stock of domestic dwellings in the UK, 10 per cent is currently at risk of flooding. In the summer of 2007, the UK experienced the most intense rainfall known since records began, giving rise to widespread floods.

The strongest storm to hit Western Europe so far occurred in Shetland in the early 1990s. It was as violent as a category five hurricane, and continued on and off for more than three weeks. Because of the normal rigours of life in Shetland, buildings there are constructed to a higher standard than in other parts of the UK. Were such a storm to occur in densely populated areas further south, there could be massive property damage and widespread loss of life.[4] Another major worry concerns dams, likely to be affected if intense downpours increase. Dam failures have become more frequent in recent years. About two million properties in the UK are potentially vulnerable to flooding alongside rivers, estuaries and coasts; and a further 80,000 from flooding resulting from heavy rains with which urban drains cannot cope.[5]

Recent studies have been able to demonstrate a link between increasing flooding risk in the UK and global warming.[6] A group of scientists studied the floods that happened in the UK in October and November 2000. The floods damaged some 10,000 properties and created insurance liabilities of some £1.3 billion. The researchers ran several thousand computer simulation models of the weather patterns, both under normal conditions and conditions as they might have been had greenhouse gas emissions not existed. In 90 per cent of the simulations the results showed that humanly induced global warming increased the risk of floods occurring in England and Wales by more than 20 per cent, and in two out of three cases by 90 per cent. In other words, the probability is high that the floods were influenced by climate change.

For about 40 years, from 1961 onwards, the UK insurance industry had an agreement with the government that cheap flood cover would be provided for all homes without regard to risk.[7] The result was large-scale moral hazard. State projects proceeded as though flood insurance could be taken for granted. Governments felt able to proceed with major building programmes in areas of flood risk – such as the Thames Gateway – without reference to insurability.

The agreement was abandoned by the insurance industry in 2002, and a new partnership between government and the industry was introduced in its stead. Private insurers agreed to provide cover to home-owners and businesses where the annual risk of flooding is put at no more than a 100:1 chance. Beyond that level, the state has to pick up the costs. The insurance companies agreed to the plan on condition that the government reciprocated by taking on board a range of preventative measures for the future. These include, for example, new investment to counter flooding, especially in areas of high vulnerability; placing restrictions on new building in areas without adequate flood protection; and improving programmes providing information to the public about local flooding hazards.

For future building to be covered under the agreement, areas vulnerable to extreme weather and rising sea levels must be avoided, or arrangements set up to incorporate insurance costs into home and business pricing. Solar panels should be installed on the roofs and façades of all new buildings, since the relative cost is insignificant. Roofs should offer a surface that gives a good reflective signal for radar satellites, allowing the buildings to be monitored for movement. A high standard of insulation for walls and roofs is necessary. Low-energy electrical fittings must be installed, which also reduce fire risk. Buildings must be constructed of materials that are robust in the face of floods and storms.[8]

The rise in the number and intensity of flooding incidents in the early 2000s in shoreline areas led the government to alter its pre-existing coastal management policy. A key necessity was to develop a more integrated approach to planning, since, until recently, coastal management was in the hands of a heterogeneous assortment of different authorities and groups.[9] There was little coordinated thinking about what forms of coastal management would best serve current and future citizens.

A new policy was introduced which ruled that coastal protection should be guided by the relationship between risks and costs. Not everywhere can or should be protected – for instance, low-lying and sparsely populated areas will no longer necessarily be defended. The policy was introduced without consultation with local interests. Property prices immediately dropped in areas where protection was to be withdrawn. The result was huge protest in those areas. In response to these difficulties, some local authorities established funds to protect parts of the coastline under threat, even where national policy had opted for no intervention. The idea was to provide time for the local communities to develop adaptive policies of their own, or find ways of coming to terms with the fact that there would be no more state aid. Local community workshops were set up to discuss the future of the coastline.

The whole system of coastal management is in a transitional state. A number of major issues remain to be resolved.[10] Even with recent changes, planning regulations are not strong enough to stop houses and business premises from being built in areas of substantial risk of coastal erosion and flooding. Buildings are still being constructed in potentially hazardous areas. Since the state no longer recognizes an obligation to defend all people and property along the coastline, some property-owners are providing their own protection, even though it might be inappropriate and out of line with wider policy – a further recipe for conflict. The situation where neither the state nor private insurance provides cover, which applies in some coastal areas, is inherently unstable.

So far, national policy is well ahead of local and regional thinking, at least on most such issues. At the same time, a new system of governance is emerging, albeit one marked by struggle and divisions of interest. Research shows a growing realization among local groups that the coastline cannot stay unchanged. It is necessary to plan ahead for a period of at least half a century, against a background of uncertainty, not just calculable risk. Neither perspective has been part of coastal policy and thinking until quite recently.

No risk without opportunity: this theorem applies to the evolution of coastal governance as in so many other areas. Rather than defending the status quo, it is far better to think creatively about what sustainable and resilient coastal communities should be like. The practical difficulties that stand in the way of such a transformation in outlook, however, are considerable. For instance, properties have to be protected from major flood risks in the here-and-now, even though the measures may not be sustainable in the longer term – such as building 'hard defences' by increasing the height of the flood walls.

Insurance, hurricanes and typhoons

Innovations in insurance are going to be of key importance as far as adaptation is concerned. These will have to span the state and the private sector, since the state's role as insurer of last resort will come under great strain. However, once more, innovations pioneered here could prove to be of wider application than only in the field of climate change.

The most difficult forms of adaptation to manage will inevitably be those related to weather changes that take a catastrophic form. When one looks on a world level, the number of 'natural' catastrophes has risen significantly over the past 30 years. Most catastrophes are weather-related, implying that there is a connection between this increase and rising world temperatures. One way of indexing the increase is via levels of insurance claims.[11] Such analysis suggests that a sharp increase in the number of natural catastrophes has taken place over the past 10 years in particular. Since 1970, of the largest catastrophes, 34 occurred between 1988 and 2006. For understandable reasons, the insurance industry has been very active in promoting research into such trends.

In one study, some 16,000 natural catastrophes over the period from 1980 to 2005 were analysed.[12] They were grouped into six categories, depending upon the degree of insurance losses they led to. The categories were:

1 Small losses (up to $10 million).
2 Medium-sized losses ($10–$60 million).
3 Medium-sized to serious losses ($60–$200 million).
4 Serious losses ($200–$500 million).
5 Devastating losses ($500 million–$1 billion).
6 Extreme losses (more than $1 billion).

The smaller categories were fairly stable over the dates in question, but there was a steep rise in each of the three larger ones. The research showed that fully 85 per cent of claims in all categories were for weather-related natural catastrophes.

The insurance claims made in any specific year are mainly determined by the number of catastrophes that occur – those in categories 5 and 6. The record for claims thus far is 2005, the year in which three damaging hurricanes occurred: Katrina, Wilma and Rita. In terms of insurance claims, Katrina produced the highest level ever, while the others were the sixth and seventh highest recorded. Over the period 1970–88, total damage amounted to more than $10 billion in just one year. Since 1989, however, totals of more than $15 billion have been submitted in 10 separate years.

Insurance claims are skewed towards the richer countries, since the insurance industry there is more developed and hence has more liabilities. Looked at in terms of death rates, the highest levels of catastrophic damage occur in Asia, but not because of the intrinsic frequency of natural disasters; rather, because that continent has the highest number of large population centres. Between 1980 and 2005, some 800,000 people died in Asian countries as a result of such disasters, 90 per cent of them as a result of category 5 and 6 events. North America and Europe experienced more or less the same proportion of natural disasters, but the amount of damage suffered was three times as great in the former as in the latter.

The above studies do not by any means cover all insurance claims and losses. They do not include, for example, the consequences for liability insurance and life insurance; or damage to roads, railways and other forms of public infrastructure, which are hardly ever insured. Real losses more generally may be many times higher than insured losses. The insured losses in hurricane Katrina amounted to about $49 billion, compared to estimated total losses of $144 billion. The difference in the less developed parts of the world is greater, since insurance cover is nothing like so advanced. In the two major cases of flooding that happened in China in the 1990s, the cost of the damage, in one case, was 30 times higher than the sum covered by insurance and, in the other, nearly 50 times higher.

A whole range of weather-induced disasters happened around the world during the course of 2010, although there is no way of knowing how far each or any of them was influenced by climate change. They included massive floods in Pakistan, as a result of which hundreds of thousands of people were displaced from their homes; large-scale flooding in Queensland, Australia – following on from a number of years of extreme drought; unprecedented high summer temperatures and drought in Russia, which produced forest fires that the authorities struggled to bring under control; widespread flooding in parts of China, leading to landslides; and prolonged drought in the area of the Amazon in Brazil.

Weather-related risks create enormous problems both for private insurers and for the state. Progress with adaptation will depend a great deal on how far both parties can come up with feasible new policies. It is crucial that the insurance industry pioneers new ways of dealing with the rising scale and frequency of catastrophic risks, since otherwise the burden on government will be insupportable. The option that private insurers have of simply pulling back from insuring certain hazards is not available to governments, which will have to pick up the pieces. It is therefore in the interests of both parties to cooperate.

Risks associated with climate change, as I have often stressed in this book, shade so far over into uncertainty that they often cannot be calculated with any precision. A single episode can cause large-scale damage, but the extent of likely damage is not readily predictable, since so much depends upon context. The damage done by a storm or hurricane, for example, depends vitally upon the path it takes, not only on its strength. It is hard to even up premiums over a period of time, since the level of damage varies greatly from year to year.

The capital requirements are large, since, in a year of high losses, the pay-out all has to come in or close to that period. This fact means that the insurer must constantly have liquid capital to hand. The amount of money needed to cover the costs of a catastrophe can be as high as 100 times the premium income in the year in which it takes place. The insurer therefore has to look for a way of spreading risk through reinsurance – against a backdrop of the probability that natural catastrophe risks will lead to much greater damage in the future. Moreover, the reinsurers face much the same risks as the original insurers, because of the high element of uncertainty.

New thinking will be needed to push back the boundaries of insurability. Until recently, catastrophic insurance was based upon somewhat traditional models of risk management. That is to say, it depended upon calculations derived from previous catastrophic events. Such a practice was no longer possible after hurricane Andrew, the predecessor to Katrina, which caused a level of damage greater than had previously been thought conceivable.

Work has begun on the construction of sophisticated catastrophe models, with the objective of reducing areas of uncertainty. These make use of some of the same techniques of computer modelling involved in attempts to predict the likely progress of climate change. For a hurricane of a given strength, 1,000 or more different potential paths through a specific area can be mapped. The point is to make the models sufficiently detailed to distinguish probabilities and hence, again, to be able to calculate premiums.

Catastrophe bonds have also been introduced to spread

risk across capital markets. They are complex financial instruments, which aim at neutralizing risk for the original insurer, but also contain safeguards for those who purchase them. Allianz issued a pioneering catastrophe bond in 2007, which provided cover against large-scale losses occurring from earthquakes in Canada and the US (although excluding California) and river flooding in Britain.

Munich Re and Swiss Re, two major insurance companies, have been exploring the possibility of applying catastrophe bonds to cover poor people in Bangladesh and other developing countries. The idea is to work in conjunction with foundations and NGOs to provide relevant insurance coverage. The Rockefeller Foundation is exploring this type of coverage in parts of Asia and in sub-Saharan Africa. The Bill and Melinda Gates Foundation has awarded $34 million to the International Labour Organisation of the UN to pursue a similar initiative. An adviser to the UN's task force on disasters has rightly observed: 'We're trying to alert public policymakers that it's much faster to get insurance payouts than to knock on doors for emergency donors.'[13]

Given that the level and extent of catastrophes will continue to mount, perhaps sharply, it is a matter of urgency to re-examine the relative roles of private insurers and the state. The cost to the US federal government of hurricane Katrina alone was in the order of $100 billion, given as direct assistance and as tax benefits. Even then, it covered no more than part of the losses incurred, especially if one includes secondary economic effects (forgone employment, for example). There is also an issue of moral hazard, when the state is known to be the insurer of last resort. Those who are vulnerable to risk have less of an incentive to deal with it themselves in advance, since they (believe they can) fall back on the state when necessary. Especial care will have to be taken to ensure that a situation does not emerge in which only the affluent can get adequate insurance cover.

The state should aim to create financial and fiscal conditions in which disaster and catastrophe cover can be expanded under the aegis of the insurance industry. It will not lose its role as insurer of last resort, but that role can be brought more within the bounds of realism. Ideally, insurance provided by the state should only kick in above a certain level, set according to the bounds of coverage by private insurance. The industry must not retreat in the face of an increasing preponderance of disasters and catastrophes, but must continue to explore ways of expanding insurability.

Adaptation: the developing world

Hurricane Jeanne made many people in the US homeless when it struck in 2004. However, it had already caused 1,500 deaths when it hit Haiti a short while earlier. During the hurricane, heavy rain fell on the island non-stop for 30 hours. Haiti is 98 per cent deforested, the result of the fact that the poor on the island harvest the trees for charcoal. As a consequence, the rain cascaded down the hillsides, inundating the capital city and other areas. Many survivors became homeless, rice and fruit harvests were obliterated and diseases spread.

The Dominican Republic shares half the island with Haiti. It is not as poor and much of the rainforest remains intact. Only 25 people died there as a result of the hurricane. An aid agency funded by the US had planted numerous trees in Haiti over a period of some two decades in order to replenish that which had been lost. Yet they were almost all cut down, mostly by people living in extreme poverty, for whom making charcoal was their only source of livelihood. In January 2010 further disaster hit Haiti when the country was shaken by a powerful earthquake. Some 200,000 people died.

J. Timmons Roberts and Bradley Parks carried out research into a large number of weather-related disasters in poor countries over the period between 1980 and 1992.[14] They made use of the Emergency Events Database, developed by the US Geological Survey. This survey contains data on 12,800 disasters happening over that period. They included events from many sources, but the researchers were able to identify those where the major cause was related to weather, which made up about half the total. They judged the evidence sound and detailed enough to make effective comparisons in some 4,000 of these cases.

CRI 1990–2009	Country	CRI score	Death toll	Deaths per 100,000 inhabitants	Total losses in million US$ PPP	Losses per unit GDP in %	Number of events
1	Bangladesh	7.33	7,849	5.63	2,068.14	1.67	259
2	Myanmar	8.67	7,124	14.33	676.35	2.04	30
3	Honduras	10.83	322	5.21	663.57	3.12	53
4	Nicaragua	16.17	157	2.80	263.33	2.05	39
5	Vietnam	19.00	457	0.59	1,861.50	1.31	203
6	Haiti	19.67	337	3.98	164.62	1.20	46
7	Philippines	26.83	821	1.08	684.45	0.34	270
8	Dominican Republic	27.67	212	2.55	185.08	0.40	41
9	Mongolia	31.00	13	0.54	308.65	5.19	30
10	Tajikistan	33.50	30	0.47	311,27	2.93	51

Figure 7.1 The long-term Climate Risk Index (CRI)
Results (annual averages) in specific indicators in the 10 countries most
affected, 1990–2009.

Source: Germanwatch: www.germanwatch.org/cri

The weather events included cyclones, droughts, floods, heat waves, hurricanes, tidal waves, tornadoes, tropical storms, typhoons, winter storms, hailstorms, dust storms, rainstorms, thunderstorms and waves of cold weather – the list itself is a potent reminder of the power that climatic fluctuations have over people's lives. Roberts and Parks made tallies of the numbers of people killed, rendered homeless or otherwise seriously affected by the weather events. A single total was created for each nation covered, providing an indicator for the whole period. The aim was to help understand why some countries and regions suffer more profoundly and consistently as a result of extreme weather events than others do. Put the other way around, they studied why some seemed more resilient than others.

They found an overall connection between the level of income of a country and its capacity to withstand weather-related shocks. The most damaging human disaster of the closing decades of the twentieth century was the result of the drought in East Africa in 1984. It was concentrated in three particularly impoverished countries: Ethiopia, Sudan and Chad. About 500,000 people died, while far more suffered from malnutrition and lost their homes. The totals of those made homeless as a result of weather-related disasters over the period make sobering reading, as the authors observe. They include 62 million in Bangladesh and 50 million in China. More than 25 million people became homeless in Laos, India, Sri Lanka, Vietnam, the Philippines and Pakistan combined.

Comparison between the severity of the weather events and their consequences showed clearly that vulnerability correlates closely with economic and political weakness, with a steep rise for the very poorest countries – those comprising the 'bottom billion' in terms of population numbers (see below, pp. 213–16). Ineffective and corrupt government, dependence on low-value tropical crops, the existence of sprawling shanty towns and poor communications and transport links all play a part. It isn't poverty as such that heightens vulnerability. Where countries remain very poor, but have overcome some of these problems, their resilience in the face of disasters is much greater.

The world has moved on from the time at which many leaders and citizens in the South believed that talk of climate change was a tactic used by the rich countries to stop others from developing. Such an attitude has been replaced by a more sober realization of just how threatened by the effects of global warming the less developed countries are. There is, in principle, the possibility of closer collaboration between North and South, not only in terms of contraction and convergence, but especially as concerns adaptation.

Aid and financial assistance from the rich to the poorer nations must focus much more on adaptation than has been the case up to now. At the moment, the resources needed to help the developing countries even begin to assess their vulnerabilities is lacking. The Adaptation Fund, mentioned earlier, is only just getting under way. Finance set aside for the 48 least developed countries to prepare national adaptation plans consists of about $33 million, around two-thirds of which is provided by the industrial countries. Yet how the money should be distributed remains the subject of strident debate, with the consequence that the money has not actually been forthcoming. Proper and detailed vulnerability assessments should be the first line of defence in adaptation, since practical action is hardly feasible if the extent and location of risks are not known.

Many of the mechanisms or changes needed for the developing countries to become richer are also important for adaptation to climate change. Population growth is a major influence on both, suggesting the vital importance of a renewed drive on the part of international agencies to help bring that rate down. The main means of doing so is well established – empowering women and assisting their incorporation into the labour force. Thus far, there has been little progress in linking adaptation to existing poverty-alleviation programmes. Some of the small island states in the Caribbean seem to have been the first to make some advances.

A commodity support fund that would protect cash-crop economies from the buffetings of price fluctuations in the marketplace would help promote resilience. It is a long way from local flooding and coastal erosion in Britain to the much larger disasters found elsewhere. Yet common strategies can be forged. For instance, partnerships instituted between government and business, and government and citizens' groups, in order to tackle such problems are also relevant for poorer countries.

Serious attention should be given to extending the role of insurance in the vulnerable countries of the world. Insurance is far less extensive in the deprived countries than in the richer ones, for obvious reasons, but the potential importance of insurance is huge. For instance, climatic variations are a major threat to subsistence farmers in large areas of Africa; those variations will deepen with the progress of global warming. Two new approaches have been introduced in recent years to provide assistance to the farmers and prevent crop failure.[15] One is the use of satellite and computer-based models to provide seasonal precipitation forecasts, which can help to reduce risk. Seed varieties can be adjusted, for example, to choose those most suitable for expected rainfall conditions. The other is the use of new mechanisms of insurance cover. Thus, index-based weather insurance can be developed and linked to micro-credit for agricultural inputs.

These programmes have so far remained separate from

one another, but it may be possible to integrate them. A pilot insurance scheme has been introduced for smallholder farmers in Malawi. Those who tailor their crops to projected rainfall conditions will be able to get insurance coverage that should allow them greatly to expand the area of land they will sow for crops, as well as the yield they will achieve.

Even in the most deprived conditions, poor people are not normally without resources – they have assets and capabilities that can help develop resilience. Adaptation policies should as far as possible focus on strengthening that resilience. For instance, traditional systems of adapting to climate variability include switching crops, social networks of support and assistance or collective savings mechanisms. All can in principle be bolstered by high-tech means of providing information or creating more extensive support networks.

Farmers in the high Andes of Peru and Bolivia observe the Pleiades star constellations so as to get advance warning of possible weather conditions several months into the future. They look at the intensity of the brightest star in the cluster, its size, the date of its first appearance and its position. If the star appears clear in the sky just before dawn, abundant rain is indicated and a rich potato crop predicted. Planting processes are modified accordingly. Scientists have confirmed that the level of visibility of the cluster is related to the presence or otherwise of wispy cirrus clouds high in the sky; and that these are also associated with the warm phase of El Niño. The farmers have, in effect, been monitoring the phases of El Niño for centuries; but they could get a lot of further help from modern methods of weather prediction.

As the examples of disasters mentioned earlier show, Bangladesh is one of the countries most exposed to the effects of climate change, because of its geographical location. The country is low-lying and will be one of the first to suffer from rises in sea levels. If those levels rise by 45 centimetres, then 10 per cent of the country will be under water. Even with its pre-established climate, the country gets too much rainfall in the monsoon season, causing frequent floods, while during other parts of the year it is prone to drought. The Bangladeshis are not just sitting around waiting for the rich countries to invest and help them in preventative adaptation – although this surely will be necessary. Meanwhile, the country has set up a National Adaptation Programme of Action, involving working groups from each of the main producing sectors.[16] It has developed detailed assessments of vulnerability and suggested a range of action programmes, although the implementation of some of these will have to depend upon foreign aid programmes to be forthcoming.

Even in the very poorest areas, Bangladeshis are building dykes and embankments, changing their agricultural practices and sharing their knowledge with other poor countries in Asia and Africa. Full flood protection is currently widely practised in Bangladesh, but controlled flooding looks a necessary strategy for the future. An early warning system for cyclonic disasters already exists and could be further extended. Satellite and information technology allow for the continuous monitoring of the formation of cyclones in the Bay of Bengal.

Major efforts are under way to increase the resilience of local communities in areas under particular threat, drawing upon local expertise and involvement. One study, for example, identified 600 vulnerable households, made up of poor farmers, fishermen, day labourers and single parent households. Male- and female-headed groups developed ideas and plans for how to diversify their means of livelihood, set up training groups on the likely effects of climate change and introduce new production processes. The work produced a whole series of novel proposals, some of which were immediately implemented, with considerable success.

Floating gardens – an idea now copied internationally – were first introduced in Bangladesh. A floating garden uses aquatic weeds as a base on which crops can be grown. It can be introduced where land is otherwise unavailable to expand the productive capacities of local villages and towns. Floating gardens are inexpensive to construct and can be established on a permanent basis.

In closing the gap between the attempts of the developed nations to limit climate change and those of the developing ones, assessments of vulnerability are likely to be very important. The vulnerability of the richer countries includes the knock-on effects of climate change-induced disasters in poorer states, which could greatly exacerbate the tensions already visible in world society. In chapter 9 I will consider such dangers in some detail.

INTERNATIONAL NEGOTIATIONS, THE EU AND CARBON MARKETS

The history of international negotiations aimed at containing climate change goes back some 20 years. From small beginnings, the enterprise has mushroomed. The IPCC itself grew out of a previous environmental endeavour, the Montreal Protocol, initiated by the UN in 1987, which was concerned with eliminating the industrial chemicals that produced the hole in the ozone layer over the Antarctic. The initiative, mainly preoccupied with ensuring that the harmful chemicals, chlorofluorocarbons (or CFCs), were replaced by substitutes, seems to have been successful in beginning to reverse the harm done.

The IPCC's first assessment of where the world stands in relation to climate change was offered in 1990, as part of the run-up to the Rio Earth Summit which followed two years later. The Summit introduced the UN Framework Convention on Climate Change, which was signed by 166 nations at that point (today there are 195 signatories). The US and some other countries initially were strongly opposed to binding emissions targets, as a result of which no such targets were included. All participating nations agreed to calculate their emissions and report the levels annually. It was accepted that there should be 'common but differentiated responsibilities' among nations for stabilizing climate change. All should at some point accept

responsibility, but the developed countries have the obligation to act first.

In spite of some foot-dragging by the US and other countries, as the discussions evolved there came to be widespread
acceptance that mandatory cuts would be necessary for
progress to be made. At meetings in 1995 it was agreed that
the industrial countries would set themselves targets for
emissions reductions. The then US president, Bill Clinton,
eventually came round to accepting this view after some
initial hesitancy. The US Senate voted unanimously against
any agreement that didn't include cuts for the developing
societies.

In 1997, at Kyoto in Japan, after tortuous negotiations, an
agreement was drawn up by which the developed countries
would cut their emissions by an average of 5.2 per cent relative to 1990 levels by the period 2008–12. The Kyoto Protocol
was set up in such a way that it could come into force without
complete consensus. The rule set up for the Protocol to
become part of international law was that developed countries, accounting for at least 55 per cent of total emissions from
the industrial states, would have to sign up. Russia, which
accounted for 17 per cent of 1990 emissions, initially stated its
opposition to Kyoto, but eventually ratified towards the end
of 2004.

The administration of George W. Bush, inclined towards
climate change scepticism anyway, and influenced strongly
by industrial lobbies, was worried that China might achieve
a competitive advantage over the US, given that the developing countries were not required to make any cuts. Bush
believed that if the US were to take more steps to combat
global warming, even in the context of the Kyoto agreements
with other nations going along, the country might damage
its international competitiveness. As the world's dominant
economy, the cost of taking steps to cope with climate change
– since the US would have had to agree to substantial emissions reductions – might have affected the wider world
economy too.

Apart from the US and Australia, all the other industrial
countries, and a large majority of countries in the rest of the
world, put their names to Kyoto.

The US pressurized Russia not to participate. The Russians were initially not inclined to do so anyway. One of President Putin's economic advisers, Andrei Illarionov, claimed that Kyoto would destroy the world economy 'like an international Auschwitz'.[1] However, Russia at that point wanted EU support for its bid to join the World Trade Organization, while the EU, the leading force in climate change negotiations, needed Russian participation in Kyoto to salvage the whole thing. So, in effect, a bargain was struck.

An additional factor was that by the early 2000s Russian emissions were much lower than they had been in 1990, because of the contraction of the economy and the collapse of some of the large state-owned industrial companies. The EU countries realized that this situation could help with the carbon trading scheme that had just been established. Russia's emission 'reductions' would be available to help ease EU member–states' problems with meeting their own emissions targets. An unfortunate outcome of the whole episode was that Russia was legitimated to carry on squandering energy domestically without thought to environmental damage.

The result of compromise, the targets agreed at Kyoto bear little relationship to what is required to make a serious impact upon global warming. They were too low and contained all kinds of anomalies. Take the case of Australia, which came out of the negotiations with the agreement that its emissions could actually be increased rather than cut. Like the Americans, the Australians initially wanted only voluntary reductions. They then argued that Australia is a special case, because it is a net energy producer with a very large transport-dependent sector. They also pointed to reductions in deforestation that had been made before 1990. Given the need to persuade Australia to sign, the country got what it was asking for (although it later opted out anyway, signing up only in 2008 after a change of government).

Because the Kyoto agreements were not adopted until 2004, most countries were slow in making any progress at all towards reaching even the modest targets that had been set. The EU has been by far the most forceful advocate of proposals to limit emissions, but even its record is wanting. Quite a few EU states have met their Kyoto targets, and some have well exceeded them. However, a large part of the reason is the impact of recession, mentioned earlier. And of course Kyoto did not include the developing countries at all – even though these are now major contributors to world emissions in absolute terms.

The Kyoto Protocol initiated the Clean Development Mechanism (CDM). The CDM allows industrial countries to get credits to put towards their Kyoto targets by funding clean energy projects in developing states. The scheme took off slowly, since few countries were willing to act until Kyoto had finally been ratified. Some 850 projects had been approved by the middle of 2009, most of them located in the four biggest developing countries: China, India, Brazil and South Africa.[2] The CDM is not quite the win–win framework it seems, since it allows developed countries to relax their own emissions reduction efforts.

It is uncertain how far the CDM has actually helped to introduce renewable energy projects into the developing countries. Marginal projects dominate, such as the containment of industrial gases by bolting on filters to already existing pipes. It has been said that perhaps half the reductions claimed are the result of 'accounting tricks' and are empty of content. In one case, the projects in a specific country were all concerned with emissions of HFC-23, a by-product of the manufacture of refrigerants. The total cost of the parts amounted to $70 million, while the value of the subsidy provided through the CDM was some $1 billion. Emissions reductions were achieved, but in a cumbersome and highly inefficient way, with much of the money being swallowed up as a result of corrupt practices.[3]

Not much has been done to focus the CDM more effectively, mainly because of the political stakes involved. Environmentalists are reluctant to criticize the only means that exists for directly helping the developing countries. As just pointed out, the EU needs the credit mechanism to help meet its targets. The developing countries, or some of them, especially China, the leading recipient, do get investment. A report from the World Bank estimates that the CDM has stimulated investments of $59 billion since it was first established.

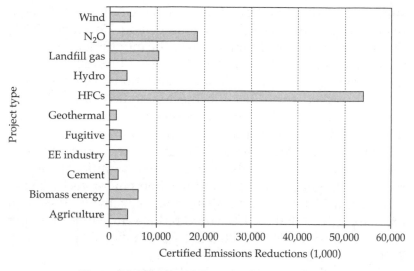

Figure 8.1 Registered Kyoto projects up to 2007

Source: 'Europe's Dirty Secret: Why the EU Emissions Trading Scheme Isn't
Working', *Open Europe*, August 2007, p. 29, graph 5

Further negotiations

A further round of climate change negotiations carried
on under the auspices of the UN was held in Bali in
2007. Some 12,000 delegates attended. Following arduous
discussions, the president of the conference, Rachmat
Witoelar, announced: 'We have finally achieved the breakthrough the world has been waiting for: the Bali roadmap!'[4]
The roadmap was designed as a new negotiation process to
replace Kyoto.

However, probably the best one can say about Bali is that
the negotiations did not collapse. The roadmap was little
more than a vague sketch. The agreements did not contain
a single specific commitment. They offered no recognition
of the problems inherent in the Kyoto framework, or any
acknowledgement of the minimal impact it has had on world
emissions. As one commentator put it: 'If this is success, give
me failure.'[5]

The roadmap arrived at in such a tortuous way in Bali was

supposed to supply a framework for the UN-brokered negotiations that took place in Copenhagen in December 2009. There were other developments over the months leading up to Copenhagen too. Following the election of President Obama, the US re-engaged in UN climate negotiations. The new leadership breathed fresh life into the Major Economies Forum – a grouping of the 17 largest economies originally convened under the Bush administration – and brought climate change within its remit. Australia and Japan, which under previous conservative governments had resisted significant carbon reduction targets, pledged to reduce their emissions by 25 per cent over a 2000 base and a 1990 base respectively. President Obama pledged that the US would reduce emissions by 17 per cent over 2005 levels by 2020 and by more than 80 per cent by 2050.[6]

The large developing countries also made significant moves. In November 2009 the Chinese President, Hu Jintao, committed his country to a goal of reducing its energy intensity by 40–45 per cent by 2020. Shortly afterwards the Indian government followed suit, introducing a carbon intensity target of 20–25 per cent reduction by the same date. At about the same time the US and China endorsed a Memorandum of Understanding, designed to promote cooperation on energy and climate change policy. The EU also held summit meetings with the Chinese and the Indian leadership in November, proclaiming the importance of reaching concrete outcomes in Copenhagen and agreeing to act together to help achieve this.

On the basis of the developments noted above, many commentators at the time were optimistic about the chances of success. Indeed, many political leaders were too, since they flocked to Copenhagen in large numbers, something that had not happened at previous UN summits. More than 40,000 delegates attended the meetings, while some 5,000 journalists were there to cover the event. There were 122 prime ministers or presidents, the largest number ever assembled together save at the UN headquarters in New York.[7]

However, not only did attendees at Copenhagen fail to reach agreement on any binding carbon reductions; the whole process was chaotic and disjointed. President Obama arrived only on the last day of the negotiations. On meeting him, Hillary Clinton commented: 'Mr President, this is the worst meeting I've ever been to since the eighth grade student council.'[8] The main reason concerned the disagreements that existed between states, especially between the developed and developing countries. However, these conflicts were compounded by strategic mistakes made by the Danish hosts, and by disagreements over tactics within the Danish government.

The Danish prime minister, Anders Fogh Rasmussen, was a supporter of the climate change sceptic Bjørn Lomborg. He and the environment minister, Connie Hedegaard, who was much more committed to the project of securing widespread carbon reductions, did not see eye to eye. Prior to the meetings themselves, Anders Rasmussen left office to become the Secretary-General of NATO and another Rasmussen, Lars Lokke, the vice-chairman of the governing party, took over. At the same time, the conflicts within the Danish government worsened. Hedegaard was committed to the UN negotiating process, which those in the prime minister's office thought too slow-moving.

The result was a twin-track strategy. The leaders of the developing countries were outraged at a document which was leaked as 'secret' to the *Guardian* newspaper, but which had in fact been in circulation for some while. Denmark was seen to be supporting only the interests of the developed nations, thus further accentuating the divisions that already existed. The whole process of negotiation dissolved into disorder.

The Danish prime minister decided to review and recast his unilateral strategy, this time bringing at least the larger of the developing countries on board. A three-page document summarizing some of the main aspirations of the negotiations was prepared. After Barack Obama arrived, a group of 26 leaders started drafting a revised text. Differences between the US and China at that point constituted one of the main sources of disagreement. Obama was trying to see Wen Jiabao, the Chinese leader, but Wen seemed to be avoiding him. Obama also wanted to see the leaders of Brazil, India and South Africa, whose delegations appeared to be stalling things. Eventually all five leaders did meet, and agreed a deal between themselves – which became known as the Copenhagen Accord.

There then followed a further set of acrimonious discussions about the document, involving the original group of 26 and other countries. The most that the states present were prepared to do was to 'take note' of the Accord, which specified that participating nations were invited on a voluntary basis to report national carbon reduction and targets and plans to the UN.

What happened at Copenhagen came as a shock to the EU countries. The EU had seen itself as being in the vanguard of climate change policy, and its representatives initially expected to play a leading role in Copenhagen. Not a single EU country figured in the discussions of the five states that agreed upon the outline of the Accord. Several European leaders played a significant part in the group of 26, but they were not there at the crunch.

Far from being the detailed, comprehensive and binding framework originally envisaged, the Accord was essentially a short statement of intent, no more than three pages long. It emphasized the need for 'deep cuts' in emissions to hold the rise in global average temperatures to 2°C and recognized that climate change is 'one of the greatest challenges of our time'. The Accord stressed the need to reverse deforestation and to provide for resources coming from the richer countries to help states in the developing world struggling with the problem. The industrial countries in addition accepted the goal of raising $100 billion a year by 2020 to help developing nations cut carbon emissions.

The meetings in Copenhagen were a failure in terms of the ambitions that originally drove them. Yet in some ways the Accord actually represented an advance over the Kyoto-style approach. For the first time, it involved the large emerging economies – China, India and Brazil – in a very central role. The states that signed up to the Accord mostly did not just specify targets for 2020, but also set out plans, in varying levels of detail, to show how these targets would be achieved. A methodology for verifying the statistics provided by countries was agreed, previously a particular sticking point. By March 2010, more than 100 countries had signed up to the Accord, accounting for over 80 per cent of world greenhouse gas emissions. Of these, 72 had set out national plans for how emissions reductions would be achieved.

The next round of UN meetings was held in Cancun, Mexico, the successor event to Copenhagen, in December 2010. Expectations at Copenhagen had been high; for Cancun they were the opposite. Few heads of state attended and it was widely suggested beforehand that the chances of making any substantial progress were negligible.

In fact, the outcome was largely positive. The Mexican hosts had done their homework. They had spent months studying the tactical errors made at Copenhagen and were determined to avoid them this time. Since expectations were in any case so low, even relatively modest successes looked impressive. The motivation to keep the show on the road was strong enough to prevent groups of states that were unhappy about how negotiations were proceeding to stop short of undermining the whole enterprise. When a set of agreements was in fact reached on Saturday 11 December, it was greeted with thunderous applause and cheering.

Essentially, the Cancun agreements consolidated the Accord and adopted a reworked version of it as official UN policy. The agreements committed a wide range of countries to targets and actions to reduce emissions by 2020. All the major emitters were involved. The 2°C target, mentioned in the Accord, was for the first time adopted officially by the UN. The procedures for the monitoring and verification of emissions outlined in the Accord were strengthened. An independent panel of assessors will be responsible for ensuring accuracy of reporting. The fund proposed in the Accord to assist the poorer countries was formally endorsed, together with the ambition of raising $100 billion annually by 2020. In spite of protests from some of the developing nations, the World Bank was named as interim trustee of the fund. The initiative on deforestation – which in fact antedated the Accord, although it was referred to in it (Reduced Deforestation and Forest Degradation, or REDD) – was given more flesh. Finally, a continuing role for the CDM was endorsed, although little detail was provided as to in what guise.

The outcome of Cancun met with widespread approval, and from disparate groups. A spokesman for OXFAM observed: 'The UN climate talks are off the life-support machine. The agreement falls short of the emissions cuts that are needed, but it lays out a path to move towards them – crucially moving the world closer to the global deal that eluded the Copenhagen summit.' Chris Huhne, the British Secretary of State for Energy and Climate Change, was even more positive: 'This is a turning point in the long-running saga of international climate change negotiations. We've got a deal here which, if I had to mark it, I would have said 8 out of 10. It's way beyond what we were expecting only a few weeks ago and, indeed, way beyond what we were expecting at the beginning of the week.'[9]

Not everyone agreed, however. Kevin Anderson, of the Tyndall Centre for Climate Change Research, compared the international negotiations to astrology. The talks meander on – now for more than 20 years – and their very continuity is perceived as a success. Targets are set and plans made, but with little or no practical consequences in terms of what they are supposed to achieve – namely, containing the impact of climate change:

> In the meantime, every molecule of carbon dioxide emitted simply adds to all those emitted over the past century, inexorably increasing the level of warming and consequently the scope and scale of the impacts. This should be a challenging and increasingly uncomfortable message for all concerned. Instead, climate negotiations continue to be informed by the astrological view, where, through either ignorance or a desire to save face, it is assumed the problem will be the same next year as this. The science, however, tells a very different story; next year the problem will have become worse – as it has done each and every day we have failed to reduce emissions since the Earth Summit in Rio in 1992.[10]

Anderson is right. There is a dislocation between the snail-like pace of the international negotiations and the implacable nature of climate change, given the continuing advance of carbon emissions globally. This is not a reason to abandon the attempt, of course, since some sort of universal, or quasi-universal, framework for carbon reductions would undoubtedly be of great value. But it does strongly imply that we have to look elsewhere for the radicalism demanded in the short term, as indeed I have argued throughout this book. Moreover, the negotiations thus far put a great deal more emphasis upon the 'what' of emissions reductions – how much and by when – than upon the 'how' of the means whereby they may be achieved.

The role of the EU

The European Union first set out an integrated strategy for dealing with climate change issues at summit meetings in Cardiff and Vienna in 1998. The objective at that time was to discuss common modes of response on the part of the member–states and to assist them in meeting Kyoto targets. Climate change became one of the priorities in the 6th Framework Programme for Research, lasting from 2002 to 2006. The EU from the beginning recognized its obligations to help poorer countries, not just to concentrate upon its component nations. It has also emphasized that climate change policy must march in tandem with that concerning energy.

In January 2007 the European Commission announced an upgraded strategy to combat global warming. The core proposal was that the EU would cut its emissions by 20 per cent by 2020; that cut would rise to 30 per cent if and when the other industrial countries came on board. Renewable energy would form 20 per cent of the energy mix by then, with (controversially) a binding minimum 10 per cent use of biofuels in motor transport.

For the next 10 years, the developing countries, the Commission proposed, should make every effort to lower their emissions and should start to reduce them in absolute terms from 2020/5. The European Emissions Trading Scheme (ETS), on which more below, was envisaged as a crucial means of allowing the EU countries to meet their commitments – the Commission anticipated at that point that means may be found to link different trading schemes into a single worldwide one.

In early 2008 the Commission put forward a new directive, setting out a framework for the EU in terms of the 2020 targets that member–states would be expected to achieve. The directive recognized that they start from different positions as far as renewable energy is concerned. Moreover, some have made much greater efforts than others in the past to get their emissions down. Differences in GDP and GDP growth are also taken into account. Member–states that have a relatively low GDP and need high economic growth will be able to increase their greenhouse gas emissions compared to the baseline year of 2005.

Only the 10 per cent target for the use of biofuels was set as a constant across the EU. The Commission recognized the criticisms that have been made of biofuels, but argued that it is possible to produce them without incurring environmental damage, and proposed that stringent criteria would be deployed to ensure that this was so. Most, however, will have to be imported.

Several leading scientists, as well as numerous NGOs, expressed their doubts about biofuels and criticized the EU's plan. They argued that it is a mistake to introduce quotas for biofuels before their effects have been fully assessed. The chief scientific adviser to the British government, John Beddington, commented that rising demand for biofuels in the US delivered a 'major shock' to world agriculture, producing elevated world food prices. Moreover, if biofuel production were to come at the expense of further deforestation, the outcome would be 'profoundly stupid'.[11]

Some major countries at the time, including France and Germany, initially expressed concern over their emissions reductions targets. Nicolas Sarkozy, the French President, at one point argued that France should not be set targets at all because the widespread use of nuclear power has already lowered its emissions levels. Business leaders from various states were critical of the EU acting on its own in relation to climate change. Higher energy costs, they said, would make European companies less competitive in the wider world and lead them to decamp elsewhere. German industrialists were especially worried about the competitiveness of their car, chemicals and steel industries. One in every seven jobs in Germany depends in some way upon the car industry.

The Commission President, José Manuel Barroso, admitted the validity of these concerns. 'We all know', he stated, 'that there are sectors where the cost of cutting emissions could have a real impact on their competitiveness against companies in countries that do nothing.'[12] There is no point in Europe setting up demanding regulations if the result is simply that production shifts to countries where there is an emissions free-for-all. International agreements, Barroso argued, would be one way to handle the difficulty, but if these cannot be reached, then the EU should look at compensation for the energy industries. Others have suggested a mechanism such as a carbon tax on imports. Nevertheless, in current proposals such ideas have been left on hold.

As the crisis in financial markets started to bite, a rebellious group of member–states in October 2008 pressed for a deferment of the date at which the EU's plans for emissions targets were supposed to be accepted as binding. Eight countries led the insurrection, including Italy and a cluster of ex-East European nations. The Italian Prime Minister, Silvio Berlusconi, commented that the targets would devastate Italian industry. He and his Polish counterpart, Donald Tusk, both used the argument that they didn't have to stick to a deal that had been struck while they were not in office. Besides Italy and Poland, the governments of Bulgaria, Hungary, Latvia, Lithuania, Romania and Slovakia all said they would resist attempts to railroad the targets through.

At the point at which agreement needed to be reached, late in 2008, France held the presidency of the European Council. Reversing his previous stance, Sarkozy pulled out all the stops to gain a consensus, and was successful. A summit of European leaders held in September 2008 agreed to the Commission's plan. A substantial price was paid, however. The EU is pinning much of its hopes for reaching its targets on the success of its emissions trading schemes. To gain an agreement, the terms of the scheme were weakened. Most companies in the processing industries, such as steel and cement, were for a period exempted from paying for carbon permits, while coal-fired power stations were allocated large discounts on the price of carbon.

As a result of the recession, the carbon output of the EU fell substantially, by more than 9 per cent in 2008–9. Consequently, the target of achieving a 20 per cent reduction in emissions by 2020 looks considerably more achievable. At the time of writing, the leaders of several EU states were pushing for the target to be elevated unconditionally to 30 per cent.

Carbon markets

The case for carbon markets was established at Kyoto, but, like all other aspects of climate change policy, was and is heavily influenced by political considerations. The European Commission originally wanted to impose an EU-wide carbon tax as part of its climate change agenda. It was unable to do so because it lacks the capability to override the wishes of member–states concerning fiscal issues. Several member–states – most notably the UK – were fiercely resistant to any measures that implied tax harmonization. However, environmental issues within the Union can be dealt with by majority vote. Carbon trading, in the shape of the ETS, could be introduced without such battles.

Designing markets to limit pollution had its origins in the US, where they were originally used with some success to control emissions of sulphur dioxide.[13] Such emissions, coming from coal-fired power stations, were the main cause of 'acid rain'. Instead of directly regulating the amount of sulphur dioxide, a market in emissions credits was created. The original proposal of Robert Stavins, the scheme's principal architect, to auction credits to the emitters, thereby establishing a market price, was blocked in Congress. It would have meant that the utility companies would have to pay large sums of money for the permits, money which would have gone to the federal government.[14] Permits were in fact issued free to virtually all companies, with a maximum total that could be issued in any one year of 8.9 million tonnes.

In spite of its limitations, the scheme produced significant cuts in emissions and at a much lower overall cost than the industry lobbyists who had opposed it had claimed it would incur. They had argued it would cost the industry $10 billion or more annually. The actual yearly sum turned out to be about $1 billion. The market forces generated helped produce quick and effective technological innovations in key parts of the industry. The scheme thus achieved a fair degree of success, sufficient to inspire some environmentalists, including Vice-President Al Gore. The Clinton administration commissioned a detailed economic modelling exercise on how it could be extended to cover carbon.

The outline of a possible international carbon market was also drawn up at Kyoto. It was agreed that the industrial countries could sell 'emissions reductions units' to one another, and could also trade them with developing countries to count towards their reduction targets. In spite of the fact that the US did not sign up to the Kyoto agreements, the idea of carbon trading did not go away. It was taken up first by business. BP set up an internal trading scheme committing the company to reduce its greenhouse gas emissions by one-tenth by 2010 as compared to 2000. It achieved this target very rapidly, in fact within a single year. The ETS started operation early in 2005. It covered about half of the EU's CO_2 emissions – those coming from fixed sources of power production, especially electricity, and from certain energy-intensive industries. It did not extend to other greenhouse gases.

The European Commission initially proposed to auction the emissions credits. As in the US, lobbying from industry sank the proposal. A hybrid creature arose from the negotiations between the Commission and member–states. An auction would have established an open market with a single price for carbon. The system that was introduced in its place allowed member–states the right to set up their own national allocation plans. These were supposed to be developed on the basis of criteria established at Kyoto, but they were vague; moreover, some states had no precise measures of their emissions in place. The result was an over-generous allocation of allowances, since it was in every member–state's interest to get the most favourable conditions it could, or at a minimum get a certain amount of wriggle room. A market was created, but one that produced very mixed consequences.

A lot of money has changed hands within the ETS, but thus far the scheme has been ineffective for the purposes for which it was set up. Early on in its history, the carbon price reached as much as 31 euros per tonne. Later it dropped so dramatically that it was worth .001 per cent of that sum. It lost its value completely as it became clear that there was a large surplus of allowances because of the slack built into the national allocation plans. In addition, some power-generating companies had made windfall profits by passing on to consumers the price of carbon credits, even though they were allocated free of charge.

The ETS has probably had some effect on emissions. Studies indicate that emissions in 2005 were around 7 per cent lower than they would have been had the scheme not been in place.[15] Yet some of that gain came from member–states' tactical exaggerations of their emissions in the build-up to the scheme. The Clean Development Mechanism is up and running, which would not have been possible without the ETS. Moreover, the ETS prompted the emergence of carbon trading markets elsewhere in the world, and these can in principle learn from the problems that emerged in the European experience.

The Commission has stated that Phase 1 of the ETS was a 'learning phase', and that ways will be found to apply a tighter cap to the market as it evolves. In January 2008 the Commission proposed a more rigorous version of the ETS, designed to overcome its earlier limitations. Allocation of allowances was to be done centrally rather than left to member nations. National allocation plans were to be scrutinized much more intensively than before. More than 60 per cent of allowances would be auctioned and other greenhouse gases included besides CO_2. From 2012 the ETS is to be extended to cover the airline industry. Ultimately, the Commission wants shipping and forestry to be included too.

Several projects for establishing carbon markets exist in the US, the most advanced being that being developed by the state of California. Governor Arnold Schwarzenegger signed bill AB32 towards the end of 2006. California has committed itself to a 25 per cent reduction in greenhouse gases by 2020 and 80 per cent by 2050, although only part is slated to be achieved through the carbon market. As of 2011, obstacles are still being encountered in instituting the legislation. Much of the opposition has come from groups that are otherwise sympathetic to attempts to reduce emissions: labour unions and environmental NGOs. Their objections do not all centre upon the use of carbon markets, but some groups are unhappy with their prominence. Of course, the bill also faces opposition from those in any case suspicious of or hostile to climate change policy.

The Chicago Climate Exchange market, a voluntary scheme, was in existence for some while. Unlike most other voluntary carbon markets, it was allowance-based rather than project-based – in other words, there was an agreed-upon market cap.[16] It was successful in the sense that a lot of money flowed through it. Its impact on emissions is harder to assess, but at best was limited.

In December 2010, the Exchange was wound up, in the sense that no new cycle was set up for companies to sign up. The allowances the system generated will continue to be traded, but only in a residual way. Its closure seemed to many 'to confirm the death of the very concept of cap and trade itself'.[17] However, the continued attempt to pass AB32 in California plus state-driven initiatives in the north-east of the US to set up carbon markets are sustaining interest in trading. The same is true of some provinces in Canada. As with Phase I of the ETS, supporters of the Exchange argue that it has been a valuable learning experience, ahead of the possible introduction of mandatory carbon markets in states or groups of states.

Carbon markets of various kinds have been established in other countries too. According to the Carbon Finance Unit of the World Bank, 337 metric tonnes of carbon dioxide equivalent were exchanged through projects in 2008, more than twice as much as the previous year, which itself saw trading rise by 40 per cent over the preceding one. The Bank estimated the size of the world carbon market at $64 billion in 2007.

Whether these figures will be maintained in a more adverse world economic situation, and where faith in markets has diminished, is a matter of conjecture. Carbon emissions trading markets are certainly here to stay, although at the moment it is an open question how well the ETS – by far the largest – will even function in revised form. Large amounts of money are flowing through such markets. Yet their capability to deliver significant emissions reductions remains uncertain. We should guard against the possibility that they take on a life of their own and are therefore seen as 'successful' simply because a lot of trading goes on. As has been shown by the experience of the ETS so far, it will not be easy to assess the impact they have on limiting emissions, even though this is their sole rationale. Although many pin high hopes on them, at the moment they are in an experimental stage. We do not know how well they will work, or how far they can be introduced on an international, let alone a global, level.

THE GEOPOLITICS OF CLIMATE CHANGE

Discussions of international relations and climate change tend to be of two kinds. On the one hand, there are many works about the mechanics of reaching international agreements to contain emissions. On the other, a growing number of studies seek to analyse the implications of climate change for geopolitics. I argue in this chapter that we have to bring these two sets of concerns much closer together than they are at the moment. Once more, energy – especially oil and struggles centred upon it – supplies one of the main points of connection.

It might seem that responding to climate change will intrinsically contribute to international collaboration. Yet the processes and interests promoting division are strong.[1] The melting of the Arctic ice provides a good example. When the area was just an ice field, there was considerable international cooperation over the activities carried out there, which were mainly of a scientific nature. The fact that navigation across the Arctic is becoming increasingly possible, and that major new oil, gas and mineral resources might become available, has led to divisions of interest and to international friction, fortunately so far of a confined nature.

For a long time the Arctic was considered as international territory, but this presumption is now under some threat. Some of the nations bordering the Arctic regions – the US, Russia, Norway, Finland, Canada and Denmark – have claimed areas of the Arctic as their own. Notoriously, in August 2007 members of Russia's parliament, the Duma, travelled in a mini-submarine to plant the Russian flag at a depth of two and a half miles under the North Pole. The objective was to symbolize Russia's claim to the mineral wealth of the Arctic, but also to establish whether a section of the sea-bed underneath the Pole, the Lomonosov Ridge, is an extension of the landmass of Russia. If it were so, the whole area could be said to be 'part of' Russia. The US government of the time responded that 'the best available evidence suggests the ridges in question are oceanic in nature, and thus not part of any country's continental shelf'.[2]

Denmark is looking at submitting a territorial claim over part of the Arctic. In 2009 the country released an all-party defence paper that proposed the creation of an Arctic military contingent, with ship-based helicopters able to drop troops anywhere. There are plans to develop a new Arctic Command. Russia has announced that it will set up an Arctic special forces unit and institute a new ice-breaker programme.

In 2010 Norway bought 48 Lockheed F-35 fighter jets, in some part because they are suitable for Arctic patrols. The Norwegians launched an Arctic military manoeuvre in March of that year, in which a fictional country, Northland, seized Norway's offshore oil rigs. The Russians lodged a formal protest. Sweden and Canada have also been bolstering their Arctic military presence. NATO and the EU have both been considering what the implications are of such initiatives. Finland and Sweden, neither of which belongs to NATO, have discussed forming a northern security alliance of their own, along with NATO members Denmark, Iceland and Norway. All the nations with interests in the Arctic are talking the language of cooperation and are signatories to the UN Convention on the Law of the Sea. Yet the worrying signs are plain to see.

Climate change issues – especially in conjunction with developing scarcities of energy – could become both militarized and dominated by security risks. The result could be a progressive deterioration of international cooperation, where security is increasingly seen as divisible. What should be an overriding goal of reducing emissions could fall prey to a competitive struggle for resources, exacerbating already existing tensions and divisions. The leaders of states, or groups of states, could exploit climate change to their own sectional ends. Several different paths to violent conflict are imaginable. For instance, political leaders might use climate change-induced strains to gain or retain power in internal struggles – for example, migrants might be used as scapegoats in such power bids. In volatile areas of the world, a country weakened by the consequences of climate change might be attacked by its neighbours seeking to gain advantage from the country's problems.

A further possibility is that armed conflicts could occur as states try to gain a hold over resources where demand is outstripping supply – the most likely path if worst-case scenarios of climate change were to prevail. This could happen if the world economy becomes 'renationalized' with a widespread return to protectionism. Yet another possibility is that 'subsistence conflicts' – of the sort that has devastated Darfur – might become commonplace. Groups living on a level close to bare subsistence could clash as their means of livelihood start to evaporate, drawing in military 'protectors' of one sort or another. Each of the above paths could overlap or intertwine.[3]

Although the sources of the bloodshed, starvation and homelessness provoked by the conflict in Darfur are complex, the situation there has been called the 'first climate change war', since the drying up of Lake Chad is one of the factors that contributed to the migration which led to it.[4] Given this influence, we see again a situation in which climate change intersects with energy resources. China is actively involved in Sudan because of the oil and minerals the country possesses. The Chinese have supplied arms and training to the government forces and for some while refused to join the UN and other major nations in condemning the role of the Sudanese government in the sorry events.

It has become commonplace to point out that most conflicts today, in contrast to the struggles of the twentieth century, derive from weak rather than strong states. However, much will also depend on how robust the links, connections and mutual interests of core regional states and groups of states prove to be. 'Pivotal states' are nations which have a significant influence on a region as a whole. If they are stable

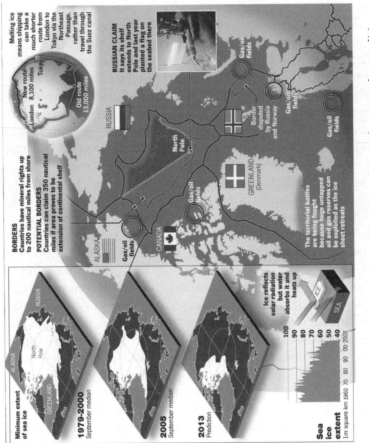

Figure 9.1 The Arctic: the interaction between climate change and geopolitics

Source: Sunday Times, 29 June 2008, p. 17

and economically successful, they tend to have a mollifying effect on that region. Conversely, if they run into difficulties, these might spill over to affect the whole surrounding area. Such countries include Brazil and Mexico, South Africa and Nigeria, Egypt, Pakistan and South Korea. Of course, if major setbacks were to occur in very large countries such as China or India, the reverberations would be that much more disruptive.

The Pentagon is already starting to see the world through the prism of a struggle for energy resources against the backdrop of damage inflicted by climate change. The main focus of US strategic and military planning, according to a recent official report, will henceforth be on a competition for resources, a competition seen as already under way. The global reach that China is seeking to establish, it argues, is driven by the demands of its economy for raw materials rather than by any specific ideological outlook. China's growing influence in the Middle East and Africa is a matter of particular concern.[5] Russia's return to geopolitical prominence has been driven almost entirely by the rising prices of oil, gas and industrial minerals. The attention now devoted to resource scarcity, Michael Klare has observed, 'represents a qualitative shift in US thinking', prompted 'not by an optimistic faith in America's capacity to dominate the world economy but by a largely pessimistic outlook regarding the future availability of vital resources'.[6]

This concern has impelled a return to investment in sea-power. The US Defense Department emphasizes that it must be able to patrol the main sea routes of the world in order to ensure its national security.[7] Overall, 75 per cent of the world's oil and 90 per cent of traded manufactured goods are transported by sea. In its budget proposal for 2009, the US government outlined a comprehensive new programme for investment in nuclear-powered aircraft carriers, destroyers carrying heavy anti-missile capability, submarines and other combat ships. The existing fleet is to be redeployed with greater emphasis on the prime routes through which most raw materials pass.

Not long ago, most US military bases were located in Western Europe, South Korea and Japan. Over the past few years, a transfer from such areas to East-Central Europe,

Central and Southwest Asia, and parts of Africa has begun. These regions contain states deemed to be supporting terrorism, but they are also home to more than three-quarters of the oil and gas reserves in the world and a large percentage of those of uranium, copper and cobalt.[8]

China and Russia are building their own security networks, in a self-conscious challenge to US dominance. As already mentioned, China's involvement in Sudan has arguably contributed to the bloodshed in that country. China is also active in North Africa, Angola, Chad and Nigeria. It has become one of the main suppliers of military equipment to some of these states. Its development and military advisers compete with those coming from the US. In Central and East Asia, Russia and China have formed a counterpart to NATO, in the shape of the Shanghai Cooperation Organization, a large military alliance. Its component states have made a strong push to assert influence over resource-rich countries. One of those countries, Kazakhstan, is a member of the alliance, together with Kyrgyzstan, Tajikistan and Uzbekistan.

An illusory world community?

Just at the time when the world needs more effective governance, international institutions look weaker than they have been for some years. The United Nations has played a vital role in the struggle against climate change, particularly in the shape of the IPCC, which has been the major influence propelling international concern about global warming. Yet the UN has few resources of its own, and can be paralysed by the actions of blocs of nations, or even single nations, especially on the Security Council. A more multipolar world could, of course, provide a better balance for cooperation, but it could just as easily produce serious divisions and conflicts with no arbiter to resolve them.

We seem to be seeing a return to a form of authoritarian nationalism, prominent among some of the key players on the world scene, most notably China and Russia, but including many smaller oil-rich nations too. Together with the policies of the administrations of the George W. Bush era – which to some extent sparked that return – the international system was redefined in terms of power and military capability. The burst of enthusiasm at the turn of the century that heralded a new world order based on international agencies rather than nations, and upon collaboration between nations rather than traditional sovereignty, seems already to have gone into reverse.

Discussing such changes, the influential writer on global politics, Robert Kagan, speaks of a 'return to normality'.[9] The title of his book is *The Return of History and the End of Dreams*. The dreams he is talking about were those of creating a new kind of international order following the end of the Cold War, and, more generally, with the advance of globalization. They were about the shrinking importance of the nation-state, the deepening of international collaboration, the disappearance of ideological conflicts and the freeing up of commerce and communications. The European Union seemed in the forefront of these transformations, pioneering a mode of organization that is not just international but genuinely transnational.

'It was all a mirage', Kagan says.[10] The nation-state remains as strong as ever, while competition between the great powers has returned. The major nations are struggling with one another for influence and prestige. China and Russia, in particular, are seeking to assert themselves, and both see international relations through the prism of great power rivalries. In each case there is a strong connection with energy. Russia's quest to return to great power status is based on its large oil and gas resources, while China is searching for energy supplies to sustain and fuel its continuing growth.

The long-standing conflict between liberalism and autocracy has re-emerged, coupled with 'an even older struggle', between radical Islam and modernity. Two of the largest developing countries, India and Brazil, are democracies. However, China and Russia are not, and are explicitly marked by a belief in authoritarian leadership as the condition of effective growth, as well as of containing the possibilities of division and fragmentation which each society faces. Prime Minister Putin's notion of 'sovereign democracy' is all about creating popular support for decisive leadership while expanding the sphere of Russia's international influence from the low point it reached in the 1990s.

The member–states of the EU, Kagan says, placed a gigantic bet at that period, that economic interdependence and the collaboration of nations would triumph over traditional concepts of sovereignty. They cut down on military spending, in the belief that the power of example would win out over the power of armed force. The EU, its leaders reasoned, has served as a vehicle for the integration of a growing number of states in Western – and now Central and Eastern – Europe into a transnational system. Why shouldn't the same model be successfully applied elsewhere?

For a brief while, the chances of success looked good. Regional associations were formed in several different parts of the world. The North American Free Trade Agreement (NAFTA) spanned the US, Canada and Mexico; a counterpart, MERCOSUR, emerged in South America; in Asia, several nations got together to form ASEAN. Yet these organizations have remained no more than loose trading groups. The EU, Kagan concludes, has lost its bet. Russia has responded with traditional forms of power to blunt EU influence in the ex-Soviet states that border it. Heavily dependent upon Russia for its oil and gas supplies – as discussed in chapter 2 – the Union has proved an easy target for a resurgent Russia, which has had no problems dividing its member–states and concluding bilateral energy deals with some of them.

According to Kagan, the decline of the UN and other such international organizations is terminal: he speaks of the 'demise of the international community'. The UN Security Council, which had a brief moment of cogency just after the Cold War, 'is slipping back into its long coma'.[11] It has been undermined by the division between the democracies and the autocracies. The scramble for energy is one of the driving forces of this division.

Kagan suggests that a 'Concert of Democracies' should be set up, bringing together the democratic nations from the developed and developing worlds. Its role would be an interventionist one. The strength of the autocratic countries, he says, is in some ways more apparent than real. Unlike in the nineteenth and early twentieth centuries, when democracy was the exception, China, Russia and other authoritarian states live in a world where it is preponderant. Hence they face problems of legitimacy that cannot simply be ignored, or not for long. Yet the democratic countries cannot expect to exert an influence just because of the values and ideas they represent. Quoting Hans Morgenthau, Kagan concludes that we should not imagine that at some juncture 'the final curtain would fall and the game of power politics would no longer be played'.

How far this type of analysis is correct will make an enormous difference to the world's chances of resolving the issues of climate change and energy security. Great powers acting in the traditional way treat resources in terms of a zero-sum game. If Kagan is right in his portrayal of the current state of international affairs, there is little likelihood of avoiding a battle for resources. As it deepens, it could very well lead to armed conflict, a potentially terrible prospect if nuclear states become involved. The UN would be powerless to intervene, since it would be rendered impotent by the very conflicts it was supposed to help overcome.

Thankfully, what Kagan says is valid only to a limited degree. Take the case of the United Nations first. It would be difficult to deny that the record of the UN since 1989 has been distinctly patchy, as even its strongest supporters concede. David Hannay, formerly Britain's permanent representative at the body, has spoken of the early 1990s as 'the crest of the wave' in terms of the UN's successes, 'the moment when it was possible to hope that the organization was set on a new path, destined to become an effective component of the system of collective security'.[12]

During those years, the UN led a number of successful humanitarian interventions – and the Rio Summit got a new and serious environmental agenda under way. From 1993 onwards, however, the UN's performance began to tip in the other direction, as the organization became bogged down in key missions in Bosnia and elsewhere. Supporters of the UN fear that it has become marginal and discredited, while its critics actively hope that such is indeed the case. Yet, as Hannay quite rightly observes, states continue to turn to the UN for help in facing common problems. It has an 'underlying indispensability' because there is no obvious alternative.[13]

The international community is not 'illusory'. It was wrong when then US Secretary of State Condoleezza Rice said it originally, and it was wrong when Kagan repeated it.[14] If we concentrate only on the Security Council, which does indeed tend to be a place of power-brokering, we get quite a misleading view of the progression of world interdependence and the UN's role in furthering it. The world is far more interdependent than ever was the case before, and the UN and other international agencies are playing a fundamental role in nurturing it. Take as an example telecommunications, which are now truly globalized, but depend upon vast networks ranging across a multiplicity of national contexts. The UN and other international organizations play an essential role in such coordination, because binding international agreements are involved.

Even in more contentious areas of humanitarian intervention and the management of health and disease, the role of the UN has been, and is, central. As far as the management of conflicts go, the UN has been more important than would appear on the surface – and more successful. The failures, such as in Bosnia or Rwanda, tend to be very visible, but successes – preventing conflicts from developing in the first place – receive much less attention and publicity.

Kagan says the world has reverted to what it was before the 'dreams' of the early post-1989 period – an arena for nation-states to pursue their power struggles. Yet this conclusion is eminently disputable. The nation-state has obstinately refused to go away, yes. I have argued for its continuing importance throughout this book. However, the world context in which nations stake their claims to sovereignty has changed massively over the past two or three decades. It is simply not the case that there is a 'return to normality' – to patterns of the past. Sovereignty does not have the same meaning as it did. This is surely obvious on an economic level, where states, no matter how large, cannot govern their economic affairs in the way in which they were able to earlier in the post-war period.

Interdependence is a part of our lives in the twenty-first century, and states which act in denial of that situation will quickly be brought to heel in one way or another. The fate of the attempt of the Bush administration to ignore the new realities is instructive. Bush wanted to reintroduce exactly the kind of world Kagan sketches out – one in which power is what counts, and where the US is pre-eminent in wielding such power. Such a world-view went along with a contemptuous attitude towards climate change.

The abrogation of international agreements which followed undoubtedly influenced the actions of other nations, including China, Russia and Iran, which, in opposing the attitudes of the US, in fact mimicked them. But look what happened to those US ambitions. The United States, the world's greatest military power, was unable to pacify a single medium-sized country, Iraq, in spite of an easy initial military victory. It was not able to fight two wars at the same time, even with the help of allies, and as a consequence the project to bring stability to Afghanistan is meeting with, at best, limited success. The US has the world's largest economy, but the country, acting alone, has very limited capacities to influence the world marketplace – as the financial crisis has shown all too clearly.

Where Kagan must be listened to is when he says that the curtain will not fall on power politics. It is quite futile to analyse what might happen as a result of international collaboration to halt climate change without setting it in the context of the rivalries that cross-cut efforts at international collaboration. For those rivalries will determine the real opportunities that exist, the points at which real purchase can be achieved. Let us consider how this point bears on the relation between the developed and under-developed worlds.

The bottom billion

The bulk of the emissions causing climate change have been generated by the industrial countries, yet its impact will be felt most strongly in the poorer regions of the world. A basic sense of social justice should help drive attempts to reduce that impact, but there are more selfish reasons for the more affluent countries to help the more deprived too. Extreme poverty is potentially very destabilizing indeed in world society. The level of risk it produces for the more favoured countries and regions, even if global warming didn't exist, would still be formidable. Among other harmful effects, poverty is one of the main influences leading to population growth; population pressures ease as countries become richer.

The Millennium Declaration of the United Nations pledged 'to spare no effort to free our fellow men, women and children from the abject and dehumanizing conditions of extreme poverty'. Over halfway to the date set for reaching the millennium goals, 2015, progress has certainly been made. The most important one, that of reducing absolute poverty by half, looks set to be reached. The same is true of those concerning education, reducing the impact of some of the worst killer diseases, and improving gender equality, employment and sanitation.

In geopolitical terms, it is essential to recognize, as Paul Collier has put it, that 'the third world has shrunk'.[15] For much of the past half-century the question of 'development' was one of a gulf between one billion affluent and four billion impoverished people in the world. The millennium goals were established with such figures in mind. Yet about 80 per cent of the five billion now live in countries that are developing, some of them at extraordinary speed. These countries have experienced rapid growth in income per capita. They have recorded an average GDP growth rate of over 4 per cent during the 1980s and 1990s. Over the early period of the current century, that rate has risen to over 4.5 per cent, although of course the fast pace of China's development alone over the period accounts for a substantial proportion of this.

These statistics drive home the importance of what I have earlier called the development imperative. Economic growth on the large scale is the only way out of poverty for the mass of the world's poor, and for many people in the world it has worked. Yet at least a billion people – located in about 60 different countries – have been left out. Most of these societies are small and their combined population does not approach that of either China or India. As Collier says, they 'are falling behind, and often falling apart'.[16] Their economies have not grown; on the contrary, their level of income has declined. It was, on average, lower in absolute terms by the year 2000 than it had been in 1970. Since then it has increased by just over

1 per cent, not enough to make any significant difference to their fortunes – they are marked not only by poverty, but by epidemics, ignorance and despair.

These societies lag behind the rest of the world because they are caught in what Collier calls four 'traps'. One is that of civil war. Over 70 per cent of the societies that contain the bottom billion have either recently experienced civil war or are still caught up in one. Susceptibility to civil war both causes economic stagnation and is caused by it. These countries face a 14 per cent possibility of experiencing a civil war over any given five-year period. Every percentage point increase in growth knocks 1 per cent off this risk. Conflict almost always affects neighbouring countries – and, as mentioned earlier, can spread to whole regions, to some extent dragging them down too.

One of the four traps is actually the possession of natural resources, especially oil and gas. Some 30 per cent of the world's poor live in countries where the economy is dominated by resource wealth. The reasons for this situation are well known. There are a few rentier states which, to some degree, have been able to escape the 'resource curse' – such as Kuwait or Saudi Arabia – mainly because their oil and gas revenues are enormous. For others, however, revenue from such sources only provides a livelihood for a tiny elite. At the same time, that revenue discourages investment in other industries, and renders the country's exports uncompetitive. Moreover, as in the past, the prices of oil and gas have been unstable, and that instability is imported into the economy.

The other two traps are, first, being a land-locked country with dysfunctional neighbours and, second, bad governance. Almost 40 per cent of the people in the bottom billion live in countries that are land-locked. The case of Switzerland shows that it is possible to be both land-locked and wealthy; but Switzerland has friendly neighbours, whose countries have excellent communications. In countries such as Uganda, Sudan and Somalia it is a different story. The economies of the land-locked societies in Africa are not integrated with those of their neighbours, but are either turned inwards or open to the vagaries of the world market.

Bangladesh ranks 134 out of 178 countries in the world

covered in Transparency International's ratings of corruption.[17] Yet it has managed to put in place fairly effective economic policies and has achieved a significant measure of economic growth. It has done well because it has few natural resources of its own and because it has an extensive coastline – (although, as discussed in chapter 7, one which puts it at high risk as sea levels rise as a result of global warming). No doubt the country would have fared even better if it had been less corrupt.

Bad governance, a matter that extends well beyond corruption as such, compounds each of the other sets of problems – producing societies in which governments are either paralysed by divisions or where there is, in effect, no government at all. One study equated failed states with countries comparable in other respects. The results showed the average cost of being a failed state, over the period during which it could be classified as such, to be £100 billion.[18]

Political reform is always, in principle, possible, and achieving it is normally the key to progress in other areas. Some of the world's poorest countries have managed such reform in the past, most importantly China. In the 1960s the country faced ruin as a result of the policies of Chairman Mao. The subsequent leadership took the decision to change direction, resulting in the economic success that is such a feature of world society today.

On the face of things, the nations that make up the 'bottom billion' are threatening to drop off the edge of world history, since they are locked into a deteriorating cycle from which most other nations have, in large measure, escaped. Ethical reasons alone demand that the rest of the world community cannot sit by while local tragedies unfold. But in the context of climate change, there are important material reasons why the more affluent nations cannot remain uninvolved. The pressures created by climate change and increasing energy scarcity, sketched out at the beginning of the chapter and throughout this book, could cause the problems of the bottom billion to be dispersed around the world as a whole. What has happened in Sudan is an awful reminder of how global struggles may play out if ways are not found to contain and reshape them.

Oil and geopolitics

The fate of the bottom billion is likely to have a major influence on how far international terrorism will continue to be a prominent feature on the world scene. The states where the poorest live frequently display a lethal combination of terrorism, international crime, drugs and money-laundering.

Where these states are also oil-producers, their history tends to be even more blighted. It would be difficult to overemphasize how important oil and gas have been in shaping world politics in the decades since the end of the Second World War. As Thomas Friedman says, when historians look back at our era, they might well conclude that one of the most important geopolitical trends was the influence of oil wealth over the changing centre of gravity of Islam.[19] In the early post-war years, that centre of gravity was located in Cairo, Istanbul, Beirut, Casablanca and Damascus, all in their way cosmopolitan cities offering the hope of progressive modernization. At that time, many Muslim nations were relatively liberal and there was widespread talk of the need to separate church and state on the Turkish model.

Yet because of the growing importance of oil, and the dominant position which the Gulf states and Saudi Arabia hold in its production, conservative interpretations of Islam have become much more prominent than they used to be. Saudi Arabia is the guardian of two of the holiest mosques of Islam, in Mecca and Medina. 'Desert Islam', aggressive and reactionary, was originally shaped by poverty; now it is in possession of untold wealth. The half-century-old pact with the US kept the ruling family in place and, in turn, helped conservatism to flourish.

'Oil is the enemy of freedom' – is it possible to make such an apparently absurd theorem stick? Without too much over simplification, the blunt answer is 'yes', and the reasons why are well known. What Friedman calls the First Law of Petropolitics brings an impressive range of cases together.[20] The tiny kingdom of Bahrain, he observes, led the way among states in the Gulf in holding free parliamentary elections, ones in which women could vote and stand as candidates. Bahrain was the first such state in which oil was discovered, about three-quarters of a century ago – but much more recently, it was also the first in which it started to run out. The leaders of the country began to think in terms of diversifying the economy, which in turn led to the beginnings of political reform.

Following Tunisia and Egypt, Bahrain was the third country in the Middle East to experience an attempt at democratic revolution in early 2011. In spite of partial reforms, up to that point little of a concrete nature had changed. When these uprisings first started, the initial response of the oil-rich states was bribery. Several rulers announced cash payments to be made to citizens to try to keep them quiescent.

Friedman has undertaken a systematic study of the relationship between the fluctuating price of oil and political change. His 'Law' states that the higher the price of oil, the more likely an oil-producing country is to turn autocratic. Political leaders get popular support from the rentier income flowing into the country and feel free to ignore what opposition groups may say, and indeed, to some large degree, what the rest of the world thinks too. Oil-rich governments use their revenues to bypass the need for taxation, thereby avoiding the pressures that come from tax-payers, who normally demand accountability.

Oil money promotes the use of patronage, creating an inner group of rulers; that self-same revenue makes possible the creation of an elaborate system of police, security services and surveillance. Michael Ross argues that it is not only conservative Islam which produces the subordination of women; it is the dominance of oil money as such. Since there is little economic diversification, there is no chance for women to join the non-agricultural workforce, which in turn has the effect of keeping the birth rate high.[21] There are 23 countries in the world which get a large part of their income from oil and gas; not one of them is a democracy in anything but name. Of course, all this might change as a result of the events that have convulsed the Middle East. At a minimum, they are likely to have a far-reaching impact on the relationship between oil and politics.

Russia is now in the grip of a small elite drawing its power almost wholly from revenue provided by oil, gas and mineral reserves. The symbiotic, yet tense, relationship between the EU and Russia has attracted a great deal of commentary. Some 40 per cent of the EU's gas supplies, 30 per cent of its oil and about a quarter of its coal come from Russia. EU–Russia relationships need to be normalized, a task that is routinely spoken about but, so far, not realized. From a climate change point of view, a major concern of a continuing EU–Russia dialogue should be a reopening of Russia's oil and gas industry to European, and then to other foreign, investment.

Large-scale new investment is needed to reduce the profligate way in which energy is produced (and used) in Russia. It has been estimated that the volume of gas flared off in the country each year is equivalent to a quarter of total Russian gas exports to Europe.[22] Leaky pipelines add substantially to this total. In the meantime, Russia won such a liberal deal at Kyoto that there is no motivation to control emissions. Russian commitments to reduce leakage should receive international support and encouragement, as should moves to raise energy prices for consumers, although neither is motivated by climate change considerations. On the back of high oil prices, Russia adopted a forceful stance in international relations.

Vladimir Putin's notion of sovereign democracy has nothing to do with democracy as ordinarily understood and everything to do with sovereignty – with the assertion of Russia's right and capability to act as a great power. The EU is rightly encouraging its former East European member–states to diversify their sources of energy supply and move towards full-cost pricing for consumers (although EU leaders objected when Russia tried to force the Ukraine to make such a move overnight), but with little impact so far. The sole exception is the Czech Republic, which has built an oil pipeline to Germany and has concluded a long-term gas deal with Norway.

These considerations show just how much there is to play for, should the industrial countries be able simultaneously to reduce their dependence on oil and lower their carbon emissions. The famous 'curse of oil' does not only apply within nations, but to the world system as a whole, since the need to sustain a steady flow of oil plays such a large part in contemporary geopolitics. If the industrial countries could break away from their wholesale dependency on oil and natural gas, it would be a major benefit not only for them but, perversely, also for the producer nations. It would help bring about one of the most far-reaching realignments of international relations in history.

One does not have to envisage a future in which the developed countries will become autonomous in respect of their energy supplies, which for most is neither practicable nor desirable. Interdependence – for example, in the shape of large-scale smart energy grids powered by renewable technologies – will continue to be a fact of life and has a clear positive side, in terms of the pooling of resources. But it will become far more possible than it is now for them to be protected from system breakdown by the capacity for significant energy self-provision. To repeat a constant theme of this book, what is important is that it should not be provided by a return to coal.

Coalitions and collaborations

The large bulk of greenhouse gas emissions is produced by only a limited number of countries – as far as containing global warming is concerned, what the majority of states do pales in significance compared to the activities of the large polluters. Moreover, only a limited number of states have the capability seriously to pioneer technological innovation relevant to climate change – rules governing knowledge transfer and investment from these countries to others will be more important than universal accords.

An approach based on agreements or partnerships between individual nations, groups of countries and regions makes sense – and could eventually act to strengthen more universal measures. The Kyoto agreements already recognized several different clusters of countries, incorporating varying provisions for them.[23] As one author remarked: 'It is increasingly becoming clear [that] the Kyoto Protocol is less a global agreement than a set of differing regional approaches.'[24]

The experience of the World Trade Organization offers a parallel. It has proved impossible to reach agreement on the

Doha round of negotiations within the WTO, but progress on trade negotiation was made through regional and bilateral agreements. More than 200 such agreements are currently in operation. Studies have shown that such deals can support the overall objectives of the WTO's multilateral trading system rather than, as might seem to be the case on the surface, act to undermine them. Regional agreements have allowed countries to go beyond what has been possible to achieve universally; but these concordats have subsequently paved the way for progress made at the level of the WTO.

It makes sense for the big polluters, especially in aggregate terms, to get together in a regular way to try to push forward climate change policy that has bite. There is a forum already in existence that can serve as one of the agencies for such a task: the Major Economics Forum (MEF), which represents the world's 17 largest economies, including therefore a range of industrial and developing countries. In 2009 the MEF set up a Global Partnership to promote low-carbon technologies and develop other means of reducing emissions – acknowledging climate change to be 'one of the greatest challenges of our time'.[25] The main focus is upon 'technology action plans' that focus upon 80 per cent of global CO_2 created by energy production.

Each of the plans supplies detailed programmes addressed to national governments. They analyse the contribution that can be made to carbon reduction in the case of each technology or programme, identify barriers and best practice strategies to overcome them, and specify government action that can be taken on a concrete level to further such strategies.

The risk of undue complexity is evident, but the G20 can and probably should have a role in active climate change policy. Prior to Cancun, the G20 leaders pledged that they would 'spare no effort to reach a balanced and successful outcome' there. In their meeting in Seoul in 2010, a robust statement about confronting climate change was made, but contained little detail.

It will be highly important to ensure that the poorer developing countries – the bottom billion – are not excluded and that their voice is heard. In a certain sense, it is right and proper that the 'developing world' is now divided in two. The days when the more successful emerging economies used to argue that the industrial countries have caused global warming, and that therefore they must exclusively be responsible for cutting carbon emissions, thankfully are over. The poorest nations, however, cannot at present be expected to engage in mitigation. For them, development is the highest priority, while adaptation takes precedence. The key issues – addressed in principle in the Climate Fund proposed in Copenhagen and Cancun – is that financial assistance and technological resources on the large scale should flow to such nations. Of course, a nest of problems and complexities is buried in such a bland statement, given the enormous difficulties the bottom billion faces.[26]

The US and China

It might be thought improbable that the US and China could collaborate in a serious way on energy and climate change issues, but there is a precedent.[27] During the Cold War period there appeared to be no chance that the main adversaries, the US and the Soviet Union, could negotiate fruitfully with one another. Yet, as Senator Joseph Lieberman has observed, such collaboration did develop, and it met with some success.[28] At the outset of the arms control talks between the two protagonists, each was extremely wary of the other. Yet an effective interchange was achieved, with concrete results in terms of arms reductions. Lieberman points out that there is something of a parallel between the arms race of the Cold War and the competition for energy resources that is getting under way now.

Michael Klare suggested some while ago that a starting-point could be the setting up of an annual top-level US–China energy summit, led by the president of each country. It could be modelled on comparable meetings held at the height of the Cold War. The main aims were to minimize possible conflicts in the hunt for resources and to work out shared energy initiatives for the future, based on the fostering of low-carbon technologies. The objective would be to create a full bilateral infrastructure, where officials, scientists and business leaders form joint committees and working-groups.

A preliminary 'memorandum of understanding' for the creation of an energy dialogue between the two nations was already signed in 2004. In October 2008 it was announced that three Chinese companies, including the country's biggest state-controlled company, China Mobile, would join the non-profit Climate Group, which is backed by some leading Western businesses. The other two Chinese corporations are Suntech, the third largest solar energy manufacturer in the world, and a privately owned firm, Broad Air Conditioning. Western businesses involved include BP, BSkyB, Nike and Tesco. China Mobile aims to reduce the energy intensity of its activities by 40 per cent by 2020. Other Chinese companies have also enquired about joining the group, whose goal is to cover more than 100 of the world's biggest firms.

At the meetings at Copenhagen, as mentioned in chapter 8, the Chinese played an odd game of 'catch-me-if-you-can' with the Americans. The Chinese leader, Hu Jintao, avoided President Obama until Obama gate-crashed the meeting that led to the setting up of the Accord. Neither Obama nor Hu attended the summit in Cancun, where Hillary Clinton represented the US. The two countries worked together much better than had been the case in Copenhagen. Clinton said afterwards that the US–Chinese cooperation was critical in forging the agreements that were reached. She added that it was time for 'both nations to translate the high-level pledges of summits and state visits into action'.[29]

In January 2011 President Obama and President Hu met in Washington and agreed to enhance cooperation on climate change policy, renewable technology and technological transfer. They welcomed a recent announcement of joint work plans to be developed under the auspices of the US–China Clean Energy Research Centre, launched late in 2009. The work plans cover energy-efficient buildings, CCS and electric vehicles. More than 150 US and Chinese researchers will collaborate on the programme. Both leaders endorsed a statement of intent signed by the US Department of Energy and the Chinese Ministry of Science and Technology on sharing data on electric vehicle projects in Los Angeles and Shanghai. As with all agreements, the test is in the implementation – what will emerge of practical consequence and when?

India and Brazil

The Indian government stands aside to some degree from China and Brazil in its attitudes to climate change policy. In the aftermath of Cancun, the Indian Prime Minister Manmohan Singh stated that the emerging nations are not in a position to cut emissions, since they must place primacy upon economic development. Singh argued that, vast though it is in terms of territorial size and population, India only accounts for a relatively small proportion of total global emissions. The observation is true in terms of emissions per person. In aggregate terms, India is the fourth largest emitter of greenhouse gases worldwide. Moreover, it has high growth rates – growth propelled at present almost wholly by fossil fuels.

However, the Indian leadership played a constructive role both at Copenhagen and at Cancun. During the Cancun meetings, environment minister Jairam Ramesh hinted that India might reconsider its current position. At the moment, it has set a voluntary target of reducing energy intensity by 20 per cent over 2005 levels by 2020. A National Action Plan on Climate Change was published in 2008, but lacked detailed proposals and contained no specific targets. Substantial investments are planned in solar and nuclear technology.

Several recent reports have stressed how consequential climate change will be for India, and are likely to prompt a more ambitious attitude on the part of political leaders. Some 70 per cent of the summer flow of the river Ganges comes from meltwater from high snow fields and glaciers. Like almost everywhere else in the world, the glaciers are shrinking. Monsoon weather affects large parts of India; as climate change proceeds, many rivers will be vulnerable to the lethal mixture of flooding and drought that global warming brings in its train in such areas. The country has some of the most densely populated coastlines in the world, threatened by rising sea levels.

What happened at Copenhagen, and then at Cancun, means that negotiations and discussions between the states in the BASIC group (Brazil, South Africa, India and China) and the US will have a fundamental impact upon climate change politics. It is certainly desirable that they be joined by the EU if it can find the means to speak with a single voice – since the EU leads the way in actually cutting back emissions, rather than simply setting targets to do so.

Brazil could be a major influence on the world scene. Under President Lula da Silva and his successor, Dilma Rousseff, the country has assumed a much more active role in pushing for effective international strategies to combat climate change. Brazil has quite a different profile from the other large emerging economies. For one thing, it is home to one of the most significant ecosystems on the planet – the Amazon basin. It is hence *the* frontline country in the struggle against deforestation. How far deforestation can be controlled in the Amazon on its own will have a major effect on how far the worst effects of global warming can be avoided. Surveys show that Brazil's population has a higher level of concern about climate change and its implications than in most of the developed countries. In a survey taken in January 2011, 90 per cent of Brazilians agreed that climate change is happening and that it is a serious issue.[30]

Unlike China and India, the energy sector in Brazil contributes only a small proportion of the country's carbon emissions – a further factor that could enhance the country's influence over other countries internationally. Only about 17 per cent of Brazil's total emissions come from energy production, a lower proportion than most other industrialized or industrializing nations in the world. Some 40 per cent of the country's energy supply is generated by renewable sources, broadly interpreted, provided by a mixture of hydroelectric power, sugarcane (ethanol) and wood-pulp (its hydroelectric power stations, supplied from the water flowing from glaciers, are vulnerable to the effects of climate change).

Beginning in the 1970s, Brazil introduced an ethanol scheme for its transport sector. The programme was extended and intensified following the oil crisis of that decade. (For an account of its influence over the later use of biofuels in

Sweden, see above, pp. 127–8). Today it is the world's largest commercial application of biomass for transport. Virtually all cars in Brazil are capable of switching between ethanol and petrol. A national biodiesel programme was launched a few years ago, aimed at progressively increasing the biodiesel content in diesel fuel. Some beans and plants that readily grow over large parts of Brazil can be used to produce biodiesel.

In 2002, the Brazilian parliament endorsed legislation allowing small independent suppliers, including households, to feed energy into the national grid. In the same year, the government proposed the Brazilian Energy Initiative, designed to increase the spread of renewable energy throughout Latin America and the Caribbean.

President Lula consistently emphasized Brazil's vulnerability to climate change. During his period of tenure in office, the country was afflicted by unusually severe periods of flooding and of drought, which, in a speech in May 2009, he said were signs of climate change: 'Brazil is feeling the climate changes that are happening in the world, when there is a deep drought in a place where there's never been one, when it rains in places where it never rains.'[31] In the run-up to Cancun, Lula pointed out that Brazil was one of the few countries with concrete results to point to in terms of reducing carbon emissions. Brazil reduced its greenhouse gas emissions by over 30 per cent from the period between 2004 and 2009 – most of this, as mentioned in chapter 4, came from a substantial reduction in the deforestation of the Amazon area. In common with the other large developing states, the country originally set itself against the principle of legally binding emissions reductions targets. However, following the meetings in Copenhagen, Brazil approved a National Policy on Climate Change and adopted a voluntary target in the Accord of reducing greenhouse gases by 36–39 per cent by 2020 over a 2004 baseline. On current trends, the target will be achieved well before then.

Latin America might very well emerge as an important region for cooperative action on climate change. Several countries, including – besides Brazil – Mexico, Peru, Chile and Ecuador, have experienced unusual bouts of extreme weather over recent times. The leaders of those depending on the Andean glaciers are becoming disturbed by clear and continuing signs of glacier retreat among other indicators of climate change. Mexico followed Brazil in being one of the first countries to set specific carbon reduction targets in 2008, with a pledge to halve carbon emissions by 2050 over 2002 levels.

Mexico of course played host to the Cancun meetings, where President Felipe Calderon stressed the urgency of the need for collective action to reduce emissions on a global scale. Costa Rica has pledged to become carbon neutral by 2021, having been for some while a leader in initiatives to do with sustainability.

In conclusion: why we still need the UN

Innovation at all levels has to be a key aspect of the world's attempts to contain climate change, and this is as true of inter-national relations as anywhere else. Somehow the slow plod of the UN-brokered negotiations will have to be energized by more immediate and practical interventions and ideas. Three sets of forces are in play in generating such possibilities. One, as stressed throughout this book, is the action of states, working individually, bilaterally or in larger groupings. For better or for worse, a great deal of power in world society still remains in the hands of states, and no other organizations approach them in terms of legitimacy. What the individual nations discussed above actually do, in their interaction with one another and with wider groups of states, will matter enormously.

So also will the responses of business, large and small. Here, as also discussed above in earlier sections, there is a very mixed picture. Some business interests, within the fossil fuel companies themselves and in other carbon-intensive indus-tries, contribute in a fundamental way to the inertia that is causing the level of CO_2 in the atmosphere still to rise. Yet the opportunities for more far-sighted entrepreneurs and innova-tors are huge.

The third influence, of immense importance, is the emer-gence of a diverse and fizzling global civil society, mediated by electronic means of communication and by the ease of modern transportation. The stunning variety of new groups, local, national and transnational, that have sprung up across the world, offer multiple possibilities for influencing climate change policy in a positive and perhaps dramatically new way.

As an instrument of global governance, the UN may fall well short of what many of us (including myself) would like. Whether or not we can limit some of the most dangerous consequences of climate change will not be settled at the UN. Yet there are very good reasons why the UN climate change negotiations must continue, with all the frustrations they entail. The possibility of achieving a legally binding treaty on carbon reductions, involving at least the large majority of nations, has to stay on the table. The distinction between 'legally binding' agreements and 'voluntary' ones is less than it looks, because there are few sanctions available to back up international law when it is flouted. But a legally established treaty would have more chance of achieving compliance than a cluster of open pledges. That underlying indispensability of which Hannay speaks remains intact.

If concern about the dangers of climate change becomes more urgent and pressing than it is now – as *must* happen, at some point because of the very advance of global warming – coping with them could be a means of rehabilitating the United Nations itself. States' leaders might come to realize that not only can they not do without it, but that lack of effective global governance is a prime reason why those dangers have become so acute.

AFTERWORD

Industrial civilization differs from all previous types of civilization that have gone before. Even the most advanced, such as Rome or traditional China, were regional – they were only able to extend their influence over a specific corner of the world. They made use of inanimate energy, such as water or wind, but only in a relatively marginal way. Their impact on the natural world was considerable, but mainly confined to modifications of the landscape.

Our civilization is truly global in scope; and it couldn't exist without the inanimate energy sources that fuel it. For better or worse, modern industry has unleashed a sheer volume of *power* into the world vastly beyond anything witnessed before. I mean here inanimate power, but also the power of human organization – the complex social, economic and political systems upon which our individual lives now depend. Power cuts two ways. The Enlightenment thinkers saw such capabilities as essentially benign. Thus Marx wrote in a celebrated phrase: 'Human beings only set themselves such problems as they can resolve.' Yet from the early days of industrial development there were those who saw the new powers as destructive or as threatening to escape the control of their creators.

The debate continues today and is unresolved. Our civilization could self-destruct – no doubt about it – and with awesome consequences, given its global reach. Doomsday is no longer a religious concept, a day of spiritual reckoning, but a possibility imminent in our society and economy. If unchecked, climate change alone could produce enormous human suffering. So also could the drying up of the energy resources upon which so many of our capacities are built. There remains the possibility of large-scale conflicts, perhaps involving the use of weapons of mass destruction. Each could intersect with the others, as analysed in the previous chapter.

No wonder many take fright. Let's go back! Let's return to a simpler world! They are entirely understandable sentiments and have practical application in some contexts. Yet there can be no overall 'going back' – the very expansion of human power that has created such deep problems is the only means of resolving them, with science and technology at the forefront. There will probably be nine billion people in the world by 2050 – after which world population hopefully will stabilize, especially if the least developed countries make significant economic and social progress. Ways will have to be found of providing those nine billion people with a decent way of life.

What hope is there that, as collective humanity, we will be able to control the forces we have unleashed? No clear-cut answer can be given, since there are so many contingencies, unknowns – and, yes, unknown unknowns – involved. What one can say is that risk and opportunity belong together; from the biggest risks can also flow the greatest opportunities, if collectively we can mobilize to meet them. Something of a quantum leap, however, is needed over the situation as it stands now.

To some considerable degree we are in the hands of our political leaders. It has become customary to be cynical about politics, but the political field retains its capacity to inspire. The use of political capacity, national and international, will be essential to coping with the dilemmas that confront us. Two countries, the United States and China, have the ability to make or break our chances of success. Of course, bilateral cooperation, even in this unique case, can only get us so far. If ever a problem called for multilateral cooperation, with every country in the world on board, climate change is it. As with the internal policies of states, the 'how' matters more than the 'what'. Target-setting isn't going to have much impact, but many other forms of collaboration can do so. The sharing of scientific findings, technology transfer, direct aid coming from some nations to others, and a host of other collaborative activities are the way forward.

Within the industrial countries there are many political battles to be fought and won. The US is in prime position because of its large-scale contribution to greenhouse gas emissions and its gargantuan appetite for oil. It will be a colossal task to turn around a society whose whole way of life is constructed around mobility and a 'natural right' to consume energy in a profligate way. Yet it isn't as hopeless an endeavour as it looks. Numerous states, cities and organizations within the country have not only been pressing for change but are leading the way in introducing it.

All governments face deep dilemmas in reconciling climate change and energy policy with sustaining popular support, especially in times of economic difficulty. Public support is likely to wax and wane, for reasons I have discussed. In order to cope, governments will have to resort to a range of strategies, while at the same time trying to foster a more widespread consciousness of the need for action. The habits and routines of everyday life stand in the way, but the key problem is the difficulty of getting people to accept that the risks are real and pressing.

Economic and political power in the international system is clearly moving from the established industrial countries of the West towards the newly developing states. It looks more and more possible that countries such as China, India and Brazil, rather than playing catch-up, could assume a leadership position in climate change policy, stepping into the vacuum left by the incapacity of the US to take the lead on a federal level. Although such nations, especially China and India, are a very long way away from breaking away from a carbon-intensive path of development, a major change in political orientation is occurring.

Technological innovation is one of the several jokers in the pack – the more so given the diversity of technologies vying for attention as we seek to shake free from our dependency on fossil fuels. Much can be done to reduce emissions without further advance. Yet the realm of technology is the most important domain where the theorem applies that the very expansion of power that has created dangers for us can perhaps allow us to meet them. A new Dark Ages, a new age of enlightenment, or perhaps a confusing mixture of the two – which will it be? Probably the third possibility is the most likely. In that case, we all have to hope that the balance will be tilted towards the enlightenment side of the equation.

NOTES

Chapter I Climate Change, Risk and Danger

1. Intergovernmental Panel on Climate Change (IPCC), Fourth Assessment Report, 3 vols and summary (Cambridge: Cambridge University Press, 2007).
2. IPCC Working Group 2, *Climate Change Impacts, Adaptation and Vulnerability* (Cambridge: Cambridge University Press, 2007).
3. S. Fred Singer and Dennis T. Avery, *Unstoppable Global Warming* (New York: Rowman and Littlefield, 2007).
4. Ibid., p. xi.
5. Patrick J. Michaels, *Meltdown* (Washington, DC: Cato Institute, 2004).
6. See Bjørn Lomborg, *The Skeptical Environmentalist* (Cambridge: Cambridge University Press, 2001). Also see the writings of the scientist Richard Lindzen – for example, 'Climate of Fear', *Wall Street Journal*, 12 April 2006; 'There is no "Consensus" on Global Warming', *Wall Street Journal*, 26 June 2006; 'Debunking the Myth', *Business Today* 43 (2006). A critical examination of Lomborg's claims is available at www.lomborg-errors.dk.
7. Bjørn Lomborg, *Cool It* (New York: Alfred A. Knopf, 2007), p. ix.
8. Bjørn Lomborg, quoted in Howard Friel, *The Lomborg Deception* (Yale: Yale University Press, 2010), p. 4.
9. Friel's book, however, can be subject to criticism. Much of it consists of showing that Lomborg doesn't represent the work of the IPCPC accurately – it is a sort of 'internalist' critique rather than a systematic appraisal of the evidence. This leads the author into one highly unfortunate oddity. Lomborg wrote that the Himalayan glaciers, according to the IPCPC, will run dry towards the end of

the century. However, Friel points out that the IPCPC report says that they could disappear by the year 2035 – the very statement that was found to be in error.

10. Bjørn Lomborg (ed.), *Smart Solutions to Climate Change: Comparing Costs to Benefits* (Cambridge: Cambridge University Press, 2010), p. 396.

11. Christopher Booker and Richard North, *Scared to Death* (London: Continuum, 2007), p. 454. For a recent addition to the ranks of the sceptics, see Nigel Lawson, *An Appeal to Reason* (London: Duckworth, 2008). His conclusion is: 'We appear to have entered a new age of unreason, which threatens to be as economically harmful as it is profoundly disquieting. It is from this, above all, that we really do need to save the planet' (p. 2). Similar ideas are presented, in somewhat less florid fashion, in Colin Robinson, *Climate Change Policy* (London: Institute of Economic Affairs, 2008).

12. Booker and North, *Scared to Death*, p. 388.

13. For an account, see Fred Pearce, *The Climate Files: The Battle for the Truth About Global Warming* (London: Guardian Books, 2010).

14. Pennsylvania State University: RA-10 Final Investigation Report Involving Dr Michael E Mann, 4 June 2010, p. 19.

15. Quoted in Les Hickman, 'Threats Leave US Climate Scientists in Fear for Lives', *Guardian*, 6 July 2010, p. 16.

16. Clive Hamilton, *Requiem for a Species* (London: Earthscan, 2010); and other publications.

17. UK Met Office, *Statement from the UK Science Community*, 10 December 2009, available online.

18. Letter to *Science Magazine*, 7 May 2010.

19. James Hoggan and Richard Littlemore, *Climate Cover-Up* (Vancouver: Greystone, 2009), p. 3. For further documentation, see Naomi Oreskes and Erik Conway, *Merchants of Doubt* (London: Bloomsbury, 2010).

20. Martin McKee, quoted in Debora Mackenzie, 'Special Report: Age of Denial', *New Scientist*, 15 May 2010, p. 39.

21. See also James Lovelock, *The Revenge of Gaia* (London: Penguin, 2007).

22. David King and Gabrielle Walker, *The Hot Topic* (London: Bloomsbury, 2008), p. 80.

23. See Michael Glantz, *Currents of Change* (Cambridge: Cambridge University Press, 1996). Over the past decade, new weather forecasting methods have been developed to give advance warning of El Niño some two years ahead, making it possible for countries affected to prepare in advance.

24. James Hansen et al., 'Target Atmospheric CO_2, Where Should Humanity Aim?', NASA/Goddard Institute for Space Studies, New York, 2007, available online.

25. James Hansen, *Storms of My Grandchildren* (London: Bloomsbury, 2009). The phrase actually appears in the subtitle of the book.
26. Ibid., p. 236.
27. Ibid., p. 269.
28. James Lovelock, *The Vanishing Face of Gaia* (London: Penguin, 2010), p. 3.
29. Ibid., p. 4.
30. Ibid., p. 44.

Chapter 2 Running Out, Running Down?

1. Richard Heinberg, *The Party's Over* (Gabriola Island: New Society Publishers, 2003), p. 31.
2. Paul Middleton, *A Brief Guide to the End of Oil* (London: Robinson, 2007), ch. 3.
3. David Strahan, *The Last Oil Shock* (London: Murray, 2007), p. 40.
4. David Howell and Carole Nakhle, *Out of the Energy Labyrinth* (London: Tauris, 2007), pp. 88–92.
5. International Energy Agency, *World Energy Outlook 2007* (Paris: OECD/IEA, 2007).
6. Stephen Leeb, *The Coming Economic Collapse* (New York: Warner, 2007), p. 1.
7. See, for example, Kenneth Deffeyes, *Hubbert's Peak: The Impending World Oil Shortage* (Princeton: Princeton University Press, 2001); Paul Roberts, *The End of Oil* (London: Bloomsbury, 2004); Michael T. Klare, *Resource Wars* (New York: Holt, 2002); Matthew R. Simmons, *Twilight in the Desert* (New York: Wiley, 2005); Strahan, *The Last Oil Shock*. Strahan's title unconsciously echoes that of Fred Pearce on global warming: *The Last Generation: How Nature Will Take Her Revenge for Climate Change* (London: Eden Project Books, 2006).
8. Strahan, *The Last Oil Shock*, p. 60.
9. William Freudenberg and Robert Gramling, *Blowout in the Gulf* (Cambridge, MA: MIT Press, 2011), p. 7.
10. David Victor et al., *Natural Gas and Geopolitics* (Cambridge: Cambridge University Press, 2006).
11. David Strahan, 'Lump Sums', *Guardian*, 5 March 2008.
12. Quoted in Dieter Helm, *The New Energy Paradigm* (Oxford: Oxford University Press, 2007), p. 19.
13. Ibid., p. 21.
14. Speech of then-President Vladimir Putin, quoted in Edward Lucas, *The New Cold War* (London: Bloomsbury, 2008), p. 212.
15. Strahan, *The Last Oil Shock*, p. 180.
16. Reported in Times Online, 11 January 2008.
17. Leeb, *The Coming Economic Collapse*, p. 77.

Chapter 3 The Greens and After

1. Nicholas Stern, *The Economics of Climate Change* (Cambridge: Cambridge University Press, 2007), p. xviii. The quote actually appears in the Stern Review in several slightly different formulations.
2. William Morris, *News from Nowhere* (London: Longmans, Green & Co., 1918), p. 280.
3. Ralph Waldo Emerson, *Nature – Conduct of Life* (New York: Read, 2006). Originally published in 1836.
4. Bradford Torrey, *The Writings of Henry David Thoreau: Journal*, vol. 14 (Boston: Houghton Mifflin, 1906), p. 205.
5. Quoted in Robert Goodin, *Green Political Theory* (Cambridge: Polity, 1992), p. 30.
6. Ibid., pp. 50ff.
7. William Rees, 'Ecological Footprints and Appropriated Carrying Capacity', *Environment and Urbanisation* 4 (1992).
8. See, for example, Ted Mosquin and Stan Rowe, 'A Manifesto for Earth', *Biodiversity* 5 (2004).
9. Peter Bernstein, *Against the Gods* (New York: Wiley, 1996).
10. Cass R. Sunstein, *Laws of Fear* (New York: Cambridge University Press, 2005), p. 4.
11. Ibid., p. 18.
12. Donella H. Meadows et al., *Limits to Growth: A Report for the Club of Rome's Project on the Predicament of Mankind* (New York: New American Library, 1972). See also Donella H. Meadows et al., *Limits to Growth – The 30-Year Update* (London: Macmillan, 2004), and many other publications by the same group of authors.
13. World Commission on Environment and Development, *Our Common Future* (Oxford: Oxford University Press, 1987).
14. Ibid., p. 326.
15. Richard North, 'Sustainable Development: A Concept with a Future?' Liberales Institute Occasional Paper (2005), p. 6.
16. William Baue, 'Rio+10 Series', *Sustainability Investment News*, 23 August 2002. Simon Dresner puts the matter forcefully: '[Sustainable development] is a concept which combines post-modern pessimism about the domination of nature with almost Enlightenment optimism about the possibility to reform human institutions': *The Principles of Sustainability* (London: Earthscan, 2002), p. 164.
17. W. M. Lafferty and J. Meadowcroft, *Implementing Sustainable Development* (Oxford: Oxford University Press, 2000), p. 19.
18. Wilfred Beckerman, 'The Chimera of "Sustainable Development"', *Electronic Journal of Sustainable Development* 1 (2008).
19. Daniel Esty et al., *The Environmental Sustainability Index* (Davos: Global Leaders of Tomorrow Environmental Task Force, 2001).
20. The website of the Global Commons Institute, led by Aubrey Meyer, provides detailed background information.

21. See Avner Offer, *The Challenge of Affluence* (Oxford: Oxford University Press, 2006).

22. Both quotes from John Talberth and Clifford Cobb, *The Genuine Progress Indicator 2006* (Oakland: Redefining Progress, 2006), p. 1.

23. Offer, *The Challenge of Affluence*, p. 19.

24. Sustainable Society Index, 2008, available online from the Sustainable Society Foundation.

25. UK Government Office for Science, *Foresight: The Future of Food and Farming* (London: HMSO, 2011).

26. *The Future of Food and Farming*, pp. 21–2.

27. John Dryzek, *The Politics of the Earth* (Oxford: Oxford University Press, 1997), p. 145.

28. See Arthur Mol and David Sonnenfeld, *Ecological Modernisation Around the World* (London: Cass, 2000).

Chapter 4   The Track Record So Far

1. See Marcel Wissenburg, *Green Liberalism* (London: UCL Press, 1998), p. 7.

2. David Shearman and Joseph Wayne Smith, *The Climate Change Challenge and the Failure of Democracy* (London: Praeger, 2007), p. 133.

3. Robyn Eckersley, *The Green State* (Cambridge, MA: MIT Press, 2004), ch. 4 and passim.

4. Yale Center for Environmental Law and Policy and Center for International Earth Science Information Network, Columbia University: 2008 Environmental Performance Index.

5. Semida Silveira, 'Sustainability in the Energy Sector – the Swedish Experience', available from the Swedish Energy Agency, 2006.

6. Paul Harris, *Europe and Global Climate Change* (London: Elgar, 2007).

7. See Axel Michaelowa, 'German Climate Policy Between Global Leadership and Muddling Through', in Hugh Compston and Ian Bailey (eds), *Turning Down the Heat* (London: Palgrave Macmillan, 2008).

8. Federal Ministry for the Environment, *Nature Conservation and Nuclear Safety: Investments for a Climate-Friendly Germany* (Synthesis Report, Potsdam, July 2008), available online.

9. I am grateful to Olaf Corry for his help in providing the statistics that follow.

10. Danish Commission on Climate Change Policy, *Green Energy* (Copenhagen, 2010).

11. European Environment Agency, *Annual EU Greenhouse Gas Inventory 1990–2008* (Brussels, 2010), p. 13.

12. For a comprehensive analysis, see Irene Lorenzoni, Tim O'Riordan and Nick Pidgeon, 'Hot Air and Cold Feet', in Compston and Bailey (eds), *Turning Down the Heat*.

13. Committee on Climate Change, *Meeting Carbon Budgets – The Need for a Step Change* (London: HMSO, 2009).
14. *The Climate Change Performance Index, 2010* (Bonn: Greenwatch, 2010).
15. President Obama: State of the Union Address, 25 January 2011 (Washington: The White House), p. 4.
16. Pew Research Center for The People and The Press, *Little Change in Opinions about Global Warming*, 27 October 2010.
17. Center for Climate Strategies, *Impacts of Comprehensive Climate and Energy Policy Options on the US Economy* (Baltimore: Johns Hopkins University, 2010).

Chapter 5 A Return to Planning?

1. John Dryzek, 'Ecology and Discursive Democracy', in Martin O'Connor (ed.), *Is Capitalism Sustainable?* (New York: Guilford Press, 1994), pp. 176–7.
2. Evan Durbin, *Problems of Economic Planning* (London: Routledge, 1949), p. 41.
3. Friedrich von Hayek, *The Constitution of Liberty* (Chicago: University of Chicago Press, 1960).
4. See, for example, David Orrell, *The Future of Everything* (New York: Thunders Mouth Press, 2006). For a critique of environmental prediction, see Orrin Pilkey and Linda Pilkey Jarvis, *Useless Arithmetic* (New York: Columbia University Press, 2007).
5. Jaco Quist and Philip Vergragt, 'Backcasting for Industrial Transformations', in Klaus Jacob et al. (eds), *Governance for Industrial Transformation* (Berlin: Environmental Policy Research Centre, 2003), pp. 423–5. Many other examples are discussed in this text.
6. Cynthia Mitchell and Stuart White, 'Forecasting and Backcasting for Sustainable Urban Water Futures', *Water* 30 (2003).
7. R. Bord et al., 'Public Perceptions of Global Warming', *Climate Research* 11 (1998).
8. Ipsos MORI, 'Public Attitudes to Climate Change 2008', available on the Ipsos MORI website.
9. Irene Lorenzoni and Nick Pidgeon, *Defining the Dangers of Climate Change and Individual Behaviour* (Norwich: Centre for Environmental Risk, University of East Anglia, 2006).
10. Quoted in Martin Patchen, *Public Attitudes and Behavior About Climate Change* (Purdue University Outreach Publication, 2006), p. 16. See also Sheldon Ungar, 'Knowledge, Ignorance and the Popular Culture', *Public Understanding of Science* 9 (2000); and John Sterman, 'Risk Communication on Climate', *Science* 322 (2008).
11. HSBC, 'International Survey of Public Attitudes Towards Climate Change', reported on the HSBC website.
12. Patchen, *Public Attitudes*, p. 14.

13. Department for Environment, Food and Rural Affairs, *A Framework for Pro-Environmental Behaviours* (London: HMSO, 2008).
14. Ron Pernick and Clint Wilder, *The Clean Tech Revolution* (New York: Collins, 2007), pp. 263–73.
15. See Ithiel de Sola Pool, *The Social Uses of the Telephone* (Cambridge, MA: MIT Press, 1977).
16. Richard Florida, *The Rise of the Creative Class* (New York: Basic Books, 2004), pp. 34–5.
17. Malcolm Gladwell, *The Tipping Point* (London: Little, Brown, 2000).
18. For a discussion of some of these practices, see Richard Thaler and Cass Sunstein (yes, the self-same destroyer of the precautionary principle), *Nudge* (New Haven: Yale University Press, 2008).
19. For this section I am heavily indebted to the work of Sarah Pralle, *Branching Out, Digging In* (Washington, DC: Georgetown University Press, 2006), which was drawn to my attention by Hugh Compston. See also Sarah Pralle, 'Agenda-setting and Climate Change', in Hugh Compston (ed.), *The Politics of Climate Policy*, special book issue of *Environmental Politics*, 2009. As I do, Pralle draws heavily upon John Kingdon's book, *Agendas, Alternatives and Public Policies* (New York: Longman, 1995).
20. Kingdon, *Agendas, Alternatives and Public Policies*.
21. D. Wood and A. Velditz, 'Issue Definition, Information Processing and the Politics of Global Warming', *American Journal of Political Science* 51 (2007).
22. Helen Clayton et al., Report of the First Inquiry of the All Parliamentary Climate Change Group: *Is a Cross-Party Consensus on Climate Change Possible – or Desirable?* (London: HMSO, 2006), p. 3.
23. Quoted in ibid., p. 13.
24. Robin Eckersley, *The Green State* (Cambridge, MA: MIT Press, 2004), pp. 243–5. However, she adopts the precautionary principle, which I avoid, and I have somewhat modified her list while, I hope, still maintaining its spirit.
25. Edelman Trust Barometer 2008 (London: Edelman, 2008).
26. For an account going up to the late 1990s, see Peter Newell, *Climate for Change* (Cambridge: Cambridge University Press, 2000), ch. 5. The quotation is from p. 98.
27. Quoted in ibid., p. 104.
28. Quoted in Peter Senge, *The Necessary Revolution* (London: Brealey, 2008), p. 77.
29. Quoted in ibid., p. 77.
30. Christine MacDonald, *Green Inc* (London: Lyons Press, 2008).
31. Senge, *The Necessary Revolution*, ch. 13.
32. Details of the company's '2020 Strategic Framework for Sustainability' is available on its website.
33. Available on Citigroup's website.
34. Charles Prince, CEO of the company, quoted on the Citigroup

website in the press release of the $50 billion programme, 8 May 2007.
35. Senge, *The Necessary Revolution*, ch. 5.

Chapter 6 Technologies and Taxes

1. Jeremy Rifkin, *The Hydrogen Economy* (New York: Tarcher, 2002).
2. Ibid., p. 9.
3. For a caustic survey of hydrogen and other renewable technologies, see James Lovelock, *The Revenge of Gaia* (London: Perseus, 2007).
4. 'Stewart Brand, an Icon of Environmentalism, Talks About Embracing Nuclear Power', *Newsweek*, 21 October 2009.
5. IPCC, *Mitigation. Contribution of Working Group III to the Fourth Assessment Report* (Cambridge: Cambridge University Press, 2007), p. 269.
6. (No author): 'Going Underground', *New Scientist* (11 October 2008).
7. Ron Pernick and Clint Wilder, *The Clean Tech Revolution* (New York: HarperCollins, 2007).
8. 'Dig Deep', *The Economist* (21 June 2008).
9. International Energy Agency, *World Energy Outlook*, 25 November 2010, p. 11.
10. The Royal Society, *Geoengineering the Climate* (London), September 2009.
11. Wallace Broecker and Robert Kunzig, *Fixing Climate* (New York: Hill & Wang, 2008).
12. Paul Hawken et al., *Natural Capitalism* (London: Little, Brown, 1999).
13. Robert Socolow and Stephen Pacala, 'Stabilization Wedges', *Science* 305 (2004), pp. 968–72.
14. Christopher Freeman, *The Economics of Hope* (New York: Pinter, 1992).
15. Nicholas Stern, *The Economics of Climate Change* (Cambridge: Cambridge University Press, 2007), ch. 16.
16. See Bethany McLean and Peter Elkind, *The Smartest Guys in the Room* (New York: Penguin, 2003).
17. John Scott and Gareth Evans, 'Electricity Networks', in Dieter Helm (ed.), *The New Energy Paradigm* (Oxford: Oxford University Press, 2007).
18. Stern, *The Economics of Climate Change*, p. 403.
19. Ibid., p. 402.
20. Amory B. Lovins et al., 'A Roadmap for Natural Capitalism', *Harvard Business Review* 77 (May/June 1999), pp. 78–81.
21. Scott and Evans, 'Electricity Networks', pp. 51–62.
22. Swanbarton Limited, *Status of Electrical Energy Storage Systems* (London: Department of Trade and Industry, 2004).

23. European Commission, *European Union Technology Platform Smartgrids* (Luxembourg: Office of Official Publications, 2006).
24. UNEP, *Green Jobs* (Washington, DC: Worldwatch Institute, 2008).
25. Michael Shellenberger and Ted Nordhaus, *The Death of Environmentalism* (2005), p. 26; available at http://www.thebreak-through.org/images/Death_of_Environmentalism.pdf. See also their subsequent book *Break Through* (Boston: Houghton Mifflin, 2007).
26. Van Jones, *The Green Economy* (Center for American Progress, September 2008).
27. Robert Pollin et al., *Green Recovery* (Center for American Progress, September 2008).
28. Mikael Skou Andersen et al., *An Evaluation of the Impact of Green Taxes in the Nordic Countries* (Copenhagen: TemaNord, 2000). See also Runar Brannlund and Ing-Marie Gren, *Green Taxes, Economic Theory and Empirical Evidence from Scandinavia* (Cheltenham: Elgar, 1999).
29. Gilbert Metcalf, *A Green Employment Tax Swap* (Washington, DC: The Brookings Institution, 2007).
30. Paul Ekins and Simon Dresner, *Green Taxes and Charges* (York: Rowntree Foundation, 2004).
31. Ibid., p. 14.
32. David Fleming, *Energy and the Common Purpose* (London: Lean Economy Connection, 2006).
33. Richard Starkey and Kevin Anderson, *Investigating Domestic Tradable Quotas* (Norwich: Tyndall Centre, 2005).
34. Mayer Hillman and Tina Fawcett, *How We can Save the Planet* (London: Penguin, 2004).
35. Simon Roberts and Joshua Thumin, *A Rough Guide to Individual Carbon Trading* (London: Centre for Sustainable Energy, 2006), p. 3.
36. Ibid., p. 31.
37. See John Urry, *Mobilities* (Cambridge: Polity, 2007).
38. Tom Vanderbilt, *Traffic* (London: Allen Lane, 2008).
39. Jean Gimpel, *The Medieval Machine* (New York: Penguin, 1977).
40. James Kunstler, *The Long Emergency* (London: Atlantic, 2006), p. 270.
41. I am greatly indebted to John Urry's *Mobilities*, referenced above, for this analysis.
42. John Tiffin and Chris Kissling, *Transport Communications* (London: Kogan Page, 2007), p. 204.

Chapter 7 The Politics of Adaptation

1. European Commission, *Adapting to Climate Change in Europe* (Brussels: Commission of the European Communities, 2007).
2. Gwyn Prins and Steve Raynor, *The Wrong Trousers* (Oxford: James Martin Institute, 2007), pp. 33–4.

3. European Commission, *Adapting to Climate Change in Europe*. Green paper of the European Commission, Brussels, 2007.
4. David Crichton, 'Insurance and Climate Change': paper presented at conference on Climate Change, Extreme Events and Coastal Cities, Houston, 9 February 2005, p. 17.
5. Tim O'Riordan et al., 'Designing Sustainable Coastal Futures', *21st Century Society* 3 (2008).
6. Padeep Pall et al., 'Anthropogenic Greenhouse Gas Contribution to Flood Risk in England and Wales in Autumn 2000', *Nature* 470 (17 February 2011).
7. Crichton, 'Insurance and Climate Change'.
8. Sue Roaf et al., *Adapting Buildings and Cities for Climate Change* (Oxford: Elsevier, 2005).
9. See DEFRA, 'Making Space for Water'; www.defra.gov.uk/environ/fcd/policy/strategy.htm.
10. O'Riordan et al., 'Designing Sustainable Coastal Futures', pp. 152–5.
11. Helmut Kesting, *Hedging Climate Change* (Munich: Allianz Economic Research, 2007).
12. Ibid., p. 202.
13. Moira Herbert, 'A New Kind of First Responder', *Bloomberg Businessweek* (28 February 2008).
14. J. Timmons Roberts and Bradley C. Parks, *A Climate of Injustice* (Cambridge, MA: MIT Press, 2007).
15. Daniel Osgood et al., 'Integrating Seasonal Forecasts and Insurance for Adaptation Among Subsistence Farmers' (Washington, DC: World Bank Policy Research Working Paper, 2008).
16. UNDP Human Development Report, *Risk, Vulnerability and Adaptation in Bangladesh* (Bangladesh Centre for Advanced Studies, 2007).

Chapter 8 International Negotiations, the EU and Carbon Markets

1. John Carey, 'Russia's Path to Kyoto', *Business Week* (1 October 2004).
2. Robert Henson, *The Rough Guide to Climate Change* (London: Rough Guides, 2008), pp. 292–3.
3. David G. Victor, 'Fragmented Carbon Markets and Reluctant Nations', in Joseph E. Aldy and Robert N. Stavins (eds), *Architectures for Agreement* (Cambridge: Cambridge University Press, 2007), p. 149.
4. Rachmat Witoelar, 'Address to Closing Plenary', UN Climate Change Conference, Bali, 2007.
5. Oliver Tickell, 'The "Bali Roadmap"', in *Was Bali a Success? Open Democracy* (online) (18 December 2007).
6. Trevor Houser, 'Copenhagen, the Accord, and the Way Forward', Peterson Institute for International Economics. Washington, DC (March 2010).

7. Per Meilstrup, 'The Runaway Summit', *Monday Morning* (a Danish think-tank), available online. I draw heavily upon this account here, because of its authoritative nature.
8. Quoted in Meilstrup, 'The Runaway Summit', p. 114.
9. Both quotes from Michael McCarthy, 'At Last, the Climate Changes', *Independent* (12 December 2010).
10. Kevin Anderson, 'Response to Cancun', Tyndall Centre for Climate Change Research (9 February 2011), pp. 1–2.
11. Quoted in James Randerson, 'Top Scientists Warn Against Rush to Biofuels', *Guardian* (25 March 2008).
12. Quoted in 'EU Emissions Trading Scheme', EurActiv.com (February 2008), p. 3.
13. See Donald MacKenzie, *Making Things the Same* (Edinburgh: School of Social and Political Studies, 2008); and 'Constructing Emissions Markets', in *Material Markets* (Oxford: Oxford University Press, 2009), ch. 7. I draw extensively upon his excellent discussion in what follows.
14. Denny Ellerman et al., *Markets for Clean Air* (Cambridge: Cambridge University Press, 2000).
15. Denny Ellerman and Barbara Buchner, *Over-allocation or Abatement*, Report no. 141 (Cambridge, MA: MIT Joint Program on the Science and Policy of Global Change, 2006).
16. For a useful survey, see Ricardo Bayon et al., *Voluntary Carbon Markets* (London: Earthscan, 2008).
17. Nathaniel Gronewald, 'Chicago Climate Exchange Closes', *New York Times* (3 January 2011).

Chapter 9 The Geopolitics of Climate Change

1. Peter Halden, *The Geopolitics of Climate Change* (Stockholm: Swedish Defence Research Agency, 2007).
2. Anup Shah, 'Dominance and Change in the Arctic', *Global Issues* (June 2010), p. 1.
3. Halden, *The Geopolitics of Climate Change*, pp. 150–8.
4. See Gerard Prunier, *Darfur, the Ambiguous Genocide* (London: Hurst, 2005).
5. US Department of Defense, *Military Power of the People's Republic of China* (Washington, DC: Office of the Secretary of Defense, 2006).
6. Michael Klare, 'The New Geopolitics of Energy', *The Nation* (19 May 2008), p. 3. See also Michael Klare, *Rising Powers, Shrinking Planet* (New York: Holt, 2008).
7. Department of the Navy, *A Cooperative Strategy for 21st Century Seapower* (Washington, DC: Department of the Navy, 2007).
8. Klare, 'The New Geopolitics of Energy'.
9. Robert Kagan, *The Return of History and the End of Dreams* (London: Atlantic, 2008).
10. Ibid., p. 3.

11. Ibid., p. 77.
12. David Hannay, *New World Disorder* (London: Tauris, 2008), p. 75.
13. Ibid., p. 300.
14. When Condoleezza Rice was set to replace Colin Powell as US Secretary of State, she remarked that the foreign policy of the Bush administration would 'proceed from the firm ground of national interest, not from the interests of an illusory international community'. Quoted in Louis Klarevas, 'Political Realism', *Harvard International Review* 26 (2004), p. 2.
15. Paul Collier, *The Bottom Billion* (Oxford: Oxford University Press, 2007), p. 3.
16. Ibid.
17. Transparency International: Corruption Perceptions Index, 2010. Available online.
18. Ibid., pp. 74–5.
19. Thomas Friedman, *Hot, Flat and Crowded* (London: Allen Lane, 2008), pp. 82–110.
20. Ibid., pp. 94–5.
21. Michael Ross, 'Oil, Islam and Women', *American Political Science Review* 43 (2008).
22. Pavel Baev et al., *Pipelines, Politics and Power* (London: Centre for European Reform, 2008).
23. Carlo Carraro, 'Incentives and Institutions', in Joseph E. Aldy and Robert N. Stavins (eds), *Architectures for Agreement* (Cambridge: Cambridge University Press, 2007), pp. 164–5.
24. C. Egenhofer et al., quoted in ibid., p. 165.
25. *Major Economic Forum on Energy and Climate: Technology Plans* (MEF, 2009). Available online.
26. Manish Kumar Shrivastava and Nitu Goel, 'Shaping the Architecture of Future Climate Governance: Perspectives from the South', in Frank Biesman et al. (eds), *Global Climate Governance Beyond 2012* (Cambridge: Cambridge University Press, 2010).
27. Klare, *Rising Powers*, pp. 244–61.
28. Remarks of Senator Joseph Lieberman to the Council on Foreign Relations: 'China/US Energy Policies: A Choice of Cooperation or Collision', Washington, DC (2 December 2005); quoted in Klare, *Rising Powers*, p. 245.
29. '"No Time to Delay" for US–China Climate Agreement', *Business Green* (17 January 2011). Available online.
30. 'Climate Change and Energy: Climate Change in Brazil', Science and Development Network. Available online.
31. Luiz Inacio Lula da Silva, quoted in 'Floods in Brazil Point to Climate Change: Lula', The ARY news (12 May 2009). Available online.

REFERENCES

'A Moment of Truth': *The Economist*, 15 May 2008.

Airoldi, Adele: *The European Union and the Arctic*. Copenhagen: Nordic Council of Ministers, 2008.

Andersen, M. S., N. Dengsøe and A. B. Pedersen: *An Evaluation of the Impact of Green Taxes in the Nordic Countries*. Copenhagen: Nordic Council of Ministers, 2001.

'A Ravenous Dragon': *The Economist*, 13 March 2008.

Baev, Pavel et al.: *Pipelines, Politics and Power: The Future of EU–Russia Energy Relations*. London: Centre for European Reform, 2008.

Baue, William: 'Rio+10 Series'. *Sustainability Investment News*, 23 August 2002; www.socialfunds.com/news/article.cgi/913.html.

Bayon, Ricardo, Amanda Hawn and Katherine Hamilton: *Voluntary Carbon Markets*. London: Earthscan, 2007.

Beck, Ulrich: *Risk Society*. London: Sage, 1992.

Beckerman, Wilfred: 'The Chimera of "Sustainable Development"'. *Electronic Journal of Sustainable Development* 1, 2008.

Benn, Hilary: 'Climate Change Bill: Update Following Passage Through the Lords'. DEFRA, 2 June 2008.

Bernstein, Peter L.: *Against the Gods*. New York: Wiley, 1996.

Biehl, Janet and Peter Staudenmaier: *Ecofascism*. Edinburgh: AK Press, 1995.

Bobbitt, Philip: *Terror and Consent*. New York: Knopf, 2008.

Booker, Christopher and Richard North: *Scared to Death*. London: Continuum, 2007.

Bord, R. et al.: 'Public Perceptions of Global Warming'. *Climate Research* 11, 1998.

Borgerson, Scott G.: 'Arctic Meltdown'. *Foreign Affairs* 87/2, March/April 2008.

Brannlund, Runar and Ing-Marie Gren: *Green Taxes, Economic Theory and Empirical Evidence from Scandinavia*. Cheltenham: Edward Elgar, 1999.

British Antarctic Survey: 'Climate Change – Our View'. December 2007; www.antarctica.ac.uk//bas_research/our_views/climate_change.php.

Broecker, Wallace and Robert Kunzig: *Fixing Climate*. New York: Hill & Wang, 2008.

Brown, Paul: *Voodoo Economics and the Doomed Nuclear Renaissance*. London: Friends of the Earth, 2008.

Bruggemeier, Franz-Josef, Mark Cioc and Thomas Zeller (eds): *How Green Were the Nazis?* Ohio: Ohio University Press, 2005.

Capoor, Karan and Philippe Ambrosi: *State and Trends of the Carbon Market*. Washington, DC: The World Bank, 2007.

Carey, John: 'Russia's Path to Kyoto'. *Business Week*, 1 October 2004.

Carraro, Carlo: 'Incentives and Institutions', in Joseph E. Aldy and Robert N. Stavins (eds), *Architectures for Agreement*. Cambridge: Cambridge University Press, 2007.

Center for Climate Strategies: *Impacts of Comprehensive Climate and Energy Policy Options on the US Economy*. Baltimore: Johns Hopkins University Press, 2010.

Clayton, Helen et al.: *Report of the First Inquiry of the All-Parliamentary Climate Change Group: Is a Cross-Party Consensus on Climate Change Possible – or Desirable?* London: HMSO, 2006.

Collier, Paul: *The Bottom Billion*. Oxford: Oxford University Press, 2007.

Combs, Barbara and Paul Slovic: 'Newspaper Coverage of Causes of Death'. *Journalism Quarterly* 56, Winter 1979.

Commission on Growth and Development: *The Growth Report*. Washington, DC: World Bank, 2008.

Committee on Climate Change: *Meeting Carbon Budgets – The Need for a Step Change*. London: HMSO, 2009.

Compston, Hugh and Ian Bailey (eds): *Turning Down the Heat: The Politics of Climate Policy in Affluent Democracies*. London: Palgrave Macmillan, 2008.

Cox, John D.: *Climate Crash*. Washington, DC: Joseph Henry Press, 2005.

Crichton, David: 'Insurance and Climate Change'. Paper presented at conference on *Climate Change, Extreme Events and Coastal Cities: Houston and London*. Houston, 9 February 2005.

Darley, Julian: *High Noon for Natural Gas*. White River Junction, VT: Chelsea Green, 2004.

Deffeyes, Kenneth: *Hubbert's Peak: The Impending World Oil Shortage*. Princeton: Princeton University Press, 2001.

Department for Environment, Food and Rural Affairs (DEFRA): *A Framework for Pro-Environmental Behaviours*. London: HMSO, 2008.

Department of the Navy: *A Cooperative Strategy for 21st Century Seapower*. Washington, DC: Department of the Navy, 2007.

de Sola Pool, Ithiel (ed.): *The Social Uses of the Telephone*. Cambridge, MA: MIT Press, 1977.

Dessler, Andrew and Edward Parson: *The Science and Politics of Climate Change*. Cambridge: Cambridge University Press, 2006.

Diamond, Jared: *Collapse: How Societies Choose or Fail to Survive*. London: Allen Lane, 2005.

'Dig Deep': *The Economist*, 19 June 2008.

Dresner, Simon: *The Principles of Sustainability*. London: Earthscan, 2002.

Dryzek, John: 'Ecology and Discursive Democracy', in Martin O'Connor (ed.), *Is Capitalism Sustainable?* New York: Guilford Press, 1994.

Dryzek, John: *The Politics of the Earth*. Oxford: Oxford University Press, 1997.

Durbin, Evan: *Problems of Economic Planning*. London: Routledge, 1949.

Eckersley, Robyn: *The Green State*. Cambridge, MA: MIT Press, 2004.

Edelman Trust Barometer. London: Edelman, 2008.

Ekins, Paul and Simon Dresner: *Green Taxes and Charges*. York: Rowntree Foundation, 2004.

Element Energy: *The Growth Potential for Microgeneration in England, Wales and Scotland*. Cambridge: Element Energy, 2008.

Ellerman, A. Denny and Barbara Buchner: *Over-Allocation or Abatement?* Report No. 141. Cambridge, MA: MIT Joint Program on the Science and Policy of Global Change, 2006.

Ellerman, A. Denny et al.: *Markets for Clean Air*. Cambridge: Cambridge University Press, 2000.

Emerson, Ralph Waldo: *Nature – Conduct of Life*. New York: Read Books, 2006.

Esty, Daniel C. et al.: *Environmental Sustainability Index*. Davos: Global Leaders of Tomorrow Environment Task Force, 2001.

'EU Emissions Trading Scheme', February 2008; www.euractiv.com/.

European Commission: *Adapting to Climate Change in Europe – Options for EU Action*. Green Paper from the Commission to the Council, the European Parliament, the European Economic and Social Committee and the Committee of the Regions. Brussels: Commission of the European Communities, 2007.

European Commission, Directorate-General for Research: *European Technology Platform Smartgrids*. Luxembourg: Office of Official Publications of the European Communities, 2006.

European Environment Agency: *Greenhouse Gas Emission Trends and Projections in Europe*. Copenhagen: EEA, 2006.

European Environment Agency: *Annual EU Greenhouse Gas Inventory 1990–2008*. Brussels: EEA, 2010.

European Union: 'Climate Change and International Security'. Paper from the High Representative and the European Commission to the European Council. S113/08, March 2008; www.consilium.europa.eu/euDocs/cms_Data/docs/pressData/en/reports/99387.pdf.

Fleming, David: *Energy and the Common Purpose*. London: Lean Economy Connection, 2006.

Florida, Richard: *The Rise of the Creative Class*. New York: Basic Books, 2004.

Freeman, Christopher: *The Economics of Hope*. New York: Pinter, 1992.

Freudenberg, William and Robert Gramling: *Blowout in the Gulf*. Cambridge, MA: MIT Press, 2011.

Friedman, Thomas: *Hot, Flat and Crowded*. London: Allen Lane, 2008.

Furedi, Frank: *Invitation to Terror*. London: Continuum, 2007.

Gardner, Dan: *Risk: The Science and Politics of Fear*. London: Virgin, 2008.

Germanwatch: *Climate Change Performance Index*. Bonn, 2007.

Germanwatch: *Climate Change Performance Index*. Bonn, 2008.

Giddens, Anthony: *Europe in the Global Age*. Cambridge: Polity, 2006.

Giddens, Anthony: *The Third Way*. Cambridge: Polity, 1998.

Gimpel, Jean: *Medieval Machine*. New York: Penguin, 1977.

Gladwell, Malcolm: *The Tipping Point*. London: Little, Brown, 2000.

Glantz, Michael H.: *Currents of Change*. Cambridge: Cambridge University Press, 1996.

Goodin, Robert: *Green Political Theory*. Cambridge: Polity, 1992.

Gore, Al: *Earth in the Balance*. New York: Plume, 1993.

Halden, Peter: *The Geopolitics of Climate Change*. Stockholm: Swedish Defence Research Agency, 2007.

Hamilton, Clive: *Requiem for a Species*. London: Earthscan, 2010.

Hannay, David: *New World Disorder*. London: Tauris, 2008.

Hansen, James: *Storms of My Grandchildren*. London: Bloomsbury, 2009.

Harris, Paul G. (ed.): *Europe and Global Climate Change*. Cheltenham: Edward Elgar, 2007.

Hawken, Paul et al.: *Natural Capitalism*. London: Little, Brown, 1999.

von Hayek, Friedrich: *The Constitution of Liberty*. Chicago: University of Chicago Press, 1960.

Heinberg, Richard: *The Party's Over*. Gabriola Island, British Columbia: New Society Publishers, 2003.

Helm, Dieter (ed.): *The New Energy Paradigm*. Oxford: Oxford University Press, 2007.

Helm, Dieter: 'Sins of Emission'. *Wall Street Journal*, 13 March 2008.

Henson, Robert: *The Rough Guide to Climate Change*. London: Rough Guides, 2008.

Hillman, Mayer with Tina Fawcett: *How We Can Save the Planet*. London: Penguin, 2004.

Hoggan, James and Richard Littlemore: *Climate Cover-Up*. Vancouver: Greystone, 2009.

Houser, Trevor: 'Copenhagen, the Accord, and the Way Forward', Peterson Institute for International Economics. Washington, DC, March 2010.

Howell, David and Carole Nakhle: *Out of the Energy Labyrinth*. London: Tauris, 2007.

Hoyos, Carola and Javier Blas, 'Investment is the Key to Meeting Oil Needs'. *Financial Times*, 29 October 2008.

HSBC: *International Climate Confidence Index*. London: HSBC Holdings, 2007.

Hughes, James: *Evidence to the Canadian Standing Committee on Environment and Sustainable Development*. Ottawa, 11 February 2008.

Intergovernmental Panel on Climate Change: *Climate Change 2007: Mitigation*. Contribution of Working Group III to the Fourth Assessment Report of the Intergovernmental Panel on Climate Change. Cambridge: Cambridge University Press, 2007.

Intergovernmental Panel on Climate Change: *Climate Change 2007: Synthesis Report*. Contribution of Working Groups I, II and III to the Fourth Assessment Report of the Intergovernmental Panel on Climate Change. Geneva: IPCC, 2007.

International Energy Agency: *World Energy Outlook*. Paris: OECD/IEA, 2007.

Ipsos MORI: *Public Attitudes to Climate Change, 2008*. London: Ipsos MORI, 2008.

Jack, Ian: 'When It Comes to Railways, the Government is on the Wrong Track'. *Guardian*, 14 June 2008.

Jones, Van: *The Green Economy*. Centre for American Progress, September 2008.

Kagan, Robert: *The Return of History and the End of Dreams*. London: Atlantic, 2008.

Kesting, Helmut: *Hedging Climate Change*. Munich: Allianz Dresdner Economic Research, 2007.

King, David and Gabrielle Walker: *The Hot Topic*. London: Bloomsbury, 2008.

Kingdon, John: *Agendas, Alternatives and Public Policies*. New York: Longman, 1995.

Klare, Michael T.: 'The New Geopolitics of Energy'. *The Nation*, 19 May 2008.

Klare, Michael T.: *Resource Wars: The New Landscape of Global Conflict*. New York: Henry Holt, 2002.

Klare, Michael T.: *Rising Powers, Shrinking Planet*. New York: Holt, 2008.

Klarevas, Louis: 'Political Realism'. *Harvard International Review* 26, 2004.

Knight, Frank: *Risk, Uncertainty and Profit*. New York: Century Press, 1964.

Kolbert, Elizabeth: *Field Notes from a Catastrophe*. London: Bloomsbury, 2006.

Kunstler, James Howard: *The Long Emergency*. London: Atlantic, 2006.

Lafferty, William M. and James Meadowcroft (eds): *Implementing Sustainable Development*. Oxford: Oxford University Press, 2000.

Lawson, Nigel: *An Appeal to Reason*. London: Duckworth, 2008.

Lawson, Nigel: 'The REAL Inconvenient Truth'. *Daily Mail*, 5 April 2008.

Leeb, Stephen: *The Coming Economic Collapse*. New York: Warner, 2007.

Levy, Joel: *The Doomsday Book*. London: Vision, 2005.

Lifton, Robert Jay: *Indefensible Weapons*. New York: Basic Books, 1982.

Lindzen, Richard: 'Climate of Fear'. *Wall Street Journal*, 12 April 2006.

Lindzen, Richard: 'Debunking the Myth'. *Business Today* 43, 2006.

Lindzen, Richard: 'Taking Greenhouse Warming Seriously'. *Energy & Environment* 18/7–8, 2007.

Lindzen, Richard: 'There Is No "Consensus" on Global Warming'. *Wall Street Journal*, 26 June, 2006.

Linstroth, Tommy and Ryan Bell: *Local Action*. Burlington, Vermont: University of Vermont Press, 2007.

Lomborg, Bjørn: *Cool It*. New York: Alfred A. Knopf, 2007.

Lomborg, Bjørn: *The Skeptical Environmentalist*. Cambridge: Cambridge University Press, 2001.

Lomborg, Bjørn (ed.): *Smart Solutions to Climate Change: Comparing Costs to Benefits*. Cambridge: Cambridge University Press, 2010.

Lorenzoni, Irene and Nick Pidgeon: *Defining the Dangers of Climate Change and Individual Behaviour*. Norwich: Centre for Environmental Risk, University of East Anglia, 2006.

Lorenzoni, Irene, Tim O'Riordan and Nick Pidgeon: 'Hot Air and Cold Feet', in Hugh Compston and Ian Bailey (eds), *Turning Down the Heat: The Politics of Climate Policy in Affluent Democracies*. London: Palgrave Macmillan, 2008.

Lovelock, James: *The Revenge of Gaia*. London: Penguin, 2007.

Lovelock, James: *The Vanishing Face of Gaia*. London: Penguin, 2010.

Lovins, Amory B.: 'Energy Strategy: The Road Not Taken'. *Foreign Affairs* 55, October 1976.

Lovins, Amory B. et al.: 'A Roadmap for Natural Capitalism'. *Harvard Business Review* 77, May/June 1999.

Lucas, Edward: *The New Cold War*. London: Bloomsbury, 2008.

MacDonald, Christine: *Green Inc*. London: Lyons Press, 2008.

MacKenzie, Donald: 'Making Things the Same', February 2008; www.sps.ed.ac.uk/__data/assets/pdf_file/0018/4860/bottom_line.pdf.

MacKenzie, Donald: *Material Markets*. Oxford: Oxford University Press, 2009.

McGuire, Bill: *Surviving Armageddon*. Oxford: Oxford University Press, 2005.

McLean, Bethany and Peter Elkind: *The Smartest Guys in the Room*. New York: Penguin, 2003.

Meadows, Donella H. et al.: *Limits to Growth: A Report for the Club of Rome's Project on the Predicament of Mankind*. New York: New American Library, 1972.

Meadows, Donella H. et al.: *Limits to Growth – The 30-Year Update*. London: Macmillan, 2004.

Metcalf, Gilbert: *A Green Employment Tax Swap*. Washington, DC: The Brookings Institution, June 2007.

Mettler, Anne: *From Why to How*. Brussels: Lisbon Council, 2008.

Meyer, Aubrey: *Contraction and Convergence*. Bristol: Green Books, 2001.

Michaelowa, Axel: 'German Climate Policy Between Global Leadership and Muddling Through', in Hugh Compston and Ian Bailey (eds), *Turning Down the Heat: The Politics of Climate Policy in Affluent Democracies*. London: Palgrave Macmillan, 2008.

Michaels, Patrick J.: *Meltdown*. Washington, DC: Cato Institute, 2004.

Middleton, Paul: *A Brief Guide to the End of Oil*. London: Robinson Publishing, 2007.

Mitchell, Cynthia and Stuart White: 'Forecasting and Backcasting for Sustainable Urban Water Futures'. *Water* 30, August 2003.

Mol, Arthur P. J. and David A. Sonnenfeld (eds): *Ecological Modernisation around the World*. London: Cass, 2000.

Morris, William: *News from Nowhere, or, An Epoch of Rest*. London: Longmans, Green & Co., 1918.

Mosquin, Ted and J. Stan Rowe: 'A Manifesto for Earth'. *Biodiversity* 5/1, 2004.

Myers, Norman: 'Environmental Unknowns'. *Science* 269, 21 July 1995.

Newell, Peter: *Climate for Change*. Cambridge: Cambridge University Press, 2000.

North, Richard: 'Sustainable Development: A Concept with a Future?' Occasional Paper. Potsdam: Liberales Institute, 2005.

Offer, Avner: *The Challenge of Affluence*. Oxford: Oxford University Press, 2006.

Oreskes, Naomi and Erik Conway: *Merchants of Doubt*. London: Bloomsbury, 2010.

O'Riordan, Tim et al.: 'Designing Sustainable Coastal Futures'. *Twenty-First Century Society* 3, 2008.

Orrell, David: *The Future of Everything*. New York: Thunders Mouth Press, 2006.

Osgood, Daniel et al.: *Integrating Seasonal Forecasts and Insurance for Adaptation Among Subsistence Farmers*. Washington, DC: World Bank Development Research Group, 2008.

Pall, Padeep et al., 'Anthropogenic Greenhouse Gas Contribution to Flood Risk in England and Wales in Autumn 2000'. *Nature* 470, 17 February 2011.

Patchen, Martin: *Public Attitudes and Behavior about Climate Change*. West Lafayette: Purdue Climate Change Research Center, Purdue University, 2006.

Pearce, Fred: *The Climate Files: The Battle for the Truth About Global Warming*. London: Guardian Books, 2010.

Pearce, Fred: *The Last Generation*. London: Eden Project Books, 2007.

Pernick, Ron and Clint Wilder: *The Clean Tech Revolution*. New York: HarperCollins, 2007.

The Pew Research Center for the People and the Press: *Little Consensus on Global Warming*, 12 July 2006.

Pilkey, Orrin and Linda Pilkey Jarvis: *Useless Arithmetic*. New York: Columbia University Press, 2007.

Pitt, Michael: *Learning Lessons from the 2007 Floods*. London: Cabinet Office, 2008.

Pollin, Robert et al.: *Green Recovery*. Center for American Progress, September 2008.

Pralle, Sarah: 'Agenda-setting and Climate Change', in Hugh Compston (ed.), *The Politics of Climate Policy*, special book issue of *Environmental Politics*, 2009.

Pralle, Sarah: *Branching Out, Digging In*. Washington, DC: Georgetown University Press, 2006.

Prins, Gwyn and Steve Rayner: *The Wrong Trousers*. Oxford: James Martin Institute for Science and Civilization, University of Oxford, 2007.

Prunier, Gerard: *Darfur, the Ambiguous Genocide*. London: Hurst, 2005.

Quist, Jaco and Philip Vergragt: 'Backcasting for Industrial Transformations and System Innovations Towards Sustainability', in Klaus Jacob et al. (eds), *Governance for Industrial Transformation*. Proceedings of the 2003 Berlin Conference on the Human Dimensions of Global Environmental Change. Berlin: Environmental Policy Research Centre, 2004.

Rahman, A. Atiq et al.: *Risks, Vulnerability and Adaptation in Bangladesh*. UNDP Human Development Report Office Occasional Paper. Dhaka: Bangladesh Centre for Advanced Studies, 2007.

Randerson, James: 'Cut in Coal Brings UK Emissions Down by 2 per cent'. *Guardian*, 28 May 2008.

Randerson, James and Nicholas Watt: 'Top Scientists Warn Against Rush to Biofuel'. *Guardian*, 25 March 2008.

Rees, Martin: *Our Final Century*. London: Arrow, 2004.

Rees, William: 'Ecological Footprints and Appropriated Carrying Capacity: What Urban Economics Leaves Out'. *Environment and Urbanisation* 4, 1992.

Rifkin, Jeremy: *The Hydrogen Economy*. New York: Tarcher, 2003.

Roaf, Sue, David Crichton and Fergus Nicol: *Adapting Buildings and Cities for Climate Change*. Oxford: Elsevier, 2005.

Roberts, J. Timmons and Bradley C. Parks: *A Climate of Injustice*. Cambridge, MA: MIT Press, 2007.

Roberts, Paul: *The End of Oil*. London: Bloomsbury, 2004.

Roberts, Simon: *A Rough Guide to Individual Carbon Trading*. London: Centre for Sustainable Energy, 2006.

Robinson, Colin: *Climate Change Policy*. London: Institute of Economic Affairs, 2008.

Robinson, J.: 'Future Subjunctive'. *Futures* 35, 2003.

Ross, Michael: 'Oil, Islam and Women'. *American Political Science Review* 43, 2008.

Rutledge, Ian: *Addicted to Oil*. London: Tauris, 2006.

Sanborn, F. B. (ed.): *The Writings of Henry David Thoreau: Familiar Letters*, vol. 6. Boston: Houghton Mifflin, 1906.

Scott, John and Gareth Evans: 'Electricity Networks', in Dieter Helm (ed.), *The New Energy Paradigm*. Oxford: Oxford University Press, 2007.

Senge, Peter: *The Necessary Revolution*. London: Brealey, 2008.

Shah, Anup: 'Dominance and Change in the Arctic'. *Global Issues*, June 2010.

Shearman, David and Joseph Wayne Smith: *The Climate Change Challenge and the Failure of Democracy*. London: Praeger, 2007.

Shrivastava, Manish Kumar and Nitu Goel: 'Shaping the Architecture of Future Climate Governance: Perspectives from the South', in Frank Biesman et al. (eds), *Global Climate Governance Beyond 2012*. Cambridge: Cambridge University Press, 2010.

Simmons, Matthew R.: *Twilight in the Desert*. New York: Wiley, 2005.

Singer, S. Fred and Dennis T. Avery: *Unstoppable Global Warming*. New York: Rowman & Littlefield, 2007.

Smith, Julian: 'Renewable Energy: Power Beneath Our Feet'. *New Scientist*, 8 October 2008.

Socolow, Robert and Stephen Pacala: 'Stabilization Wedges'. *Science* 305, 2004.

Starkey, Richard and Kevin Anderson: *Domestic Tradable Quotas*. Norwich: Tyndall Centre, 2005.

Stern, Nicholas: *The Economics of Climate Change*. Cambridge: Cambridge University Press, 2007.

Strahan, David: *The Last Oil Shock*. London: John Murray, 2007.

Strahan, David: 'Lump sums'. *Guardian*, 5 March 2008.

Streck, Charlotte et al.: *Climate Change and Forests*. London: Chatham House, 2008.

Sunderland, Ruth: 'Carrots As Well As Sticks Will Help Us to Swallow Green Taxes'. *Observer*, 25 May 2008.

Sunstein, Cass R.: *Laws of Fear*. New York: Cambridge University Press, 2005.

Swanbarton Limited: *Status of Electrical Energy Storage Systems*. London: Department of Trade and Industry, 2004.

Tainter, Joseph: *The Collapse of Complex Societies*. Cambridge: Cambridge University Press, 1988.

Talberth, John and Clifford Cobb: *The Genuine Progress Indicator*. Oakland: Redefining Progress, 2006.

Thaler, Richard H. and Cass R. Sunstein: *Nudge*. New Haven: Yale University Press, 2008.

Tickell, Oliver: 'The "Bali Roadmap"', in *Was Bali a Success?* openDemocracy (online), 18 December 2007.

Tiffin, John and Chris Kissling: *Transport Communications*. London: Kogan Page, 2007.

Torrey, Bradford (ed.): *The Writings of Henry David Thoreau: Journal*, vol. 14. Boston: Houghton Mifflin, 1906.

UK Government Office for Science, *Foresight: The Future of Food and Farming*. London: HMSO, 2011.

Urry, John: *Mobilities*. Cambridge: Polity, 2007.

Urry, John and Dennis Kingsley: *After the Car*. Cambridge: Polity, 2009.

US Department of Defense: Annual Report to Congress: *Military Power of the People's Republic of China, 2006*. Washington, DC: Office of the Secretary of Defense, 2006.

Vanderbilt, Tom: *Traffic*. London: Allen Lane, 2008.

Victor, David G.: *Collapse of the Kyoto Protocol and the Struggle to Slow Global Warming*. Princeton: Princeton University Press, 2001.

Victor, David G.: 'Fragmented Carbon Markets and Reluctant Nations', in Joseph E. Aldy and Robert N. Stavins (eds), *Architectures for Agreement*. Cambridge: Cambridge University Press, 2007.

Victor, David G., Amy M. Jaffe and Mark H. Hayes (eds): *Natural Gas and Geopolitics*. Cambridge: Cambridge University Press, 2006.

Waugh, Phil: 'Deal on Climate Change at Risk'. *Evening Standard*, 9 July 2008.

von Weizsacker, Ernst, Amory B. Lovins and L. Hunter Lovins: *Factor Four: Doubling Wealth – Having Resource Use*. London: Earthscan, 1997.

Wissenburg, Marcel: *Green Liberalism*. London: UCL Press, 1998.

Witoelar, Rachmat: 'Address to Closing Plenary'. UN Climate Change Conference, Bali, 2007; available online.

Wood, D. and A. Velditz: 'Issue Definition, Information Processing and the Politics of Global Warming'. *American Journal of Political Science* 51, 2007.

World Commission on Environment and Development: *Our Common Future*. Oxford: Oxford University Press, 1987.

Yale Center for Environmental Law and Policy and Center for International Earth Science Information Network, Columbia University: *Environmental Performance Index*. New Haven: Yale Center for Environmental Law and Policy, 2009.

Young, Stephen C. (ed.): *The Emergence of Ecological Modernisation*. London: Routledge, 2000.

INDEX